Black, White and Blue

Surviving the Sifting

Jonni Redick

Black, White, and Blue: Surviving the Sifting
ISBN 978-1-7350180-7-2   Hardbound
ISBN 978-1-7350180-9-6   Softbound
ISBN 978-1-7373694-3-1   E-Book
Copyright © 2021 Jonni Redick

Request for information should be addressed to:
Curry Brothers Marketing and Publishing Group
P.O. Box 247 Haymarket, VA 20168

Editing by Cheryl & William Greene
Formatting by Joniece Jackson
Cover Design by Alex Cotton & Nellie Crichlow
Photography by Joe McHugh

CURRY BROS.
MARKETING + PUBLISHING GROUP

TABLE OF CONTENT

DEDICATION

To the Broken Little Girl...

You no longer have to hide...

She had known her for years without ever really getting to know her. Running into her recently, she somehow seemed different. Today she wasn't sure if she was the same person at all, though she seemed the same until we began talking.

Her first instinct was to avoid her at all costs, but no matter how hard she tried, she always ran in to her. She seemed nice enough, but she was always poking and prodding me into feeling guilty about the way I chose to live my life. Right or wrong, it's how I felt like living it. I wish she'd find someone else to harass. But here she is, right in my face again.

I always enjoyed her lively stories about the things she was up to in her life. I didn't always agree with them, but they were the kind of things that sounded like living on the edge could really be exhilarating. I'd done many of those things before in my past, but had realized that they were not the best choices for me or my spirit. I'm looking forward to hearing more about what's going on with her these days. She seems, well, almost ready to really dig deep and tell me what she's been hiding all these years.

There's something about her aura. It almost makes me cringe about myself; yet, somehow want to open up to her about everything inside me. I'm so afraid of letting her see who I really am. She may then stop coming around altogether. Even though she makes me upset, she also soothes the darkness inside that keeps me from shrinking away from the fullness of my life. This may be a good day to let the veil of shame begin to fall. It might be the day that I no longer have to hide from myself.

It just might be the day...

ACKNOWLEDGMENT

My Village

"So in Christ we, though many, form one body, and each member belongs to all the others."
Romans 12:5

The Bible says we are put together, joined together, built together, members together, heirs together, fitted together, and held together. We are created for community, fashioned for fellowship, and formed for family. We are not alone on our life's journey.

My Lord and Savior, I am grateful, blessed and highly favored.

As the scripture describes, we are designed to be connected through community with one another. Looking back over my life, I could never have imagined all the amazing moments of grace I've experienced. Grace is the help given to us by God just because he wants us to have it, not because of anything we have ever done to earn it. I'm grateful to how each of you in my "village" has come alongside me and been an extension of that grace. In so many ways you have been influential directly or indirectly on my path of leadership and overall personal journey. Many of you know your imprint, many of you may never know, I do.

To my husband Kevin, my children Sean and Emily, there are truly no words to describe the power of your love for me and the way you have been my champions.

To my extended family and friends, I see you. I always will. Thank you.

Remember, surround yourself with love and those who love you on this journey of life. It will transcend all else and give you the patience, perseverance and hope you'll need to be better for yourself and for others.

FOREWORD

As this book is being completed...

The current global and American landscape is painted in social unrest with divisive narratives constantly rising between communities and the police who are supposed to protect them. It is mired in the ravages of COVID-19 with its tentacles of death, severe illness, and economic paralysis - some of which have spawned and amplified political camps with deeply embroiled divides. Divides that are devastating to the fragile tapestry of our country and our world. All of this has brought virtually every person to pause and to experience the gravity of both the Coronavirus pandemic and the social unrest - all within the same 86,400 seconds that make up our day. However, within this chaos, resilience has risen - from the vacant streets, the empty restaurants, the abandoned pews and most of all from the goodness of people.

There are endless stories of good works being accomplished by ordinary people who have become suddenly extraordinary – each somehow finding their "Kairos" moment. A "Kairos" moment is an ancient Greek phrase that means the right, critical or most opportune moment and one that can best be described as a "moment for action or decision." It is a moment to do or say the right thing - a moment born of action that can significantly alter the future. Within one of my devotionals, I was reading a story about a Kairos moment. It was pointing out that the difference between a significant moment, one that might 'wow' us, and a "Kairos" moment, lies simply in the call to action.

Seeing these things was so important to me. For weeks I had awakened each day with a feeling of deep sadness because of the growing shift in our humanity towards one another. I was honestly heartbroken, sitting both literally and figuratively on the fence of blue and black lives mattering, yet in a moment of our history that should speak to both our humanity and our collectiveness, not our separatism. This is far more than taking political positions and the "us versus them" that exists in almost every arena. Somewhere amid the degrees of chaos and tragedy, we, as people - humans in our own humanity, have lost our ability to see one another.

It is one thing to recognize a significant moment, but it may not be a moment for change if it does not lead to action. It necessitates taking a risk and, with it, facing fear. So I ask you, "What would you do differently if you weren't afraid?" Often, we spend time admiring the amazing heroes of our faith in their 'finished' or final heroic state forgetting that they, like us, were just ordinary men and women.

But something in that moment set them apart and that something was the ability to find within themselves the humility, strength and courage to take action and thus making that moment a "Kairos" moment.

We must take a stand. I must take a stand and not dwell silently amongst those who speak hate and lack any sort of humanity towards their fellow human beings...

It is time for both you and me to stand in our "Kairos" moment.

Prelude

Mirror of Dreams and Realities

Her little eyes danced, and the curves of her mouth were smiling so big as she looked at her reflection in the mirror. As she was deep in her moment, she faintly heard a voice in the distance. She focused even harder on her present moment until she heard the voice getting louder and closer. She exhaled and yelled back, "Yes! I'm coming!" She slowly took her beautiful long hair off and folded it back up and put it back on the towel rack uncovering her real hair underneath which was more of a fuzzy little mess on her head. The coarse coifed hair oddly sat on her pale scalp and didn't match her fair skin and hazel eyes. She knew her mom was waiting for her, but she took one last moment to look in the mirror and be in her imaginary place where she was free to be whoever she wanted to be. It made her feel like she fit in, like she was special. Though only in the 5th grade, she understood her acceptance in the world outside of her mirror at home was not as kind and inviting. The world was filled with a masquerade of people that would shape her paradigm in ways she could not possibly understand or imagine.

This all came flooding back to me as I was conducting a mental inventory in preparation for an upcoming personal interview. The mirror was reflecting a duplication of me that was almost identical... almost. Recalling those moments as a young girl spent in front of that mirror gave me a flicker of innocence and reminded me of the dreams of the person that I had hoped I would and could become. It was so long ago yet seemed so vividly clear.

It was early in 2018 that I had the opportunity to be interviewed by a young woman who was writing a doctoral dissertation on the subject of why African American women were not entering the law enforcement profession and why they were not ascending the ranks once they were hired. More specifically the subject of her dissertation was, "Factors Impacting African American Women, Underrepresented in Executive Law Enforcement Positions." Immediately drawn to the subject matter due to my long history of recruitment, leadership development, coaching and mentoring in this field, I quickly agreed to be interviewed and to share some names of other women who might want to assist her in her research.

As we sifted through the questions of this seemingly straight forward interview, I found myself going through a tempest of reflections and responses. My responses to her simple questions became visceral entanglements, and I had to carefully balance the weight of what I would share with her. Not far removed from retirement, I had the feeling that divulging anything too personal could reflect negatively on my previous employment. This was somehow making me a bit hesitant. Remembering that little girl looking in the mirror as she played with her long, beautiful hair made me vulnerable in that moment as well. An incredible researcher, educator and renowned author, Brene Brown shares her thoughts on such a moment in her book "Daring Greatly."

> *"As children we found ways to protect ourselves from vulnerability, from being hurt, diminished, and disappointed. We put on armor; we used our thoughts, emotions, imagination, and behaviors as weapons; and we learned how to make ourselves scarce, even to disappear. Now as adults we realize that to live with courage, purpose, and connection – to be the person whom we long to be – we must again be vulnerable. We must take off the armor, put down the weapons, show up, and let ourselves be seen."*

Our sense of value and belonging originates early in our lives and for some of us, it takes a long time to feel that we are worthy of love and good things for ourselves. I thought of all of these things as I reflected on that little girl who used to laugh and play yet was already feeling ashamed that she was so, so different - chubby with short, nappy hair. How she desperately wanted to be someone else, anyone other than who she was in those early years and in a good many that followed.

Naivete in a child is one thing - to think that simple imaginary moments can erase reality. It is normal at a young age to harbor what I consider this form of escapism or self-deception. The long towel I would wear on my hair was symbolic of the long, beautiful locks often found on white girls. I couldn't understand why mine didn't seem to look the same way. In my young mind that small difference could change it all.

I would then somehow fit in. But alas, my naivete was not allowing me to understand how my whiteness was harnessed to my blackness. Thus creating my biracial status that was inseparable from me and who I could or would become. That moment in that seemingly harmless interview became my new mirror – one in which I could finally begin to see myself for who I really am.

Chapter 1

Remembering How it All Began

As my interviewer, a powerful professional black woman, started asking me questions, she remarked how privileged she felt to have the opportunity to interview me. Incredibly humbled and flattered by her comments, I was floating in this surreal space of past and present. The initial conversation was simply light banter designed to get us both comfortable. She started with softball questions that were relatively easy. Yet even so, the journey of fading in and out of the past with moments of remembrance had begun.

Around her third or fourth question, she asked me, "What were your career goals as they relate to advancement to executive leadership? Was that it or were you aspiring to do even more?" My inner voice echoed her question through my mind's eye, "Was there more?" Outwardly, I responded, "Actually, no. When I started, I had no high visual horizon. I was just seeing the next promotion or hood ornament was my view for many years." Because I didn't want to rob her of any details and hoping this would ultimately end the interview, I began to share my story.

Like most good stories, it should have an origin. Almost every good comic book that I've ever read always provided an origin or background story for its superheroes or characters. As I was growing up, we would move from city to city virtually each school year. While living on this traveling bus ride of new cities and friends, I was always able to find beauty and escape in comic books. Comics seemed to transport me to an almost serene place that was far away from my reality. My favorite comics were a mix of *Archie* to *Wonder Woman* to the *Justice League*. I'm not sure why these stories were so important to me - none of the characters looked or lived like me or my family, especially *Wonder Woman* (WW). But I found a sense of excitement and wonder in their cartoon lives. The silly tiffs they'd get caught up in or the cute romantic antics that would abound between Veronica, Archie, Reggie, Betty and the gang would transport me to a safe and serene world of almost unreal innocence. The powerful essence of *Wonder Woman* and how she balanced her strength with her femininity along with the colors used in the graphics lifted her story off the page in a way that made it fun, exciting and adventurous. Learning about the backdrop of the characters and their origins gave me context. Where they each came from and how their lives intersected became the basis of the stories that sprung to life in those comic book pages.

My Law Enforcement Origin Story

When I joined the California Highway Patrol in 1988, it was more of a personal challenge to see if I could do it. I had no family members in law enforcement. No one had recruited me and I only had a high school diploma and a little junior college. I found out about the job quite by chance. One day I was reading a comic strip in the local newspaper – yep, a real newspaper and yep, the comics. Across from the comics were the classified ads where there was a quarter page ad that read "California Highway Patrol – NOW HIRING." The ad listed the annual salary at "$40,000 a year," along with the benefits of health, dental and vision insurance and an opportunity for a secure a retirement. As a 20-year-old, the salary was the biggest draw. It was significantly more than I was making at the time. At that moment, I was working full time as a clerk typist for a small unit of women social workers (HR). I was making just a bit more than the minimum wage which was about $3.75 an hour at the time. The benefits were exciting to me as well. I'd never really had health benefits before as my mom was often on government assistance or, as most know it, welfare. We didn't go to the doctor or the dentist unless lifesaving treatment was absolutely necessary. Basically, if there were no detached limbs or profuse bleeding, she would stitch me up or pop the dislocation back into place. If there was significant pain, she would give me some aspirin and tell me to take a nap. Mom was always tough love. Born in Seagraves, Texas in 1933, she grew up in Leon Junction, Texas. Starting at a very young age, she picked cotton and took care of her younger siblings. As a result, she didn't have a lot of empathy for "small" problems.

As I continued reading the ad, the minimum requirements to apply were all pretty basic. I met the age requirement, had a valid driver license, 20/20 vision, no misdemeanors and a high school diploma. My inner thoughts were, why not apply? I loved watching *CHiPs*! How cool would it be if that were me, you know, hang gliding? Looking sexy in a tight-uniform and laughing with my pals as we did our job. I really gave little thought as to what it would really take to be a CHP officer. What a transparent moment…now to even say this out loud. Most youth are so naïve.

My inner curiosity about the advertisement was not earth shattering. I was simply bored with my current job. I wanted to make more money and do something that was really exciting. Not wanting to grow up struggling like my mother was a subliminal thought as well. We never had any real security or stability. Although I loved her incredibly, I just didn't want to be sad, lonely, depressed and addicted to prescription medications as she had been. I didn't want to live with nothing and not know where I or my kid would be living from day to day. And more importantly having to live each day almost without hope.

Before my mother Sara became broken, she had been a strong woman. Educated and licensed as a registered nurse, she had enjoyed a beautiful life somewhere in her past. However, our life together – as mother and daughter - was like waves crashing in the ocean. We seemed to always be in a leaky canoe praying we'd just make it to someone else's shore for a while. It always felt as if she was searching for something. It was a void no person or child of hers could ever fill. When she was in those moments, it left me feeling almost rudderless. I knew she loved me and was doing the best that she could but I always felt I needed to find my own way - a way that would give me independence and hopefully financial security. The CHP was my escape.

Once I applied the next steps were exciting but also distracting. While my attention at that age span wasn't very long, the testing and hiring process seemed to me to take forever. There were so many steps that I had to go through and I didn't understand any of them. I just worked to show up to where and when I was directed. It was also tough to turn off the noise from the naysayers. My inner monologue was already one of doubt and trepidation and I was feeling lackluster support from most of my friends and co- workers as well. I don't know how many times I heard people say, "Why would YOU want to be a police officer? It's more for guys, isn't it?" I didn't know! I never thought about who it was for because the newspaper ad didn't say it wasn't for me. Geez, such haters!

Those faded faces from my old tying job and my shallow friend group are still etched in my memory as I shared with them that I was applying for the CHP position. The guys laughed at me and the women would look at me like, "What the hell? You're not tough enough to be a cop. It's stupid to even think you could do that job." When I recall this part of my story, the memory of some of my co-workers at HR not believing in me always makes me smile. They always seemed to be mockingly reminding me that my job at HR would be there when I returned. Ironically, I did go back. Every time I was in town, I would make it a point to stop by the old HR site to say hello. As an officer, a sergeant, a lieutenant, a captain, and ultimately as an assistant chief!

I suppose they never really thought that I could do it, or that I should do it or that even would do it. I'm glad their pessimism didn't rub off on me. Perhaps they thought I was too cute – yep, I said it – too damn cute. The nappy headed little girl in the mirror had blossomed. Outwardly, she was considered a "looker." Allowing myself to explore the newness of it all, modeling was a path I had attempted for a couple of years after high school and even while I was working at HR. I took some modeling classes, did a few local modeling gigs, and even took a trip to New York for a competition. Because of this, maybe they felt I was too soft to be a police officer and didn't fit the stereotype of a police woman. I'm not exactly sure what that stereotype looked like but I imagine it goes along with many of the other underlying biases that prevail to this day.

It never really crossed my mind that I "couldn't do it." It was more did I really want to do it. At 20 years of age, I felt physically fit. I had played basketball all four years of high school and had planned to play at the local junior college before having to begin my work career. So I didn't think physical fitness would be a problem.

Though many people tried to discourage me, my mother would tell me all the time that there was nothing that I couldn't do if I set my mind and heart to it. Her favorite words were, "Jonni Lea, I believe in you." Whatever I wanted to do, she was always behind me all the way.

When I was younger, Sara's support for me was always important in spite of the brokenness of our life and love. While I truly loved her, needed her and respected her; I also despised her, couldn't stand her and was ashamed of her. Why were the two of us so incapable of having a "normal" life? Why can't my address be the same year after year? Where was my father and why didn't he come around more often?

The spiritual warfare of our relationship was a heated battle for most of our lives. It was sometimes fought openly, but most of the time raged silently within me. I just wanted her to stay steady and get her act together. Stop crashing into depression, prescription drugs and chaos. For once, I just wanted to finish a school year in the same school versus attending two or three.

She had the ability, education, and intelligence to stay employed as a registered nurse. I had seen her in action when I would visit her at some of her work places. I would be so proud when they would call her to the front desk because she was often the head nurse or a director of the facility. I just didn't know why she couldn't do it. For some reason it mattered so much to me that she thought I could do it. It made me feel very brave that she was not afraid of the type of work I would be doing. So, I went for it.

As a sign of my immaturity during the hiring process, the day of the written test I was trying to hurry up so that I could get to Los Angeles to go the beach with my boyfriend. It sounded like a lot more fun than taking a four-hour test at home in Bakersfield, California. The test time flew by for me and as I was leaving, there were still lots of people still plugging along. And by the way, the beach was awesome that day!

Several weeks later, I got a notice in the mail informing me that I had passed the test. Yikes! I had no idea what was supposed to happen next. It turned out the process was relatively simple. I had passed the written test, the physical ability test and had completed the background interview. I had completed all of the medical and psychological examinations as well. I hadn't been too sure how I'd do on the psychology exam. There were lots of questions from assessing the regularity of my bowels to the type of relationship I had with my mother. I just figured there had to be a method to the madness, literally and figuratively.

Shortly after the last background piece, a background investigator visited my house. At 20 plus years, I didn't quite know what to expect so it was good to have my mother by my side. The white male background investigator went through some brief expectations and the next steps to accepting the invitation to the December academy class in Sacramento, California. It was literally in just a few months as it was already September. He said the academy would involve a lot of physical training (PT) and so I might want to step up any exercise program I was currently doing. What did that mean exactly?

Not a big fan of PT slash physical education (PE), dreadful high school memories sprung up in my mind. Ditching PE had been my mission as a freshman because I was ashamed of my body. Ugh! Anyway, I had no idea what I was getting ready to embark upon, but I started getting up before work and running a couple of miles each morning. Remember the boyfriend I went to the beach with on the day of the written test? Well, he became my ex-boyfriend shortly afterward. He just couldn't wrap his head around me being a policewoman, so we decided it was for the best. We still had a nice friendship outside of our relationship. He still wanted to help me get ready with strength training in the afternoon and occasionally drive by the route of my morning run in order to give me encouragement. He even attended my graduation.

The Academy Experience

My arrival at the Academy was like a very small blip on the old radar screen from every submarine movie you have ever seen. Pulling in through the front entrance of the Academy, you arrive at a security building where you must stop and show your identification. (Once you pass through, the grounds are spacious with trees and green grass and off in the distance you can see the driving track).

As you begin to take the roundabout, you notice the flagpole in the center flying the American and California Flags. Simultaneously while taking in this new environment, I was feeling proud, excited and scared. Yet even more unsettling, from somewhere deep inside me, I wasn't sure how I would ever fit in.

On that particular day, the parking lot was full of cars as a scurry of new reporting cadets were unloading their bags and walking across the lot. I tried to find some parking close by but ended up parking what felt like a mile from where I needed to be. The atmosphere in the parking lot was busy but the Academy campus appeared to be so inviting or at least it did so initially. I remember hurriedly walking with my suitcases to the location where everyone else was standing.

Me in my very cool, new, grey two-piece suit that had a skirt that fell below the knees and a matching jacket with a white linen collared shirt underneath. The large rectangle silver earrings I was wearing were sharp, my makeup was "poppin," and my hair was freshly "permed", styled, and had a light bounce to it as I walked. Having a fresh perm or relaxer for those who may not be familiar with the term gave my hair a feathered 'Farrah Fawcett' vibe. Feeling pretty confident that my personal presentation was on point had me completely unaware of the paramilitary police environment around me. Aww, such naivete.

I instantly became the target of unwelcome attention. The staff officers singled me out immediately and began barking at me and calling me 'Darlin'. "This ain't no fashion show princess! Where do you think you're going, cupcake?" Those comments quickly morphed into "Throw your trash over there and get lined up! Did I tell you that you could look at me maggot?" I was feeling shell shocked. What the hell was happening? We were all given just minutes to go and change out of our business attire into the Academy Blues - basically baby 'Smurf' outfits. My sixth sense was telling me something wasn't right. The imagery of hang gliding and surfing on the beach quickly dissipated with the cold, damp sting of Academy blues.

Gee, I wish I would have kept a list of all the lovely lines used on us cadets by the academy PT (physical training) staff. A few will never fade and are forever imprinted on my conscience. "You "cain't" wear all that long hair around here princess! This ain't no beauty pageant missy! "You'll need to get that clown makeup off your face darlin." And my absolute favorite, "You probably just need to go on home and bake cookies with your Momma!" On this last one, if they only knew, my momma didn't even bake cookies, so Ha!!!

As expected, physical training was grueling. We were up at "O' dark thirty" each morning to do floor exercises and run. Odd days we'd swim, but most of the time the pool needed maintenance. It was so weird having to use a high dive. When on earth was I ever going to jump off of anything high into a body of water while I was a highway patrol officer?

Um, how about never? I know I hated it as much as regular PT. Again, not being good at blending in, one day my hesitation to jump lasted so long that a member of the cantankerous PT staff kept yelling at me from below, "Calloway (my maiden name) if you don't jump your princess-self off that platform I'm comin' up there to push you myself!"Well, luckily, my classmates were "supportive" and pushed me off for him so he didn't get the satisfaction of doing it!

Never being the best at running, push-ups, sit-ups or pull-ups, I seemed to always find myself in the front row of our PT workout every morning. Basically, the more fit you were or became, you were migrated to the back rows and the PT staff didn't seem to harass you as much. However those who remained in the front row, well, it appeared to be the PT staff's life's mission to see and note every sagging push-up, lackluster sit-up, and lame attempt at a pull-up.

They had a designated area right in front of the front row PT regulars called the "morgue." The "morgue" participants were those the PT staff had deemed as poor performers during the floor exercises. Usually the problem was poor performance with either sit-ups or push-ups. As a "permanent" resident of the "morgue", I always felt embarrassed, incompetent, and somehow less capable than the rest of my fellow cadets. Over time, I realized it was just part of the game - the pressure and the stress - always trying to break you down, to build you up, or some other mind controlling crap, at least that's how it felt to me at the time.

Anyway, I managed to survive. I honestly got used to the front row and the "morgue" embracing the daily abuse yet never giving in. I was proud of my own personal milestones that kept me showing up each morning at "O'dark thirty" singing our morning company song, "Early in the morning before the break of day, highway rangers leading the way...blah, blah, blah." On those early mornings as we made our way around the Academy trails, the song became the cadence for our runs in the darkness. Over time it developed into a catchy beat and I found pride in the chant as I began to adjust to the patterns of my new life.

It was a different daily grind at the Academy especially if you were a woman and even more so if you were a woman of color. At the outset, our Academy class contained over 145 cadets. Over twenty of these cadets were women of which two other were African American. Most didn't know my ethnicity, and it took a while for my classmates to figure it out. I'm not sure what gave it away. It could have been how quickly my hair lost its Farrah Fawcett feathering and became a frizzy, nappy little bun on my head. Honestly, it wasn't something I thought too much about as I was just trying to survive the academy experience. My focus was on keeping my emotions in control and telling myself "Do not cry!"

Navigating the Academy on a daily basis became a strategic way for me to manage my emotions and my interactions. Almost weekly, I wanted to quit because I didn't think I could do it. Within the first week, several women did quit after shooting their guns for the first time at the range. For many of us women it was the first time we had ever experienced firing a weapon. That moment along with the cold reality of actually having to use a gun to take someone's life was, no doubt, overwhelming. I remember just wanting to go home and bake cookies with my momma! But when I would call my mom on the pay phone, she would tell me that I was not coming home, that I could make it another day, another week, another month or whatever it took. Oh, and she would always tell me to take a nap when I could. It took me years to understand the significance of the nap for life management.

Although it was hard for the men, it was harder still for the women. There were just more of them and they kept each other going. Not to say that they didn't want to help us women – some truly wanted to help in the right way but others in ways that were completely inappropriate. I even had one classmate that wanted to take all of us single ladies out for pizza. It took me a minute to realize he was chasing all of us, not just me. We would have our midweek liberty or night off and everyone would be heading out to go to the local pubs for a drink and dinner. The ladies would look completely different out of class and the guys, well, they'd "oogle" all the women. I'm not here to reveal people's escapades but it sometimes got a bit messy during some of those "liberties."

The women's dorm quads were set up with two cadets to a room with two rooms on one side of a two-toilet / two-shower cluster with two rooms connected similarly on the other side. My roommate was ten years older than me and was prior military. She was, quite simply, just tougher than me. I was still wondering why everyone was yelling at us so much. We all could hear them clearly, yet she just kept handling her business totally unfazed.

I had never experienced anything remotely close to a military boot camp and I must say it was every second an emotionally draining experience. My roommate's wisdom, experience and patience helped me to learn how to balance the physical challenges with the mental toughness needed to be successful at the Academy. Instead of looking at the overwhelming magnitude of the entire Academy experience, she urged me to focus on the small things that I could work on every day. For example, I was always late getting back to the room to shower after PT, which made me late to breakfast and then late to marching. As a result, I would be just barely on time to classes, and even more importantly, I would be exhausted all day. She recommended that I work on improving my running in order to avoid being a part of the last group. She told me that it would help me get to the showers sooner and to breakfast and marching in a timely manner. All of this, of course, would enable me to be more alert in class.

When I'd start to get in a rhythm in one area, there was always an area I was exposed. It never failed that I would receive a disciplinary report, a Blue Card, for one thing or another. After a while, these disciplinary report cards would accumulate and you would lose a privilege of some freedom or liberty would be lost. I'd have to say I was one of the best brass polisher in our class as that was often my task on those libertyless nights.

What I appreciated most about my roommate was that she took the time to help me to be successful and to survive the Academy. Many of the women didn't survive. In fact, the power structure couldn't wait for your failure. It was an important lesson for me on how women can be successful together. And why on earth would we even want to see each other fail in law enforcement?

In the United States, women are estimated to make up only about 12.8% of all police officers. I learned later when I was in recruitment that women in my department made up less than 7%, and African American women made up less than 1%. When we "chocolate Chips" could sit around and name all of the African American women out of roughly over 7,000 officers, well... you get the picture.

The Field Training Experience

After being sucked into the vortex called the California Highway Patrol Academy, I emerged 6 months later ready to get to work. To work where, you might be asking? Well, during the latter part of the Academy, you signed up for your location "wish list" of sorts on assignments throughout California. Of course, I assumed I would be able to go home to Bakersfield, so that was #1. After that, I really put little or no effort into my other selections.

The final assignment list was posted in the classroom near the front and one of my classmates yelled out, "Calloway (Fenner), you're going to Ontario." He continued to list all the other names after mine and yell to them where they were going but Ontario just did not ring a bell for me. A little awkwardly, I asked out loud, "Is that in California? I've only heard of it as a city in Canada." Really, where in the heck was Ontario, California? After they laughed and ridiculed me, someone was nice enough to blurt out that it was in southern California.

Oh, ok. I thought "I'm going to be near the beach. Nice." Well... not really. It turns out Ontario is about as far east as you can go from Los Angeles without being in the desert. Leaving the sanctity of the Academy was a big adjustment. Transitioning from doing police work scenarios to contacting and arresting real people was going to be a big deal.

However, telling myself how prepared and trained I was helped me fight the anxiety and fear starting to lodge in my throat. Academy role players give up when your arrest control twist lock starts to hurt, but real arrestees won't. It was becoming very real and I had to put on my big girl pants, game face and toss any notion of baking cookies out the window.

My transition from Academy to the field included a 3-4 month period with a series of field training officer (FTOs). In this paramilitary environment, the on-boarding into the organizational culture of the office to which you are assigned isn't very personalized. You are a badge number and a maggot until you graduate. After graduation, you're not called a maggot any longer but you feel like one as you enter the gauntlet of field training phases. Depending on how you're doing in the process, the training phases occur in intervals with three to four different officers who are assigned to you as your field training officer (FTO). This experience can be mind-blowing to a new officer especially if you either get a FTO from hell or one from lah-lah land. While neither extreme helps you grow and get better, they do actually begin to introduce you to the nuances and sometimes unsavory organizational office culture. And, in a power dynamic profession, many FTOs use this time to assert their small bit of authority over "newbie" officers. In some ways, it's very similar to hazing.

Reflecting on this experience, I realize as a new officer you are just loosely floating through these phases with no one really assessing or identifying you or your potential. It's really sink or swim. I felt like they just saw us as robots or widget makers. Even though we are in law enforcement where critical thinking and effective communication skills are critical, no one was making any real concerted effort to cultivate important quality standards of effective communication, emotional intelligence, resilience, problem solving and leadership capacity. I mean for goodness sake, we have the authority to take someone's civil liberties and their life yet the ideology at the time felt like it was to train as you go, or "build the plane as you fly it." The difference was that we were not flying planes.

Finding My Way

For the first five or six years, there was absolutely no mentoring. In fact, as a female and despite your race, you had to work with men who still discriminated against you. Women had only begun to be hired on to the CHP in 1974. It had only been a little over 15 years that women had been working alongside men in policing. Police history shows that women were initially only allowed to work as matrons in jails. In 1905 Portland, Oregon hired Lola Baldwin as one of the first woman police officers in the U.S. Her primary duties were as a social worker. However, in 1908, she was sworn in as an officer with the power to conduct arrests. Subsequently, there was Alice Stebbins Wells. In 1910, Ms. Wells was hired by the Los Angeles Police Department to do social work with women and children, but she did have a badge number "#1."

Wells went on to create a movement of what some would call "social unrest." Officer Wells was sworn in only after she, along with many others, had petitioned the LAPD to make her their first female police officer. The petitioners created a groundswell of support and the LAPD had no choice but to acquiesce. During Wells' career, she founded the International Policewomen's Association which advocated for women in policing, nationally and internationally. However, it wasn't until the 1970s that women began to be increasingly accepted and/or tolerated in policing. The passing of Title VII of the Civil Rights Act in 1972, outlawing gender discrimination in public agencies further broadened opportunities for women in policing. And let us not forget the popular TV shows, 'Get Christie Love' and 'Policewoman' which helped foster increased public awareness and support for women in policing.

Now we were in the early 1990s and the older male officers absolutely refused to work with women on graveyard shifts (9:45pm to 6:15am) or respond to "female" incidents. I was not about to be considered someone's "matron" or "social worker." I particularly remember this older, white, male officer who would go home sick every time he was scheduled to work with a female as a car partner on a graveyard shift. As young officers at the time, other female officers and I would laugh it off and try to make the best of it.

That particular memory is so clear. He would sit in the back row of the briefing room to where all of the senior officers usually gravitated. They would look at all of us females with a "stank" eye. The white male sergeant would be going over the briefing items for the night. Invariably one of the female officers wouldn't have a beat partner. I would immediately think, "Oh boy...here we go..." We already knew the old officer was going to pack up his stuff and head home "sick." However on this particular night, the officer didn't just leave like he would usually do. No, instead after the sergeant assigned him to work with the female officer, he got up and muttered, "This is fucking bullshit and I ain't working with her or any other woman!" He left out the back door in a huff. The sergeant didn't skip a beat as he was reading the briefing items and assigning people to their shift beats. This happened night after night, usually without the profanity, but always with the disgusted attitude. There is so much to unpack in this one incident, but the complicit silence and lack of response by the sergeant made him just as discriminatory and negligent as the older white male officer.

This type of behavior is still pervasive and prevalent in many police agencies. Moral muteness allows for the spread of complicity which has become the norm. When someone does try to have a voice in these or similar incidents, they are often beaten back by their peers and threatened with retaliation themselves if they continue to speak out. Retaliation looks like many things in policing. For me, whenever I spoke up in a way that may have been considered out of place, it was met with the lack of assistance by my white male beat partners. Or if I were to question the sergeant on why I was being picked out for something over someone else, he would just do it more often. He may also make comments on my performance evaluations that were less than positive and those words, his words, would follow me throughout my career.

Most of the women I worked with in those early years tried extremely hard to become good police officers with only a few making me embarrassed to acknowledge that I had worked with them. I was always hooking and booking DUI drivers just as much as the next guy, but still, most men didn't want to ride with me or the other female officers. The male sergeants were either heavy-handed with us or too personal. When I was brand new and in my first assigned area, Ontario, I recall an older white male sergeant always calling me in off my beat to go over what I had done for the day. It was always in the evening and I was always the only one he called.

My beat partners and classmates working the area with me teased me about being the sergeant's favorite. Being very naïve, I thought I was going to get fired most of the time. One day I asked this sergeant for a special day off to travel back home to Bakersfield for the weekend. The sergeant asked me what I would do for him if he gave me the day off. Unsure of what that meant, I said "Work really hard when I come back." Nothing overt from that comment transpired right away until our holiday party a few months later. My date for the party was a fellow classmate. Why not? He was a genuinely nice guy. We had been friends in the Academy and now we were working the same office. While sitting at the table, the sergeant who had given me the day off stumbled over towards me. He had been drinking. He leaned over and whispered in my ear, "You sure look pretty" and then he tried to give me a kiss. It made me so uncomfortable. I told my date, "He just won't take his drunk ass away from our table." My date intervened and asked me if I wanted to step outside for a moment. That was a big intervention.

It was so awkward. We were both new officers and didn't want to make a big deal out of it and perhaps lose our jobs. I thought about sharing it with the female supervisor, the only one in the office, but she was dating one of the other sergeants. It was a beehive of overlapping relationships with an office culture submerged in a "good ole boys" culture. "Good ole boys" includes the "good ole girls" right along with them. It was such a weird vibe. Because of that and other things, I was almost ready to quit. It may seem like a pattern with me, but this is my story and my narrative. It's really how I felt. Those people sucked, big time. I was tired of being treated like a maggot, spoken to like I was invisible, and told to do things that were simply wrong.

A Mustard Seed is Planted

I survived my break-in training and my early years on the job though just barely. My initial assignment in Ontario lasted exactly one year and then I voluntarily transferred to Ventura, California. This was an office where you could see the ocean and the beach. I was excited about the change of scenery in every way feeling that perhaps the new command would bring a fresh organizational culture change. Not so much. It was very similar to the office I had just left. With the same Adam Henry (code for asshole) cliques and the unnecessary nonsense, it disgusted me to the core. I had to find something to distract me from another cesspool. My saving grace was that the ocean between Malibu and Ventura was so beautiful to patrol.

Most of the time, I worked the graveyard shift. It was fun but left me out of sync with my circadian rhythm. Only 22 years old, I found myself working "the yard" and on my days off partying in Los Angeles. My apartment was in Thousand Oaks which placed me halfway between the office and Los Angeles. It was the first time I had lived on my own. Stretching my "being adult" to the limit was what I specialized in during this time. Endless partying became as hollow as the guys I would encounter – none of it had any depth. Although drinking, smoking and drugs were not something I had ever explored, my promiscuity was a pattern I carried with me from childhood.

I started feeling lonely, used, and began to slump into a slight, depressive state. I was sleeping longer than I needed. I stopped going out and was really only engaging with other humans during work hours.

When at work, I was agitated and either too quiet or too loud. I hated the "clique" and they hated me. Luckily, there was a small squad of folks that hated them too. We instantly connected and would rotate being graveyard partners. It helped but something was missing. I felt so off.

I never realized how dark my days had gotten until one day I was sitting on the couch in my apartment. All the furnishings had been carefully selected from Rent-A-Center. Why not? I wouldn't be taking them with me anywhere. The repetitive nights of arresting drunks, handling fatal collisions, pursuits or foot chases was wearing on me. As I sat there, the eight straight days of working and having very little sleep was sucking me in. Always returning home to an empty well-furnished apartment, I was feeling so desperately lonely, lost, and sad. I wondered what it would be like to just die. Who would know other than maybe at some point, my mother? My gun is here. I'm here. It began to cross my mind more than I wanted and that scared me. I couldn't tell anyone or I could lose my job. My mother would have me institutionalized. So, I stayed silent.

Eventually, my mother would be relocating from Los Angeles to Oakland, California to take a new position as a director of nursing at a senior living facility. She had struggled on and off for years with staying consistently employed, so I was really excited and proud of her. My mom was my heroine. Despite all of her brokenness, she was the one person I needed. How was I going to make it staying in Ventura, so far away from her in Northern California, almost 400 miles away. I was 22 years old, grown, but not. I decided to transfer to Hayward, the closest my seniority would take me to her.

The change to my new office helped me to somewhat lift the cloud of loneliness under which I was living. I was slowly finding my way back to my relationship with God. I had been introduced to Him at age13 through baptism, but I was never really living life as if I knew him. I now found myself seeking Him more. Not perfectly, but more. Those early years were hard on my immature mind and spirit. Trying to understand the carnage at crime scenes, having to interact socially with difficult people and being separated from all that was familiar to me was truly overwhelming. There was no peer support, employee assistance or even compassionate leadership. Like the Academy, it was a "suck it up, buttercup" and keep it moving mentality. And we wonder where cumulative trauma comes from, and why we end our careers with health issues, high divorce rates, addictions, and suicides? Just trying to balance work and all its gory details with your personal life is hard... incredibly hard.

Chapter 2

The 1st Promotion ~ Sergeant

As I matured in my job as a CHP officer, I noticed that a number of others around me were starting to get promoted. I thought to myself, "If that blankety-blank can get promoted, then so can I!" Yes, when I was younger, I certainly had an attitude about a lot of things. I grew up with it. That young girl inside me was still filled with anger, frustration, shame, and pain. It was always bubbling just below the surface wanting very much to get into a rumble with someone - anyone.

I had been on the force for about seven years and was working in Hayward when I first got the bug to take the sergeant's test. My captain at the time was an old relic who today reminds me of the senator from Kentucky, Mitch McConnell. He had pale skin and eyes that were cold and unkind. When he'd walk down the hall, a hall that was similar to the one in the Tom Hanks movie *The Green Mile,* he would never make eye contact or speak to me. While it was only figurative for me, it was not unlike the walk a prisoner takes before he is executed (there's that *Green Mile* reference again). It killed a little something in me every time he would walk past me, as if I wasn't there.

Over time you begin to grow a thick skin or, at least, you think you do. You begin to try to adapt to the surroundings of which you are a part. The gruff and tough environment somehow becomes ordinary. You start to take on some of this gritty attitude so you can bite back when you need to and I certainly would. Though it really didn't do me a lot of good to mirror those behaviors, I just didn't know what I didn't know. The first time I had even a passing interest in taking the sergeant's test, I realized very quickly that I would have little or no help or support. I had no one actively mentoring me or willing to provide any sort of encouragement. Needless to say, I didn't take the test.

Not long after that, a new Asian captain took command of our post. He was in his mid-thirties and his arrival created a big ripple of interest throughout the command. He was so different. Not just because he was Asian or because he was young, but more importantly, because he didn't look or act like the relic we had before. On top of these obvious differences, his leadership style was so different. I mean, he actually had a leadership style. One thing that stood out for me is how he would come to the briefings or training days dressed in casual attire just like we were dressed in jeans, collared shirt and actual tennis shoes. It humanized him and stripped away some of the rigidity of his rank and responsibility. He'd perch himself on the edge of a table or sit amongst us – totally opposite from his predecessors who would look down at us from a podium in the front of the room. He'd look you in the eye and you felt he was really seeing you.

Another thing that was very different from the three previous captains was that he wanted to get to know us individually. While we were on patrol, he would go on personal ride-alongs with each of us. Many of us were not in favor of this idea initially, at least, not openly. I remember being resistant to him riding with me because I now had some seniority. My attitude and voice were starting to echo the collective culture of the command which was one of complaining and cussing. To this day I'm not proud of it; it was just a fact. On one particular day, our new black female sergeant (a real "unicorn") was giving the briefing. She mentioned that the new captain would be riding with each of us during our shifts over the next few days. As if my mouth had a mind of its own I blurted out, "Not with me he isn't. I have way too much to do to be carrying the captain around." With my arms folded, sitting in the back of the briefing room, where all of my seven years of seniority had promoted me, I felt completely entitled to my comments.

Others in the room felt the same way and I knew it. We had talked about it in the locker room, at lunch, out on the beat, and in the parking lot. But in this briefing room...on this morning, not a word was said other than what came out of my big mouth.

Well, our "unicorn" sergeant was nobody's pushover. She didn't get here by anybody's handouts and she had a mouth that rivaled anyone's. In the instant my mouth spit out those words, she cut me right off. It almost seemed that before the words had completely left my mouth her voice and tongue eviscerated me. "You better get your fucking act together and make sure your narrow ass is ready for the captain. In fact, you'll be in the first rotation. Go get your car ready and wait in the parking lot until he comes out. One last thing, I better not hear another fucking word out of you about what you're not going to do. You will do it and you will behave. Get going!"

In that moment, I felt parented and immediately complied with my tail between my "narrow" ass. Sitting in the parking lot waiting for this new captain, I was already planning on how little I was going to say. I just wanted to get through the ride. Running through my head was what Brenè Brown refers to in her book Rising Strong as my "shitty first draft" (SFD) - also known as a "stormy first draft" for a rating appropriate for a younger audience. This is the draft where you let out all that you're thinking and feeling in a place where no one can see or hear you. It's intended to create more wholeheartedness in ourselves if used correctly. However, the initial drafts are where you don't necessarily engage your wholeheartedness; it's just plain having an adult tantrum. And since I already had one outwardly during the briefing, this one was raging internally.

He came out to the car looking sharp in his uniform and carrying his "go bag." A "go bag" is what we officers carry in our patrol cars that contain all of the forms, resources, and equipment we need for the day's work in the field.   I was really curious as to what was in his and what he might do on any of our impending calls. I thought, "Management thinks they're still road dogs." Either way, he threw it in the back of the cruiser and jumped into the passenger seat. It was then I noticed it. It was an aura or presence that emanated from him. You just seemed to know that he was a really nice guy. Not a threat or someone that would put me on the defensive. He was not at all like the last captain and very quickly I felt much more at ease.

As I made traffic stops, he would get out and cover me. He would help by calling in on the radio or assisting me on our calls to traffic collisions. He never once critiqued my work but worked alongside me as a decent male partner officer. In between the calls, we'd ride and he would casually share thoughts about his family and his career path. He asked me easy questions that I felt comfortable answering. Before I knew it, my time with him was up and I had to transfer him to another officer.

He was charismatic, kind, and authentic. He left me, in some ways, a changed person by just being himself. Though neither of us realized it at the time, he was planting seeds that would help me begin to see my own potential. It was the first time that I was able to start seeing a glimpse of my own possibilities. At the same time, the old mirror that I used to play before as a child started to have a new reflection. It began to reflect my own bad habits and behavioral characteristics, most of which I had long needed to resolve, but hadn't recognized. He did not directly mentor me, but he inspired me through his leadership style by being engaged, professional and authentic. He made me feel like I was being seen in the right way. My "SFD" had disintegrated as I rumbled and reckoned with my feelings through that experience. My wholeheartedness was emerging.

It was around that year (year seven) that I decided to take the sergeant's test for the first time. I had no idea what the test would be like and there were no real guidelines or study groups to help me. It was the very impetus for me later writing *The Survival Guide to Law Enforcement Promotional Preparation* when I retired. The guide was self-published to provide a framework for law enforcement professionals trying to navigate the process of promotions including assessing readiness, understanding how to study and what to study, along with sharing strategies for success in all aspects of the examination process. It had been a secret for me, but now it would be available to everyone, not just the fortunate. When I was trying to figure out how and what to do in my examination journey, there were no people, processes, or institutional framework available to assist officers in preparing for promotion. You basically had to figure it out on your own or be connected to the right people. Back then that meant connected to men because they were in over 90% of the leadership positions in the CHP.

On top of those challenges, I really had no idea what being a sergeant meant or was supposed to even look like, but I still wanted to do it. By this point, I was a married mother with a young son. I was commuting to a new home 60 miles from Hayward. It took me over two hours round trip to get to work each day. My best friend, my soul patrol "sista", my graveyard shift partner and associate in crime, asked me one day on our daily ride, "Why do you even want to take the test and become a sergeant?" Back then, I didn't really have a good answer other than that I wanted to do it and believed that I could. Somewhere inside of me, I felt like I was supposed to do more and become more than I thought I could as a child. My partner was good about not trying to kill my dreams. Instead, she was always one of my biggest champions and still is to this day. In fact, she is one of the first women to remind me how to show up for work. I use to wear sweats and house shoes into the graveyard shift. The second night we were working together she told me, "Jonni Lea, there will be no more of those "slipper" shoes and sweats. Nope. We can't be like everybody else." She was my senior classmate in the Academy and I always looked up to her so her words mattered. I never wore those sweats or "slipper" shoes again.

Although I did receive support and encouragement from my partner and a few others, I still didn't know what I needed to know about the sergeant's examination. Neither did I take the time to immerse myself in a disciplined study practice or really understand what information I should be focusing on to properly prepare. Needless to say, I was not ready. The day of the examination is a blur but what stands out...the test questions. As far as I was concerned the questions were in a different language because none of them made sense. It was a random guessing game as I sat in the room with others who had come prepared. Afterwards, I really didn't want to run into anyone and have to have any light banter about anything that I had just experienced. Ugh! Why did I even think that I could or should try this?

My examination results were not surprising, but I was still really frustrated and disappointed with myself. It unhinged me to see several mediocre officers make the sergeant's list. Embarrassed with myself that I hadn't made the list, I sulked awhile but kept doing my job, or at least I thought I was. Looking back, I realize that I was not only unprepared for the written examination, but I also wasn't really mature enough to be a supervisor. I needed to get a grip on my emotions, learn the meaning of discipline and most importantly, how to really do my job with excellence.

I had to learn to figure out what having a high visual horizon meant both personally and professionally. If you think of it in the context of driving an automobile, having a high visual horizon means to be able to see beyond the hood of your car. It means to be able to anticipate what's ahead, both to avoid hazards and to be prepared to take evasive action should it become necessary. Early on, I had no idea of how to navigate the nuances of my career path. My high visual horizon consisted of looking no further than the tip of my nose - not even beyond the hood ornament of my patrol car.

A couple of years later, I ended up transferring to a new command closer to my home in the valley. Once again, I decided to take the sergeant's exam. The culture in the new command was nothing like the one I had experienced in Hayward. For starters, there was no back row seating for me as I had zero seniority. As a matter of fact, among some 65 officers, I was right next to the K9s (police dogs) in seniority. The top two rows of officers literally had snow white hair and looked like they were from an old 1950's movie. Additionally, there were only two other female officers in the command - one was pregnant and the other was an acquisition from a merger with another state agency.

Shortly after I arrived, two more females joined the command. However, it was still an uphill battle to prove my own womanly value in the mostly male "old school" and "good ole boy" office. While inconspicuously battling their power plays, I was also trying to learn my new environment. Patrolling in my last command was a cake walk compared to the complexity of the calls in this mix of both rural and urban areas. The calls for service had you busy from the moment your shift started to often well beyond your 10-10 or sign-off time. The traffic collisions were more complex and chaotic with overturned big rigs, closed lanes and dead bodies. Pursuits were like hell on wheels. They often included speed racing on the freeways until sometimes literally wheels would come off and many times end with weapons being drawn.

Most of my calls in those early months after my transfer, I handled myself unless they became highly risky or dangerous. The sergeant would sometimes roll up to the scene, take a look around, bark a few commands, and then drive away. It sucked for quite a while until some of the senior officers began to appreciate my work ethic and gave me the "she's okay" nod. One night as I was getting off, one of the "white" hairs invited me to have a "soda" with the shift in the parking lot next door. I told him I didn't drink "soda" but he simply said, "You should come on over, it'll make a big difference." Hanging on to his offer, yet half wanting to balk at it, I went with him. My "soda" was literally a soda, but the impact of sharing that soda was far reaching. My calls now came with helping hands other than my own.

As I was trying to find my place in this vastly different sub-system, I still wanted to pass the sergeant's test. At that time, we had a relatively new sergeant in the office. He reminded me of Potsy from *Happy Days*. He was always smiling, friendly and wanting to be helpful to everyone. He had arrived having just been an instructor at the Academy so he was fresh on policy and working hard to remain on his own upward mobility track. He did try to put together a study group with a few of us, but he didn't seem to know exactly what it would take to make it successful or if he even had time for it. He seemed distracted with his own promotional track, and honestly, we weren't the easiest of students to help prepare. It was such a fractured study process. I could never really grasp or retain a lot of the information. However, I took the test again. And again, I did not pass. Not making the list by two tenths of a point was even more humiliating. Yes, back then, the scores came out in fractions of a fraction.

Through all of this, there was a learning point to be determined if one could just recognize it. In order to get better, to be better and to be better prepared, I would have to take a closer look at the process and try to determine where I was failing to grasp what was keeping me from being successful in it. The notice informing me of my examination failure provided me with a breakdown of my scores. My oral panel interview scores were better than my written scores, but noy by much.

As I reviewed the study material from the previous exam and the one I had just taken, I realized that I had buried myself in minutiae and had no proper organization for my study process. By deciding to structure my study activities more efficiently, I ended up creating an effective framework for my future success.

In addition to improving my study efficiency, I still had to go to work, be a wife and a mother. This experience was so overwhelming and disjointed that it left me with a feeling of incompetence and a lack of certainty about myself. Yet, the seed of wanting success and fulfillment had been planted and passing that test was my next step. I refused to be denied even if I was, at times, my own worst enemy. One Sunday, the pastor at the church that I was attending delivered a sermon entitled "A Slow Leak." I was half paying attention to his words as I tried to get my kids seated next to me. He started off talking about how there are slow, spiritual leaks in our Christian life. He continued, "You know you're leaking when you are too proud, too impulsive and without prayer." He used Biblical examples of Peter to demonstrate how these issues affect your relationship with God.

Impulsiveness made Peter try to get a head of God's plan and left him feeling distant and frustrated. The message explained how you must go through a three-step process of rebellion, repentance, and restoration to overcome this problem. As I listened to him speak, the hair rose on my tingling forearms and chills sent ripples through my body. Instead of tuning out, I leaned in mesmerized by his words as if he were speaking directly to me. There is no way he could have known my situation so it had to be God speaking to me through my pastor. "Our failures don't have to be final. God doesn't see you as you are but as you're going to be. So, when you are going through the trials, He is making you a better person. Better prepared for what He has in store for you."

I am a true believer in the concept that each of us can rise to our own level of expectation if we have someone who believes in us as much or more than we do in ourselves. The pastor was speaking words of vision and blessing. Those words were pushing my spirit to go further towards my destiny. The point of his sermon was how it would glorify God to be using my blessing to be a blessing. It was more than just about me and my inward desire to be promoted "just because" but more about how I could use the opportunity to do greater things for others.

The third time taking the test was no easier than the first two. My two children were both under 5 years old. My husband was working the swing shift for the local police department. I was taking classes at the local community college with the hope of acquiring my Associate of Arts degree. All of this while continuing to work the graveyard shift. Finding the time to attend classes was especially challenging since most colleges at that time simply did not have many online classes for general education requirements. As I fought these battles, a lot of resistance was rising up in me as well. The department didn't require a college degree and neither did the sergeant's promotion. I was in my early thirties, what did it matter and what if I failed? All these whispers and thoughts circled in my mind endlessly. Forcing myself, I registered for two classes a semester. Initially awkward because most of the students were a fraction of my age, I found myself, almost imperceptibly, starting to enjoy the classroom environment.

My favorite class was English 1A. The teacher was a 70s hipster cased in Berkeley professorial attire. He was very laid back, friendly and easy going with all of his students. One of his first assignments was to have us write about an experience that we'd had recently and to be creative, detailed, and descriptive in our work. It sounded interesting. It had been a long time since I had taken an English class but this class was fun. Just to be free to simply write something I enjoyed writing about versus the report writing or shorthand ticket writing that I'd been doing on the job was a new and exhilarating challenge. I chose to write about spending time with my mother and her love for playing bingo. It was a unique space to explore. As she got older, it tickled me to watch her get so excited about going to play bingo. The paper earned me a big, bright, red A with a circle around it. A few words followed as well, "You are a very gifted writer and I enjoyed reading your paper." Having anyone say I was good at anything in almost forever felt great. I like an "atta girl" occasionally - I really do.

Writing these papers challenged me both creatively and academically. One night in class, the teacher gifted me a book, *The Bluest Eye* by Toni Morrison. Unfamiliar with the book, I made a point to read it as soon as I could. I found the book to be a complex mix of racism, womanhood, personal and sexual feelings. There was such a richness to Ms. Morrison's language and a bold vision in her writing. Her pages, paragraphs and narrative drew me in. I saw myself in so many places in her story.

My English teacher told me that he found a great deal of talent in my writing and felt that the Morrison book would help me nurture and improve my writing skills. I'm not sure how much my writing ability has improved, but that act of kindness created a desire in me to want to write better and say more meaningful things in my work. That book still sits on my bookshelf as a reminder of all of those lost moments of my self-discovery when I wasn't sure where God would lead me. What I know now is that God was sifting something in me and ultimately cultivating a new me as I worked through my journey. God was teaching me both in the classroom and in my life. As a result, I was becoming more spiritually mature. I was finally able to begin using my heretofore unrealized leadership skills to find my place in both the CHP organization and the world.

As I began to embark on my third attempt at the sergeant's examination, I realized that working closer to home had its perks but it did not come without its challenges. Often, I'd end up working large scale incidents and as a result, my days would be extended because of the endless reports I would be stuck with writing. Trying to balance school and home life, I had to use every ounce of my spare time to study. The new approach I took was more organized, systematic, and consistent than the ones I had taken previously. Going back to school helped me to build better study habits and broaden my learning lens for information.

With my head up and refusing to take no from that darn exam again, I showed up and took the test. Many days later, I was at home washing clothes (such a good therapy for me) and hanging out with the kids. The phone rang and as I picked it up, "Hello…" a voice said. I heard my captain's voice on the line. My heart was suddenly in my throat as my peaceful laundering vibe had shifted to the fight or flight feelings.

His voice was rattling off words, none of which were filled with my results from the test. He made a few quips and then shared the names of people who had made the sergeant's list. After he mentioned the last name from our command that had made the list, he asked me how I was doing. I was silent. It was just me and him when he blurted out, "you're number 123!" I waited for the other shoe to drop, like him saying "but unfortunately the list was cut off at 122.99." But he didn't. The list stated that 125 people had passed the test and were now eligible for promotion. I was 123. I did it! I finally passed that test! Finally!

Passed the Test, Finally! What Now?

Again, my emotional pendulum swung from peaceful bliss, to extreme surprise and excitement, to the worry of what happens now. Everything associated with the promotional process was about choice, what opportunities would be available, which ones would be of interest to me. Now that I passed the exam, the next step was to be assigned. Being lower on the list meant there was a possibility that I might not even get an opportunity for promotion and, at best, my options would be limited and take a bit longer. Still I waited patiently. It took almost a year and a half but a divine opportunity finally came my way.

I had continued to work on the road in my valley command. I must admit that as I was waiting, I began to think that I might never get that promotion. As international speaker Jim Kwik says in his book *Limitless,* those "automatic negative thoughts" or "ANTS" began to surface.

Mr. Kwik's concepts always resonate with me because he not only acknowledges the existence of these negative thoughts but, in turn, shares methods to get beyond them and jump start your productivity, while unleashing your super brain power. "ANTs" are one of the primary game changers in shifting your positive mindset and momentum. And that's exactly what was happening to me at that time. The negative thoughts swept in and overpowered all the positive ones that I was experiencing.

One afternoon, my captain called me into his office. Nervous but unafraid, I went in to meet with him. I wasn't sure what I had done this time. I spoke first, "What's up, Captain? You're looking sharp in that uniform, Sir." Inside I was rolling my "eyes," as he always wore his uniform so snuggly. I mean, his uniform did fit tight across his arms and chest and even at his age, it was a bit much. Although he was nice and meant well, he also was a bit arrogant and strutted around the office like a peacock. I remember one day I saw him in his Wrangler jeans with a big silver belt buckle on the cowboy boots. I made a comment in passing, "Gee Captain, nice buckle," with a smirk on my face. He told me, "One day when you're a captain you can wear whatever you want." Oddly, that stuck and I surely did, but there were no belt buckles in my ensembles. On this particular day, he just smiled at me. I think he always thought of me as a bit of jokester. He motioned for me to have a seat and closed the door.

He began to ask me what my plans were regarding my promotion. I explained to him that I wasn't sure, but that once offers started to come in, I wanted to try to stay as close to home as possible. It might include a commute back over to the Bay Area, but I didn't want to move my family if I could avoid it. He asked me, "Well, have you ever thought about going to Sacramento?" Honestly, Sacramento would be ideal. It was only 40 minutes north of us and was a much better commute. The only reason I hadn't said it out loud was because you had to have seniority to get into the Sacramento commands or, at least, know someone who worked in that Division or at Headquarters. I knew nobody.

Calmly I said, "Sure, I'd love to work in Sac but it's impossible to get a position up there off the list." He smiled and said, "Well, impossible looks like it has become possible. You've been requested to put in for the Recruitment department. The catch is that they want you there next week." Before I could even measure my response, I blurted out, "I'm not going." There went that darn mouth of mine again, speaking before thinking. I had just had my second child and my husband was still doing shift work for the local police department. How in the world was I going to flip my family upside down in a week? I was also starting to feel really comfortable thinking I would have the time I needed to consider my options before accepting an offer. A disruption this jarring was not in my game plan. I was really drinking my own weird blend of Kool-Aid because with a state agency the size of ours. Over 11,000 employees, over 7,000 sworn members and around 700-800 sergeant positions all by seniority, the odds of my getting promoted any closer was just not going to happen.

The captain didn't flinch at my crazy response. Instead he said, "Listen, go home and talk about it with the hubby. Let me know what you think tomorrow. Remember, it's only a temporary assignment for 30 days. If you don't like it, you can always come back." Before I left his office, he also said, "By the way, when a commissioner asks for you, you don't say no." As He usually is in my life, this is how I know God was involved in this matter. Still being a bit naïve about executive leadership, I said, "Who is this Commissioner?" He smiled and answered, "Let's walk to the front lobby." So, I followed him to the front lobby, an area I'm never in because I always come through the back door of the office. He pointed to the four pictures on the wall the second picture from the top was of an African American man. He said, "This is the commissioner. He's the first African American to be Deputy Commissioner of the patrol." Baffled, I couldn't understand how he would even know about me. Unless you take a really close look, I'm so light that I pass for white most of the time. Surely, he must be thinking I'm darker than I really am because I'd never met the man. I thought I'm going to be a big disappointment. It seemed to me that the Recruitment department must be looking for someone who looks a lot blacker than I do, right?

Once again, the thoughts of not being "good" enough, those haunting insecurities, those "ANTS" were rising in me again. I was a bit sassy and indignant in my response saying, "There must be some other African American females that he could request." That was just my armor rising to protect myself from embarrassment and disappointment. Not backing down, he replied, "There might be, but he's asking for you specifically." I was beside myself because I had never met the Deputy Commissioner. Other than seeing his picture, I wouldn't have known who he was if he had walked into that building right then and there. What on earth will I be able to do in Recruitment?

What I discovered was that there was a divine intervention taking place. It turns out that a friend of my girlfriend, my old graveyard partner, who I had met at a dinner one night worked at headquarters with the Deputy Commissioner. This friend of a friend had mentioned to the Deputy Commissioner that I was working in my field command and was on the sergeant's promotion list. There are no coincidences - absolutely none. So, I took my sassy self on a 30-day temporary assignment as a sergeant. Why not? Sometimes we just need to walk into our wins, go with the flow, and stop trying to justify them.

Coordinating the details of my new commute, my husband and I had to work out a plan to navigate childcare for our kids that didn't interfere with either of our work schedules. Once we were able to do that, I was off to Sacramento. It was quite an experience going from working in the field for the last 10 years and now, all of sudden, working in an office, in a real office building, not a patrol car. The people were very friendly, and though I was feeling like a fish out of water, it didn't scare me into going back home. As I later found out, the current sergeant in the Recruitment unit was planning on transferring to southern California in a few months and her position would become vacant. It turned out that it wasn't as easy a transition as it appeared to be and my 30-day temporary assignment ended up lasting 6 months. I was eventually promoted into her spot about 10 months later. Ultimately those 10 months extended into 4 years.

What a 30,000-foot View Can Do...

My world was forever changed, again. This opportunity elevated my growing visual horizon beyond anything that I could have ever imagined. I was assigned to a headquarters position where I coordinated all the department's statewide recruitment and community outreach. Did I say all? Yes, the entire organization which spans across the entire state of California and over 100 commands. I was working with all levels of personnel from officers to chiefs and commissioners. I was involved in developing strategic planning and innovative ways to broaden recruitment and community outreach efforts. It included managing programs and grants with millions of dollars in funding, allocating resources to commands throughout the state, and providing training and vision on a scale that I could never have imagined. I don't know if anything as unique as this could have ever been planned. In this position, I worked directly for the chiefs which normally you would have at least two other ranks in between. The two star chief in the division was a stern but fair older white man in his late 50s. I always appreciated the autonomy he gave me and how he gave space for people of color. We had a diverse team and he always supported my program development ideas to try new ways of doing business. Wow, what an eye opening moment it was. My limited view in the field would have encumbered me from reaching any of the potential that God would have for me. This experience changed my mindset from always saying no first to at least keeping an open mind to future opportunities.

One of the most noticeable observations from my new 30,000-foot view was how all of us were in separate silos throughout the organization. In this statewide coordination role, I was able to see a much clearer view of the challenges that lie ahead in trying to diversify the CHP workforce both externally and internally. Never really having a large scope of understanding or even really caring about one, the sudden realization of these things was quite striking. Although I met and saw more people of color than I ever had previously, I still was not prepared to find out that, at that time, there were less than 23 African American women in the entire 7000 plus ranks of our organization.

My old graveyard partner from Hayward had always referred to any African American officer as a "unicorn." I'd laugh because I got it, but yet, I had no idea the level of scarcity. I really didn't get it. In my new position, when I'd see another "unicorn," I'd scurry so fast to go meet them that it probably scared them a little. Most of the time, I was really just making sure they were real and not a mirage. Reaching out to my fellow African Americans allowed me to connect and create relationships that I could use to encourage, to mentor or be mentored, or to just simply be kind.

The mantle of breathing life into our efforts to be more inclusive in recruitment and succession was a large and exciting responsibility. It was an amazing assignment. We did some wonderful work building bridges into the community and creating better pathways for diversified recruitment. One highlight of which I was extremely proud was establishing and holding the first annual Black History Month Open House for the CHP. It was a strategy to build trust, communication, and partnerships with communities of color by inviting faith based and other community leaders, along with young adults to the Academy for a day.

The agenda for the day included a tour of the academy in Sacramento, a luncheon, hear from the commissioners directly and have an opportunity to network with their local executive chiefs and staff. It was always such a powerful day. Members of the department were so proud, they cried, and couldn't stop saying, "In my time I never thought I'd see anything like this." The theme colors of the day were black, red, green, yellow, blue and gold. It was a regal, polished, and classy event. It felt like a big step toward dismantling the armor of military rigidity in which the department had often been veiled. However, there were many people disturbed by the audacity of such an event. Their negative response became the only real down-side to what was going to be an annual event to being the only event. I really don't know if those people just weren't concerned about equity for the non-white cultures involved or that they were just systemically racist.

The disparity in how the CHP organization was structured both internally and externally did not reflect the racial makeup of the communities it was serving. At one point, I became overwhelmed by the responsibility. I quickly remembered that God had aligned this situation perfectly. I now believed He was planning to use me to build new pathways. Pathways that could help to develop understanding that, in turn, could help lead to upward mobility for the diverse population already in the organization and for all of those to come. He showed me that it starts with planting seeds of hope and vision for those within the organization and for those outside of it as well. And just as important, was being able to provide aid and support to those who were just beginning their journey of discovery and recognition in a tough and racially fractured world.

On one of several occasions, my recruitment team and I had the opportunity to go over and speak with the female cadets at the Academy. Even though this sounds like a relatively minor event, we had to overcome some big hurdles regarding EEO perceptions. My being there in my role as a sergeant, along with the other team members, was saying 'Come on in' to the female and African American cadets. However, most of the women's concerns were about how to get through the Academy as women. In the group, there was an African American female who was a little bit older than most of the cadets and had gracefully just met the age requirement threshold. Although, she had a great deal of experience in life and other career paths, she needed encouragement that would remind her of her power, promise and capacity to be able to make it through the Academy and beyond. She and I had spoken several times over the months while she was at the Academy. Today, many years later, she is one of my best spiritual, soul sisters in Christ and was recently promoted to lieutenant. Our journey together is one that would need more space to tell, but suffice to say that she is a testimony to perseverance and commitment in succeeding and claiming your just victories.

There is nothing wrong with women helping women within an organization. Nor is it wrong for us to advocate for help and support and to both, individually and collectively, stand for something so valuable. We must not allow the excuse of regulations and "optics" to ruin the richness and importance of mentorship.

This assignment was a pivotal point in defining the future of my pathway to executive leadership. Here I was learning how to create new statewide programs, developing recruitment "firsts" and expanding the scope of women in the CHP. I was tasked with not only statewide programmatic responsibility, but developing both innovative leaders and new technologies, while building a network of associates that I would be able to draw from over the course of my career.

During my time in this assignment, I was also starting to get a lesson in political positioning and in understanding its global implication on desired outcomes. Politics is a dirty word. Back then, the thought of politics evoked uneasiness in the pit of my stomach and choked my spirit. But I knew that I had to either learn to navigate the political landscape or be overwhelmed by it. I decided to keep pushing forward

- always advocating for change, in our management, in our people and within our purpose for bringing diversity to the CHP. Often, I would be met with lackluster support from a management team somewhere in the state that didn't see the priorities the same. I began to grow frustrated with the stone walling and was often reminded of my position as "just" a sergeant. Yet, they had given me all of this responsibility. How could I do a good job and not take these issues seriously?

There were several people who would "flit" in and out of my professional life attempting to give me guidance. More often than not, their attention was critically divided as they were concerned about building their own careers. I didn't take it personally. After all, we weren't really friends. Yet, it did bother me to see these folks, mostly men, regardless of their race, brought into the circle of trust, all the while women were not. There was a specific moment when I witnessed a female two-star chief go to the commissioner's office for a meeting. As one of her staff, I accompanied her in case specifics were needed on the subject matter. When we got to the third floor office, the secretary waved her to go on in, "He's just shooting the breeze." As we approached the doorway, you could see the commissioner, an older white male in his very late fifties lean back in his chair. He began to laugh with another white male chief who was sitting across from him. She crested the doorway with a greeting and smile. The commissioner, without even acknowledging her or even turning his head, tersely said, "Wait outside until I call you in." She stopped short in her stride and didn't say a word. We went and sat outside his office until we were called. I was seething inside and I'm sure she was too. But she never let me or anyone else know how she felt. When we were called in about 30 minutes later, she handled the business at hand without skipping a beat. It was a moment in which I learned the strength that was needed as a woman in order to survive in a male dominated world at a management level. Here I was thinking about how to thrive when survival was still a thing.

However, to this point and prior to taking the lieutenant's test, I had not had any formal mentoring relationships. I had known certain people here and there who would help me to expand my capacity to do more and be more. Mentoring isn't one single act. Mentoring is continuous engagement and giving someone the platform, knowledge, experience, and encouragement to help them succeed. Thankfully, many women and men are willing to offer some nuggets of wisdom and "real talk" about how to navigate the work and management landscape. My favorite nugget was constantly being told to "balance my field time with my administrative time." Though it was on my mind, no one was specifically suggesting that I take the lieutenant's examination. After four years of headquarters' politics, I was in need of some balance. I was tired of having to smile outwardly while suffering through comic book imagery of explosions in my head every time someone said something ridiculous. It was then that I knew it was time to go back into the field. It was where I felt safe and comfortable. At least that's how I remembered it the last time I had been there. Fortunately, I was able to transfer back to Stockton, the Valley Command, which to me was home.

Reflecting on my promotion to headquarters, I never had to move my family or disrupt them like I had been as a young child. When I was young, my mother moved all of the time. I was a hot mess emotionally because of it. My mother and I would live in several different cities or sometimes different states within one school year. I was always trying to figure out how to balance being new, trying to fit in and yet, looking different. I just never wanted to do that to my kiddos. So, instead, I commuted over 45 minutes one way, each day. A small sacrifice for what I felt would keep my family sane, solvent and placated. It was just another area that God was revealing to me slowly.

Seeking Excellence is a Choice

Once returning close to home again, I gave serious thought to not attempting to get promoted again. I kept thinking about the pain of studying, the pinch of previous test failures, the struggle to commute and all of the politics involved. I was getting comfortable with the absence of a lengthy commute, getting into the routine of the work (if there ever really is one with policing), and still not feeling as though I was being constantly stretched to my limit. Yet, I still felt an occasional tug at my spirit. One Sunday, my pastor was preaching a Bible topic about not living our lives in mediocrity, but to always seek excellence in everything that we do. The teaching was from the Charles Swindoll book, *Living Above the Level of Mediocrity, A Commitment to Excellence.* In covering this material, he mentioned this statement, "But in the small corners of life, in those areas of service that will never be newsworthy or gain us any recognition, we must hammer out the meaning of obedience." That statement stood out as it wasn't from the literature designated for Bible study but from another book, *Money, Sex, and Power* by Richard Foster.

The correlation was to get our attention focused on those things that we prioritize as important in our lives and how we often live just above mediocrity in the process of achieving them. He went on to say that living for service, we somehow, often settle for mediocrity and all that is the consequence of those actions. The rest of the sermon continued to resonate with me and my spirit. In the final comments he shared, "Never take your cues from the crowd. You have the God-given drive because you have God-given dreams. What are your hopes, your dreams? Why are you trusting God? Make sure that the kind of dreaming you do results in character building - the kind that cultivates God's righteousness. And if you advance confidently in the direction of your dreams and endeavor to live the life that you imagined, you will meet with a success unexpected in common hours." These final thoughts were a beautifully crafted statement sourced from both Henry David Thoreau and my pastor who, on that day, made a lasting impression on my spirit.

Carrying that sermon around with me helped in my transition back to the graveyard shifts in Stockton. Although I had worked it not that long ago, it was nothing like I expected. As a supervisor, it was much different. I had a responsibility to others, to the organization, and to the people that my officers would be in contact with on a nightly basis. Remembering my experience as an officer there, with my picture next to the K9 on the picture board, was both humbling and yet empowering. As I sat in the sergeant's office, I was now a peer with those who used to supervise me, however fairly or unfairly. Having almost eleven years as an officer before being promoted to sergeant, it took a minute for me to get acclimated to the "road" again. Initially, it felt like I was almost brand new to the position, which in many ways, I guess I was.

Many of my officers were new at working the "yard," but there were some who had worked with me as partner officers. Finding my inner voice of confidence and competence helped me to generate an outer voice that was able to demonstrate leadership to my all male shifts. Some of the officers were my age; some were younger. Many were older with a great deal more service time than I had. I'm sure you can remember those moments in your life when you experience a maturation point or growth spurt both in leadership and in life. This time back in the field and on the road, was for me, one of those moments. As an officer, I had several experiences that involved incidents with pursuits, foot chases, physically wrestling with someone in custody, multi-death collisions and harrowing near miss hits by vehicles, while working a traffic scene or writing a ticket. You name it, I had experienced it. Supervising them was an entirely different ball game. In the area office, we were often short staffed, or staffed just enough that I would often have to pair up with one of my officers and be their partner for the evening. If I wasn't paired up with them, I rode solo throughout the shift.

The city of Stockton sits within San Joaquin County and the County covers over 1,400 square miles. According to the US Census Bureau, it has an estimated population of over 700,000 citizens. It is an enormous area of jurisdictional coverage for the Stockton command. For clarifying of authority, the CHP covers all county and state roadways and those roads within unincorporated portions of the cities within the Stockton jurisdiction. Although there was some outside allied agency support, which was greatly appreciated, it was the sheer amount of geography to be covered on a graveyard shift with such minimal resources that kept most nights extremely busy. Some nights, responding to a fatal collision 20 miles out east and then having to get to a freeway closure on the west side would take over 20-30 minutes to get from call to call.

In one month, we experienced six multiple fatal collision scenes with several involving children or teenagers. We had four officer involved incidents where officers under my command were involved in physical altercations that resulted in injury, motor vehicle collisions with injury or shootings with suspects. Even though these incidents all happened in just one month, most of the months that followed mimicked one another over the next couple of years. The things that I was now responding to and handling had become sort of routine or at least I had to make myself feel like they were. I mean, when I would check in with my officers to see how they were doing on a shift after some of these incidents, they'd always say, "We're good, Sarg. Thanks for checking. What else do you need us to do for this one?" We'd meet up later at the local early morning restaurant, the only one that would be open at 4 a.m. where we would have breakfast or a cup of java. It was mostly banter and frivolous conversation with no obvious residual effects from the events of the night before, or at least any they would let me see. It's our defense mechanism to armor up our emotions so we can keep pushing through each day and the next. Not realizing the damage cumulative trauma causes.

For me, I found that I was going home almost in a fog. I would arrive home just in time to get the kids up and get them ready for school. I would then walk them less than 500 yards to their elementary school, shower and get into bed. I would set my alarm to get up 30 minutes before they needed to be picked up from school. That would give me enough time so that I could tidy myself up and not look like a tired, crazy lady. They'd come home, we'd laugh, play, do a little homework and then I'd nap late in the evening before starting it all over again. Somewhere in the midst of these days, I found myself sitting alone on the couch unable to make even small decisions such as what to watch on TV. I would often just sit and watch sitcoms trying to get lost in the simplicity of their story lines. There was no death, sadness, chaos, or violence, just the sounds of Sheldon, Wolowitz, Kuthrapoli and Leonard, or some other cast of similar characters on another sitcom.

A small crack appeared in my armor when I was asked to be a statewide instructor for First Line Supervisors' class, instructing hundreds of new supervisors in the organization. Another instructor and I co-taught the 80-hour class on a myriad of subject matters. One of them happened to be on the human side of critical incidents and utilizing departmental resources through the Employee Assistance Program (EAP). As I was sharing the type of cumulative experiences that you could have, we referenced some situations from *Emotional Survival for Law Enforcement* by Kevin Gilmartin. In this book, the author talks about the "Hyper-vigilance Biological Rollercoaster" which he describes as being the day-to-day work cycle of high emotional elevation followed by detachment, social isolation and exhaustion at home all in the context of how it redefines life's daily patterns for many police officers. Within this scenario is something called the "Magic Chair" which for me happened to be a couch.

Mr. Gilmartin describes some of this in his book, "After returning from work as if by "magic," all of their blood instantly turns into lead. They can't talk; they can't answer even the most basic questions. All that they can do is sit in a vegetative state, usually situated in front of a TV." Reading this was a big "aha moment" for me. My emotions began streaming down my face as I shared how lost I had felt over the last several months. After having experienced all of the senseless death and near death incidents that had involved both me and my officers, I realized the burdening weight of being a supervisor. It had left me mentally and physically exhausted. I felt as though I was on autopilot which didn't leave much for me to muster up for my family. I thought perhaps that was all they really needed. After all, they weren't in danger or at least the danger of being directly or indirectly involved in policing. Or were they?

During this unarmored moment, I shared details of some of the recent incidents in which I had been involved. As I was sharing one incident in particular, the correlation of that incident to my emotional fragility dawned on me. A quick summary was as follows, the call came in late, around midnight, from a rural part of the county. My officers were just finishing up on another collision several miles away. I began responding as the 911 dispatcher indicated that it was a multiple fatal collision with the vehicle on fire. While traveling on the two-way road that would get me to the scene, visibility was decreasing due to light fog in the area. Fog is often an insidious veil in the valley during the winter months.

Arriving on the scene, I could see the fire department had already started putting out the fire as it appeared to be more smoke than flames. Just finding a good place to park was a challenge as the location was on a narrow road with ditches on both sides. As I walked up, I was briefed by fire personnel. The vehicle had apparently traveled off the road at a high rate of speed and broadsided one of the trees in the orchard before bursting into flames. What I was not prepared for were the details regarding the occupants of the vehicle, or what I was about to see as I walked down to the crash site. There had been four teenagers in the vehicle, probably 16-17 years old. The acrid smell of burnt flesh mingled with the smell of the burnt vehicle. The remains of the driver were only bones of the spine from the ribs down the rest had been burnt like molten lava into the rest of the ashy vehicle. One of the other bodies had burned in the backseat as well. The other two had been ejected, one across the backseat through the windshield and the other partially out of the passenger window. It was a horrifying incident, absolutely scarring.

As a sergeant, it was my responsibility to take photographs of the incident and to help my officers with the investigation. As I was sharing the story, it was the pain of the senseless loss of those young lives and the potential correlation to my own young son and daughter who would one day be that same age that haunted me. How does a parent recover from such devastation? While we go about dutifully doing our jobs on scene, how do we not shed a tear?

My vulnerability in the moment of sharing this incident with the students in this class forced me to exhale and also opened up a flood gate of interaction. It was apparent that many had been holding in their own experiences of trauma for years.

They needed what author and speaker Simon Sinek refers to in his book, *Leaders Eat Last,* a "circle of safety" so they could release their emotions and thoughts. They also needed a place that would not make them feel ashamed or weak for having these feelings. It was a way to help them channel their experiences into new leadership roles in a more positive and productive way. It felt good to feel the rush of energy as the weight of my armor was being laid aside. The even bigger revelation was the blessing of being able to empower others to acknowledge and share their own stories. I felt that this is what it feels like to allow God to use you. I was growing and discovering more each time I allowed myself to be seen.

God is Stirring Me

After experiencing this open and vulnerable moment while teaching and having just experienced a number of recent revelatory experiences, I felt as though I was in a much better space to keep pushing forward. I could have totally misinterpreted the pastor's message, but I truly felt like it was the first restorative call on my life to consider becoming a part of something bigger than myself. Reading Dr. Gilmartin's book and going through what I experienced during this teaching assignment, I realized perhaps just a taste of what the future may hold. However, He was not going to let me get comfortable. God was truly stirring my spirit. He was pushing me to strive to do more than I would have ever believed I could on my own. I was being pushed even beyond what my mother could have imagined for me. He was also shaking me up deep within my spirit in this internal battle for my soul. It sounds a bit dramatic, but all of the numbing darkness that had caused me to isolate and retreat was just part of this raging, spiritual warfare, just as it was when I was 22 years old sitting on my couch thinking about taking my own life.

Those years in Stockton felt like dog years, each year like seven anywhere else. Yet, it made you feel proud that you worked and survived in such a tough environment. All the while building your mettle and honing your skills. However, the years there also had a fraying effect on my soul. After returning to the field and having experienced all of what I had gone through as a sergeant, I realized that the lieutenant's examination process was forthcoming. I wasn't completely sure if I wanted to take on the beast of preparation again but there was a female lieutenant who was holding study groups in headquarters. I had met her a few times during my recruitment assignment. She was very energetic, like a tiny tidal wave of positivity and "can do" attitude. I wasn't sure if she would remember me, but I reached out to her via email and asked if I could attend her study group. These study groups had gotten rave reviews, but I thought you may need some secret handshake to participate.

She didn't hesitate and emailed me back exactly what the expectations were for the group. It was refreshing to see another woman willing to help other woman, because it just doesn't happen all the time. Jealousy (that ugly, green-eyed monster) still existed. But she was different. She was all about helping people - all people. Her study groups were very regimented. She taught you how to study and how to prepare. She differentiated between taking an exam and how you should develop as a leader. In order to attend the study group I had to commute 45 minutes each way twice a week for 10 weeks in preparation for the written exam and an additional 8 weeks for the oral panel interview. All of this while balancing children, school, work, and marriage. While none of it was going to be easy, I felt it was something that I had to do. It was a challenge, but I made it work, or at least it felt like it was working most days.

My days were much longer and it seemed like there was never enough time to sleep, so I never felt rested. My kids were so young. They were fun, but always busy. They always wanted attention, saying "Mommy, look at this. Mommy, look at me. Mommy, isn't this funny?" However, in those special moments, no matter how tired I was, they truly helped anchor my spirit. Children have a way of transporting us to a place we often take for granted. A place where we don't always realize that we need to spend time, but one that is absolutely necessary for a healthy mind and outlook. Harry Chapin's song "Cat's in the Cradle" rings in my head, and those missed moments you can never recapture.

During this time my husband was working a swing shift which meant we often didn't see each other very much. His day was filled with getting to the gym for several hours and then off to his shift where he often had to work overtime. Our lives were lived separately but together. When I'd look around the living room or in our photo albums, many of the pictures, at least the ones that were taken professionally, would be of the children or just me and the children. Unfortunately, we just got used to these cavernous spaces in our marriage. Over time we all settled into this new routine of work, study, family, and rest. It was a twisted priority list for me, but I convinced myself that it would all work itself out. There were a few times I almost stopped myself during the process, not really sure of why I was pursuing this next promotion. But I'd shake those feelings off, likening it to my getting those old feelings of self-doubt bubbling up again. Little did I realize that some of the most important shaping of our character takes place in those moments of doubt and self-deception.

Chapter 3

The 2nd Promotion ~ Lieutenant

All of the commuting to the study group and grinding it out in the weeks prior to the exam paid off. I only had to take the lieutenant's exam once. Thank God! The study group experience was spot on in keeping me disciplined and focused in my preparation. I had stored the process in the back of my mind and with some modifications as I went along, it became part of the solid framework for my future.

Placing at dead center on a list of 45 out of the hundreds who had taken the exam was an awesome feeling. It was especially so for me after having passed the sergeant's exam on my third try while still being near the bottom of the exam list on all three of my attempts. In this process, gaining a mentor, a solid mentor was also priceless. What she did for me and for so many others were to develop, mentor, and invest in people, personally and consistently.

Over the years, I mirrored her study group format and paid it forward to many others which, hopefully, planted seeds for them to do the same. In many cases, it only takes one person to make a difference. Living and working in this new space above mediocrity and striving for excellence was becoming more a part of who I was becoming and wanted to be. I was finding it to be a profoundly rewarding experience as well. I began to really see other people, my children, and my staff for who they really were. God was showing me that how He was blessing me was not just for the selfish me but for the selfless me.

Like the promotion to sergeant before it, the promotion to lieutenant was about timing and choosing the right assignment. It was going to be a tough decision, as the kids were a little older. Their father and I had been separated once or twice over the last several years, and it had been a disruptive time. Considering how the promotion list works which is from the top score to the bottom one in the first three ranks, I felt that I had time to consider whatever offers might be available or offered to me. As important to me was that I wanted to stay as close to home as possible. As a result, I decided to pass on many of the offers.

After a good amount of time had passed, I felt it was getting to the point that a decision would have to be made. So with the concurrence of my husband, I decided on a position in San Jose in the South Bay Area. It was exactly 81.1 miles one way from my home, not including the atrocious commuter traffic. However, it was going to be the best option. It was a good decision, right? Only I had to make the small sacrifice of driving 2-3 hours each day. The kids wouldn't be disrupted by having to move. My husband wouldn't have to commute or be inconvenienced.

This should work out, right? We invested in a newer small commuter car (with a stick shift of all things, it was cheaper) and off I went to my new lieutenant's command. I had my library of CDs from gospel music to favorite books to help cover the time in that little car. My husband put the CDs together for me which was thoughtful. On these commutes, I often wondered how I would get from point A to point B over 81 miles away.

Excited about the promotion, it was disheartening to discover undermining happening already. The new assignment I accepted was supposed to have gone to the current white male sergeant in the office who had been there forever. I say "supposed to" because that's what he and several other sergeants in the office thought should have happened. Well, not this time. In actuality, that's just not how the process works. It's really hard to rig the system for field promotions to anyone's advantage. That's one of the nice safeguards for fair promotional placements. Promotions really can't be withheld from you based on a single interview or "how you may fit" in a position. The promotion is strictly based on how well you scored on the exam and whether you put in for that particular opening. So, "like it or not," they got me. As the talk show host Wendy Williams would say, "How you doin?"

The captain of my new command was a big golfer. He and the other male lieutenant and sergeants would go golfing once a week. I was offered the opportunity to play golf in the larger fundraising tournaments, but not in their private outings where they'd drink and smoke cigars. I found it hard to try to make myself a part of this "good ole boy" system because basically, I wasn't part of it. Most of the time, I felt like I was on the outside looking in. It made me feel as though I was just a regular officer again walking the long hallways and being looked through rather than really being seen.

Another Divine Intervention

After a few weeks at this new post, the captain began to loosen up a bit around me. I want to think it was because he saw that I was competent and a hard worker. However, he never really let me know. The work wasn't too complicated and again, my time in the previous field commands had been great preparation for just about anything and everything. All commands are not created equal and even though it was busy, it was manageable. I learned a lot while I was there, but the commute was grueling.

After about three weeks, another divine intervention took place. A position for a lieutenant in the headquarters office opened up. Yes, a 45-minute commute versus my current two-hour commute was on the table. Feeling instantly excited to becoming quickly deflated is an interesting rollercoaster. It's the moment when that little voice inside you pricks your bubble of hope. Remember, "ANTS." Could I even put in for this position? Should I put in for it? I'd only been a lieutenant less than a month. What makes you think you can put in for something back at headquarters? Adding to that voice was the actual voice of my captain recommending that I stay in the field so that I could learn more. Figuring he knew best, I left it alone and kept doing my thing.

Out of the blue, an African American female sergeant, one of the few "unicorns" in place at the time, called me at the office. She started off casually checking in with me but then quickly jumped to how she was getting ready to interview for a lieutenant position. She was nervous and excited. Then without a pause, she told me that I should put in for the advertised position at headquarters. After I shared what my captain had recommended, she told me that the current assistant chief would really like me to consider the position. I asked, "Who is the assistant chief?"

The words that came out of her mouth left me stunned. You mean to tell me that my former "unicorn" sergeant who would bark at me to get my narrow ass here or there was now an assistant chief and asking me to put in for the headquarters' position? Let this be a reminder to everyone. Be obedient, be disciplined and be careful how you respond to and treat others. One day, one of them may be your saving grace!

After we talked a bit about the opportunity, I decided I would submit my application. Reflecting on this moment, I greatly appreciated my peer reaching out to me and not As shared in the book *Break Your Own Rules,* by authors Flynn, Heath & Holt. Unfortunately, this feeling of being threatened is a reality in promotional environments among many female colleagues and friends. Some experts assert that because the workplace is so male dominated, women often feel the need to compete against one another for the few opportunities that exist for them. This subsequently creates an atmosphere of jealousy and resentment. However, women need to remember this quote by former U.S. Secretary of State Madeleine Albright, *"There's a place in Hell reserved for women who don't help other women."*

The assistant chief that I'd be reaching out to had been one of only a handful of African American female sergeants in place when I had joined the CHP. She had moved through the ranks quickly. We only got to work for her briefly as she rose to the position of assistant chief before she retired. We absolutely loved her grit and gravitas. To this day, I am so grateful that the door had opened and I was wise enough to step through it. She and my peer sergeant who called me are conceptual models of two levels of group support as described in the book *Break Your Own Rules*. These two levels are needed so that women can support each other. The exact quote reads, *"If women are to ever pave a path to power, we must close ranks and stand together."* Standing together is simply about giving other women sincere moral support and genuine assistance: pulling for each other, networking, and lending each other a hand. Closing ranks is true solidarity: women promoting other women."

In my preparation for the interview, I would need to be vitally aware and be fully informed of the critical areas that would need problem solving. As importantly, I would have to be able to share with the interviewer what unique qualifications I would be bringing to the table and how I would best address these issues. I truly felt my understanding of the nuances along with the technical elements of these issues set me apart. Interviewing for the position was nerve wracking but I was able to draw upon my previous experience as a sergeant overseeing many of the same issues and programs.

During the interview, my responses and delivery were on point and focused on not only the policy and processes, but the people. While I may not have known all of the exact details in each of the issues discussed, I wanted the interviewer to know that I would be able to acknowledge and prioritize them based on their impact and importance. This was another defining experience in the development of my understanding of leadership and being able to demonstrate and implement it – proof that for me it was more than just a group of cool buzz words. Truly, who you are is how you will lead.

More and more, my authentic self was emerging and because I was allowing it to happen, doors were continuing to open. Even though I had only been in my new position of lieutenant for a few months, I was once again overseeing statewide programs for community outreach, grant management and development of new traffic safety programs. What was not mentioned when the opportunity for the assignment was shared with me was how I would be inheriting a very dysfunctional team. Most of the staff were not sworn police officers and that would be new for me after having been working in the field for the last several years.

Additionally, a couple of the supervisory positions were vacant. So it would be crucial that I hire the right people not only for the mission of our work, but for the mission of our people.

After spending many days peeling back the layers of staff, I discovered pain and disappointment in their not feeling valued. They didn't feel as though they were truly being seen or heard. Many others might have selected different people to come in and supervise the team, but I was seeking people who had a natural affinity for people, specifically, these people. They were broken personally and professionally.

A "Jerry McGuire" Moment

Over time, morale increased, productivity improved, and we galvanized as a unit. The team went from being ostracized and unrecognized to one that created some notable programs that received national recognition and awards. Instead of being just another unit on a sub-standard project log rife with missed due dates, failed attempts at satisfactory submissions, absenteeism, and lack of organization, they now felt like people who mattered. People who would finally be seen for their individual value and ability to make a contribution. As a result, they began to feel more confident of their place in the organization. They finally felt as though they had someone to mold them and champion them.

Holding them accountable while giving them flexibility to be innovative, I was all in for them. It's amazing what happens when we slow down enough to serve our own people as we work to support the outward mission of our organization. It makes me think of a moment in the *Jerry Maguire* movie when Jerry is accompanying his only client, Rod Tidwell. The only client he's able to retain after he was fired for distributing his mission statement. Tidwell had been feeling hurt and under-appreciated because he hadn't been getting any "love" from his Arizona Cardinals team or what he felt was proper media limelight. And then in a Monday Night Arizona home game, he plays a phenomenal game that gets his team into the playoffs. When he comes out of the locker room, instead of the media looking for other players and ignoring him as they had usually been doing, they were all waiting for him. Light bulbs were flashing, everyone is calling his name and he is finally experiencing the moment he'd been waiting for. Not to mention the fact that he may now have a chance to achieve his financial goals as well. As you remember at that point he yells out, *"Show me the money, Jerry!"*

During that moment, it is the personal connection he has with Jerry that is pivotal. Remember, Jerry Maguire's "breakthrough, not breakdown" is where he finds his heart for service and writes *"The Things We Think and Do Not Say: The Future of Our Business."* In an excerpt from that "mission statement" he wrote, "We are losing our battle with all that is personal and real about our business. Driving home, I think of what was not accomplished, instead of what was accomplished. The gnawing feeling continues. The feeling that families are sitting waiting for a call from us, waiting to hear a word on the contract, or a general manager's thoughts on an upcoming season. We are pushing numbers around, doing our best, but is there any real satisfaction in success without pride? Is there any real satisfaction in a success that exists only when we push the messiness of real human contact from our lives and minds?" Authentic personal connection with our employees resonates deeply, well beyond the constant hammering of performance metrics. Good leadership is a continuing delicate balance. I'd like to think that as result of these efforts, many of these staff members went on to be promoted and continue to be promoted throughout their careers.

Time for the Field Again

After a couple of years of working in these arenas of community outreach, marketing, and recruitment, I decided to transfer back to the Stockton office as the field operations lieutenant. My team gave me a very thoughtful and powerful departing gift. It was a beautiful plaque with the following inscription, *"The capacity to shape a vision of what can be achieved and to share the vision with others so that it becomes their own is one of the most important elements of leadership."* That moment was yet another defining one in my leadership growth and capacity to serve others.

The decision to transfer was my own. Sensing that I needed a change, I didn't want to become complacent. It was a tough transition leaving the healthy and thriving environment that we had created to once again go into an unknown space. Despite my knowledge, skills, and experience, I had only completed a couple of months in the field as a lieutenant. Nervous, excited, and a bit insecure were some of the feelings that were seeping their way into my thoughts. Stockton is well known for being at the top of many crime lists. The city is noted for violent crime, auto theft, and homelessness to name just a few. The work there had been challenging as an officer, a sergeant, and now I'm sure it would be as a lieutenant. Coming from being immersed in efforts to diversity our workforce, being back in Stockton came with a greater awareness of the scarcity of people of color within the CHP organization. Within the entire 130-person command, there were only a couple of African American officers, a few female officers and very few people of color in other civilian positions. Luckily for me, though we had only a few women in the uniform ranks, it turns out the captain was a female. She was soft spoken but carried a big stick. Her reputation for fairness and tough love was well known. I enjoyed working for her. She taught me a great deal in a short time. What I always appreciated about her was her ability to command a room without being loud or rank heavy. She was highly respected and good at her job. It was no wonder that she quickly was promoted to the rank of assistant chief and left our command. Once she had departed, my peer lieutenant and I shared the load of leading the command.

Being a woman in leadership, I always felt as though my every action, direction, or conversation was being monitored. Returning to Stockton was strange and awkward. I would be working with folks that I had previously served with as an officer, supervised as a sergeant, and now I would be back as their lieutenant while balancing commanding the office. The more opinionated sergeants would try to leverage their seniority and work around my direction. They would potentially be scoffing, stonewalling, or hoping that I'd give up, forget or just move on. Despite their attempts, I dug in. With the reasonable ones, I found that listening to their concerns, compromising on issues that were not too problematic and always explaining why we would be doing things differently if a change was necessary seemed to work best. For the old timers who didn't want to change, I found that simply holding them accountable to be better supervisors and to do their job took about 90% of my time. My tolerance was really low for the old BS and these "fossils" would often tell me, "Lieutenant, you don't have much of a poker face, do you?" Nope, not really.

Unicorn Times Three

My three years as the field operations' officer was much different than when I was a regular officer or a sergeant. I had matured, been exposed to more and understood this bigger umbrella of liability and my role in being a risk manager. The multitude of officer-involved, critical incidents during the three years that I was incident commander was extraordinary. It felt as though I was living a sequence from the movie *"Groundhog Day"* only amplified many times over.

I remember getting a phone call from another "unicorn," an absolute BOSS of a woman. She understood the weight of the work my partner and I would be doing until we were to get our next captain and she wanted to check in on me. In our conversation, she allowed me to vent and then she quickly reminded me, "That's all good, but remember to do your job." She gave me some useful tools to help streamline the commander duties. All of which helped me to focus on using my leadership skills to take care of people, to follow policy, and to be sure to ask for help when I needed it. As time passed, she always kept me focused with a call here and there along the way. She was modeling the way for me as we often hear in so many leadership books and I was paying attention.

Amid the day-to-day turmoil of the managing the command, the leadership team was continuing to evolve. We now needed not only a new captain, but also a new lieutenant. My fellow lieutenant and partner in handling the duties of captain would be transferring so he could be closer to home. I had enjoyed working with him. I had liked our banter and the way we had ended up sharing our co-captains' roles. Not long after, we finally found out who our new captain and lieutenant were going to be. What?!? Was it to be an African American female captain and lieutenant in the command? Yes! Three women "unicorns" leading a predominately white male law enforcement agency command. It just hadn't happened before, or at least, maybe only once before. It might have been the second time. Let me think...no, I don't really think so.

Let me just say, if we could have been a fly on the wall in any of the male locker rooms, I can only imagine what they might have been saying...LOL! There's always the chance they weren't saying anything, but boy, I know I was having a lot to say! Our new captain was a "Shut Your Mouth" and take care of your business type woman. She taught me the importance of being strong in my command presence and never being ashamed of being a woman in the role of leading men. Let me clarify what I mean by being ashamed of being a woman. Often women in policing feel we must be more masculine in order to be worthy of our leadership positions. In trying to achieve this, we often veil some of our natural feminine traits in order to be taken seriously. We talk tough, walk tough and well, even act like the "fellas" when we're hanging around them. She demonstrated, however, that you could adhere to the constructs of who you are as woman and still boldly stand in your own heels, or combat boots, all the same.

She was very straight forward and constructive in her criticism. She created opportunities for me outside of the command that helped me to broaden my knowledge, experience and exposure. All of which would help to make me more qualified for future promotions. She was awesome at pushing you to be better because she loved helping people. Because of her advocacy, I became part of the teaching cadre for the entire department. In addition, I was assigned to high level committees and was volunteered for special assignments. She made a point of creating ample opportunities for me to perform as acting commander whenever she was out of the office. These opportunities were preparing me and putting me in position for the next promotion.

When Life Throws You a Curve

What I didn't know was how my life was going to take some very devastating shifts. My mother died suddenly just as I was going through my divorce after an 18 year marriage. The phone rang one Friday morning as I was getting ready to leave for work. I almost didn't pick it up as I was rushing to avoid being late. Snatching the phone from the cradle on the fourth ring, the voice on the other end verified who I was by asking my name. "Is this Jonni?" "Yes," I replied. It was then I realized that she was calling from my mother's assisted living facility. She told me in a steady and detached voice, "Your mother is unresponsive and we've called the paramedics." I had several of these emergency calls before and usually she would be transported to the hospital for precautionary reasons. It had gotten to the point that the ambulance personnel knew her by name as wondered if many of those calls were for mere attention. These incidents would have me tossing the day upside down so I could be there and each time she would be just fine. So, my almost automatic response was, "Ok, what hospital are you taking her to?" She hesitated for a moment and then told me, "We are not transporting her because she is unresponsive and there are no vital signs. In response to my silence, she went on to say, "The coroner's office was called and they are here now." Though I heard the words, I could not really comprehend what she was saying. All I could mutter was that I would be there as soon as I could. My inner tremors were growing into an outer shakiness. I could hardly focus well enough to call any other number. I overheard my 16-year-old son getting dressed. Normally, he's not up that early in the morning. With a stoic look, I told him, "I need you to drive me to Grandma's while I call your father." He didn't hesitate, but I could tell he knew it wasn't good. Of course, he had heard me speaking earlier on the phone and as I began making other calls. I just remember in those moments, who do I call? What do I do? Yes, the lieutenant who usually knew exactly what to do, this time, did not know what to do.

In those first 20 minutes it was only God that kept me from completely crumbling. I could only think to call my soon to be ex-husband because the kids would need him. I was hoping he would be able to help me sort through what needed to be done. He was the first call, and after the clarifying questions, he said he would be on his way. I felt relieved.

My next call was to my captain. She quickly went into action assuring me she would take care of whatever my work responsibilities were for that day. She truly made me feel safe in that moment and that it would somehow be alright to be a broken woman, a broken daughter, and maybe, a broken human being. What I had not stopped to realize was that while I was going through the divorce process, I had buried a good many of my feelings. I had been attempting to channel all of my emotion into work and trying to parent my kids. Actually what I really had been doing was not placing my trust in God. Instead of leaning into Him, I was trying to control my own level of trust and doing things to occupy my pain. When this devastating call came, the very walls of "togetherness" I was outwardly displaying began to crumble like a sandcastle struck by a harsh wave. My armor was disintegrating.

By the time I got to the assisted living facility, I was totally numb. I got inside and rounded the doorway into her room. I saw her lying facing the window with her back to the door. The blanket was pulled up to her shoulders and it appeared as if she was simply sleeping. I went over to touch her. Her body was rigid and cold, very cold. The flood of emotion and tears cannot be adequately described in mere words. The numbing pain and sense of loss that I was experiencing startled and scared me. I was audibly heaving and trying to catch my breath.

I had almost forgotten that I was in the presence of my son and some deputies. I recognized one of the deputies as we had just met while on duty the week before at a fatal traffic collision. He recognized me as well and gently explained what had occurred. My son was sitting silently nearby with a blank stare of shock and confusion. He had grown into a tall young man, standing over 6'3" and fit from being a three-sport athlete. Yet, when I looked over at him, I saw his little face smiling with his Grandma as a young boy. His father, an off-duty local police officer, knew the deputy and they briefly spoke at the doorway before he came all the way into the room. He walked over and I could tell he had been crying as he gave me a hug. His words and the strength of his presence were needed and appreciated. My son buried his head into his dad's broad shoulders and began to cry. His large frame seemed small as he let go of what he had been valiantly trying to hold back. It was as though he needed to be strong for me just long enough to get me there and then for someone else to help carry the weight. That someone was his dad.

The divorce had been hard on all of us. We had been married for over 18 years and had been together for 20 years. I could go into all of the reasons that the marriage failed. However, that would really be irrelevant to the focus of how God used our circumstance and situation to strengthen our resolve and through it all made us better people. Our relationship was not easy. It had been turbulent from the beginning. The shards of our journey were painful, but we had also found blessings along the way. Despite all that we had been through, in this moment of pain and suffering, we came together as a family. Our daughter, who was 12, was still at school. I had forgotten to make arrangements to have her picked up, so my husband drove our son home and went to get her.

In that immediate time alone, I found myself searching for what I could have done better as a daughter. We had just spent her birthday at the Red Lobster the week before. Still I was racked with guilt for having not called her recently because I had been so busy. Shortly after her death, I came across a card she had given me earlier in the month. It was a "just because" thank you card. It was stuck in one of my bible study journals. It read, *"Jonni, Thanks for being so sweet and loving. You've helped me so much and I do love you. You're such a good mommy to Emily and Sean and such a good person all around. You are my angel. Love Always, Mommy (Grandma for Emily & Sean) xxxxx."* If we can just be still long enough, God's beauty will speak to us in so many ways. I continue to occasionally come across this card. Just recently, I had been looking for something completely different and there it was still a source of love and comfort. On what would have been her 87th birthday, it spoke to me again quieting the underlying insecurities that occasionally resurface as I reflect on her.

As finishing up with the deputies, I was slowly moving from heavy tears to an off and on trickle. I truly didn't know what to do next. Then the phone rang. It was my captain. God was working once again. She was going to bring some food over to my house and was sending someone to pick me up and drive me wherever I needed to go. She didn't ask me many questions as that was not her style. Remember, she was about "the business" whatever that may be. I needed that. God knew what I would need before I ever knew I would need it. Around the same time, my girlfriend arrived. She was an administrative executive responsible for several care facilities. A few years prior she had helped me transition my mother from an out of state intensive care unit to this assisted living facility in town not far from me. During this dark time of mourning, she comforted and consoled me. She helped me navigate the paperwork involved and in dealing with the facility, the coroner, and the mortuary.

The days after that call were filled with so many emotions. My girlfriends, sisters and family came together and guided me through all that needed to be done as I felt like I was floating above all that was happening. I spoke at her funeral. I don't know how I did it, but I knew it was something that I had to do. It was important for my children to know what their grandmother meant to their mother and how she changed my life through her own. They adored her and she adored them. She had become someone different in her later years for her grandchildren, and me, than she had been during my childhood. She was not perfect, but she was my mother and you only have one mother.

It was hard for me to recalibrate for many months after her death. The divorce was final the following month. During all of this, I was broken inside. I would sit in my bathroom in the dark with the door shut, on the floor, crying into a towel. The same "towel" I had played with as a child while imagining my long, beautiful hair in my safe imaginary space. The towel was now suppressing my sobs of grief and loss of hope so that my children wouldn't hear me.

Gates of Change, Save Your Strength

During this time, I again began doubting who I was. Who was I supposed to become? Who did I even matter to in the world? What it took me a long time to notice was that God was undergirding me while I was at my lowest point. I was still managing to go to church with the kids. All of the church folk knew that my husband and I were divorced. At least I thought they did until a couple of people asked me, "So where's your other half?" The question took a while to register. I didn't want it to be awkward for me or them.

One particular Sunday, the pastor was preaching a message like any other Sunday. On this day, my heart must have been more open to what he was saying. I distinctly recall feeling that something was different from what I had been feeling. The message was on the "Gates of Change, Save Your Strength." It was a message about victory within the context of defeat. Save your strength for the real battles, the real relationships. He talked about new beginnings. We cannot change the beginning, but we can change the end. It was a reminder that we must forgive to have freedom. My freedom had been slow to return. I was trying to close the gates on so many fears. I was trying to overcome the fear of starting over and the fear of not having my mother's voice to ground me in reality. I was facing the fear and anxiety of running a household alone. All the while trying to forgive myself and my ex-husband for what we had wrought. Above all, I wanted to free myself to trust God through the process, the circumstance, not just in the outcomes.

As time passed, I decided to re-establish my footing both personally and professionally. The first time I took the captain's exam, I thought it would be like taking the lieutenant's exam. No one had ever said that it wouldn't be anything like that exam, no one. On my first attempt, I ended up in the fifth rank, the very last tier of eligible candidates for the list. I was furious with myself for not having paid more attention on how to prepare for this exam, an assessment center test. I thought I had this process down, never feeling as though I needed to ask for any real help. However, the old me was still waiting for someone to help me. I knew better, so I had to do better.

Not far removed from my mother's passing, the finality of the divorce, and trying to harness my new restorative process, I was feeling like I still managed everything pretty well. I was buried in running the command, reviewing and overseeing investigations along with responding to critical incidents. If that wasn't enough to keep every plate in my kitchen cabinet in the air, I decided to go back to school to get my bachelor's degree. Looking back, I must have been insane. I guess it depends on one's perspective. I realize now that my grieving process was all jacked up and this was my way of convincing myself that I was striving for excellence while still trying to work through my grief. Having this mindset often led me to over-compensate in both my work and my studies for something I was either, visibly or invisibly, lacking. I was exhausted but didn't know it. I just kept pushing myself. It also didn't help that I assumed that because I was doing the job of a captain that I would be able to pass the test for that position easily. Well, that approach didn't pan out so well.

In addition and unbeknownst to me, the process had changed to an assessment center and thus, the dynamics were quite different. This is where I became aware that my network of associates must have some holes in it. You know the mentoring network that helps you fill the leadership and promotional gaps along your career arc, that one. This exam was like nothing I had ever experienced. I felt that old familiar feeling of complete failure. Especially when all of the folks in the command are cheering you on and constantly telling you that you're going to do great. Ugh! I was feeling that old familiar pinch.

When God Shakes You Up

For a hot minute, I threw my own pity party. After which I realized I needed to overcome the bigger issues of my own fears and unhealthy defaults during a crisis. As a result of my fear of failure, I would temporarily forget my faith. This fear had me acting like someone other than myself. It was reducing me to less than I felt that I was called to be. I found myself becoming bitter. I was complaining because I saw those less than mediocre guys making the list, again. I was still in the field working myself into the ground, pouting, "Why not me?" But just like that, God shook me. He silenced my nonsense when I received a call out of the blue from an assistant commissioner.

I probably should give context to this call so you can glean the full capacity of God's grace. At this point in my career, I was one of three African American females among several hundred lieutenants throughout the state. The assistant commissioner who called me was a first in many ways for the department. I had crossed her path several times when I was in my headquarters' position or during training. She was so impressive, sharp, and extremely kind. Her phone call was brief, but it was powerful. She did not commiserate with me about my position on the promotional list but simply asked me, "Have you ever thought about going to a class to learn about how the assessment centers work?" I replied, "Well, no." She shared with me that there was one upcoming in Sacramento and emailed me the information to sign up for it. She said, "I think it will be really helpful to you." The phone conversation ended with her reassuring me that my opportunity would come but I needed to do some work in the meantime.

In the midst of my fear and anxiety, He had sent me a reminder of His promise. Not His promise about the testing and promotional processes, but how He will never leave me or forsake me. Trusting God needs to be ongoing and intentional. It would be the only way that I could get through this journey of discovery in my profession, and in my personal life. It was the only way that I would be able to find my way through the hills and valleys in front of me. Considering the recommendation from the assistant commissioner, I signed up for the class.

The class was held in old Sacramento on a dinner boat on the river. Yeah, kind of weird, but true. The riverboat is a popular attraction for tourists visiting Old Sacramento Historic District and was definitely an interesting place to hold the training seminar. The riverboat was originally built in 1927 and had been restored for entertainment, lodging and nightlife purposes. The inside of the boat smelled old and dank but had a converted dining area and meeting rooms. The students at the seminar were mostly all white males. Many were my peers but a number of them had several more years as a lieutenant than I did. Have you ever felt like a fish out of water? Well, I felt like a "unicorn" fish out of water which was really ironic as I sat there looking out at the Sacramento River through the riverboat's large fishbowl windows.

Nervously, I sat in the class feverishly taking notes. I was really just trying not to make any type of eye contact with the presenters. By the way, that never works. They still see you even if you feel like you're invisible. Like a honing beacon, I was called to come up to the front of the class to do a role play of what my response would be during a scenario in the assessment center. What happened as a result isn't as important as what I discovered. Hey, I know you're probably curious as to what happened, but it's my story. The big revelation was discovering the intense anxiety and insecurity that doing this role play brought me. My command presence and verbal responses were totally disrupted. My ability to string more than two sentences together without fumbling my words was completely lost. My heart was pounding so loud in my ears that I felt it was rattling the boat deck beneath my feet. Feeling anything but confident, my body language altered my physical command presence to the point that I didn't really have any. Standing in front of the class, I felt small and inadequate. The others in the class gave me that look of "It will be okay, we've all been there." As my internal spirit hung low, I tried to keep my outer spirit flawless. Never let them see you sweat or even glisten. It was such an unhealthy and dumb way of thinking.

Although the presenter had put me on the spot that day, God called me out of my shell. That one pivotal experience helped reshape my understanding of not only the testing process but how I needed to work to build my confidence in my own potential and capacity for success. He showed me that just doing the work was not necessarily acknowledging the additional work that I would need to do for my leadership acumen. The busyness of being in the "trenches" doesn't always give you a high visual horizon when you're focused on putting out daily fires instead of effectively managing priorities.

Additionally, working in the field is not necessarily always working by the letter of the law versus the spirit of the policy. We all know that we nuance things between the lines, not necessarily unethically or illegally, but just brushing beyond the line when it is needed. However, to achieve success in the examination process, I would need to know how to command the position I was seeking. I would need to understand the policy, the people and the processes and how they all interrelate. And perhaps more importantly, how my leadership lens should be sharpened to the point of being able to encompass it all and add my own unique perspective as well.

That moment, that day, it wasn't what others didn't see in me; it was what I couldn't see in myself. I replayed the moment in my head over and over. It made me think of how I was possibly creating an Upper Limit Problem (ULP) in myself through barriers from my past and current experiences. As author Gay Hendricks explains in his book *The Big Leap*. These ULPs are psychological barriers that come to fruition in the moment-to-moment interactions between a person and those around them which prevent that person from soaring beyond their self-imposed limitations. Mr. Hendricks' powerfully simple book is all about overcoming these barriers to success in your life. It explains how to develop a clear path to your true potential in spite of how the reality of our lives twists its very simplicity.

Each time I heard myself saying, "If they can do it, so can I." But what I needed to be saying was, "If God says I can do it, I can do it. But I have to do the work!" Not looking to the left or right but straight ahead towards elevating my own readiness through preparation for the next position. It was about working on me and not making any comparisons to anyone else, just me. It was also my first real tangible attempt to understand my career path and to be able to recognize the anxiety I had as a result of that understanding. It would be an anxiety that I would carry with me for the rest of my life.

What the training also revealed was the process of testing within an assessment center. It is an intricate web of correlating your work experience to your contemporary readiness demonstrated through your knowledge, skills, and abilities. It also discussed how the assessors would evaluate your actions by using a scoring matrix that incorporates decision making, interpersonal skills, communication, judgment, and leadership. What? I had no idea that all of this was part of the process. It's basically learning how these various facets combine to help you translate your individualized experience in conjunction with your acquired knowledge into positive action when having to respond to various scenarios and questions. I found it absolutely fascinating! It was fascinating to the point that I bought additional study material, examined it, researched it and applied it. I even stopped along the way to share it with a few other people that were lost in understanding this new testing paradigm. The funny thing, but not so funny thing, was that I would have never figured out these missing links without God's divine phone call - the call that came from that assistant commissioner, a truly inspiring woman. She was a pioneer who found her voice along the way and retired some years later as another first in our department. She was and is a rock star!

Chapter 4

The 3rd Promotion ~ Captain

Navigating the role of daily operations and understanding leadership is more than being engaged and balancing plates. It is balancing competing priorities while having a high visual horizon. Before I knew it, I took the captain's assessment center exam again and passed it. I was in rank 1. This might have been a good spot for me to drop the mic, but there is so much more to share. I was both humbled and pleased with my placement. My faith had been tested on both a large and small scale. Yet my personal growth throughout this process was the most amazing facet of it all. My pride and ego were reshaped and my capacity to see beyond myself was truly realigning. I had made myself believe that getting promoted was about having greater positive influence and continued ability to give back to others. However, in ways I had not understood, I was still moving forward to prove to others my own value and my own worth as both a woman and a black woman. And perhaps, most importantly, to prove it to that broken little girl who had stared into that mirror so many years ago.

The Promotional Acceptance Dance

One might think that if you test well and score in the first rank, that a promotion would be pretty quick and easy to obtain. However, that wasn't the case for me. A large state agency has a massive responsibility to create fair and consistent hiring practices. Therefore, there is a layered process involving several steps after an exam that include advertising vacant positions, interviewing eligible candidates, selecting a candidate for the position, and then offering that candidate the position.

The job bulletins for the available positions are usually worded in such a way so as to include other qualifications that allow for a sliding scale of selection criteria based on who is conducting the interview. The interviewers is where the slope can get slippery as they have great autonomy in deciding what candidates from the most recent promotional list they will interview - incumbents or new candidates.

It is an interesting dance. Unfortunately, I had to subject myself to several of these dances. After I had completed an interview, I would get the obligatory, cookie cutter phone call shortly thereafter. It would go something like this, "We just wanted to let you know that we did not select you for the position. You did a great job on your interview, but it was very competitive. You are going to get a spot soon so just keep doing the great work that you are doing." After I would get my internal monologue and emotions under control I would ask, "Is there any feedback you could give me that will help me do a better job on the next interview?" More often than not, they wouldn't provide me any feedback and would awkwardly try to get off the call as quickly as possible. I was in rank 1 but what did it really mean?

After being interviewed and rejected several times, I found myself shrinking inward again. I was outwardly becoming less engaged. I was still stable, but hope was fading. The days were long and the summers were blisteringly hot in the valley. There had been so many critical incidents that required my standing on the hot asphalt watching the heat waves rise from the ground. There were many days it was so hot the soles on the bottom of my combat boots literally melted. Some days I was physically drained, heavy, and exhausted. I started experiencing intense pain in my lower abdomen and heavy menstrual bleeding during my monthly cycles. Brushing it off, I kept up with the pace of the work. I tried to squeeze in a little rest when and where it was possible. On a day a couple of months later while I was in the bathroom getting ready for work, the pain gripped me so hard that it forced me to my knees. Not realizing what was happening, I curled up in a fetal position and rocked myself for several minutes hoping the pain would ease. Sweating profusely and still in agonizing pain, I crawled back to bed. I downed a couple of 600 mgs. Ibuprofen, and tried to fall asleep. When I woke up, my daughter was hovering over me asking if she should call her dad. With the recent timing of the divorce, I really didn't have any other emergency contacts to call. So I agreed.

After a grueling experience in the ER, the doctor recommended a hysterectomy. After researching the options and weighing the pros and cons, it was the best alternative for the medical condition diagnosed. I was only 40 years old but I knew I wasn't going to have any more children. Why would I when the two I had were pretty awesome. I think it was more about the loss of my womanhood, along with all of the other things I had lost that year. Additionally, I was just beginning to embark on the road of single parenthood. So, that, along with the possibility of dating again was a bit much to absorb. However, I decided not to fight it. The surgery was seamless and my stay in the hospital was only a few days. Recovery would take 6-8 weeks of healing for the stitches across my lower abdomen. No simple laparoscopy and pull it through a belly button for this one.

Luckily, with the help of a few of my girlfriends, my children, and my ex-husband, recovering at home was the rest that had been eluding me for months. It's funny how God will slow you down in ways you can't deny, at least not for long. The first couple of weeks were the hardest. Trying to push past the pain and trying to get comfortable sleeping were a challenge. It was tough just to stoop down to use the rest room all while trying to avoid any sudden cough or sneeze. In time, it eased and the system for taking my pain medication was rhythmically flowing.

One day during my recuperation as I was lying on the couch, the phone rang. I debated whether to answer it or not, but since I was awake, I picked up the call. The call was from the female mentor who had helped me through the lieutenant's examination process several years earlier. At that time, she had been a lieutenant. She was now an assistant chief in the Bay Area working for another female chief. Being slightly medicated from the prescription drugs I was taking, I hoped I was hearing her correctly when she asked me if I was interested in an open captain's position in the Hayward command.

Trying to sit up better on the couch and pay more attention, she asked again if I wanted to interview for this new position as the Hayward Area commander. The irony was that I had interviewed for her and the chief about a month previously for another Bay Area command position. It ultimately was given to an internal division incumbent captain. What was even more interesting was that she told me that I could choose not to re-interview and just let my last interview stand toward this new position. I was puzzled, or was I perhaps impaired from the medication? My inner voice was saying, "I didn't get the last position off that interview, so what the heck?" My outer voice responded, "Are you sure that my last interview will be sufficient especially since that position was offered to someone else? I wouldn't want to pass up an opportunity to re-interview and do a better job." In a way that was carefully worded, she let me know that my interview was more than sufficient the first time. Even more carefully, she explained that the incumbent who had interviewed was in good standing and they had moved him from the Hayward command to the new command, thus creating the new opening. Even though I was bit drowsy from the meds, I recognized the opportunity. I decided to take her up on the offer and let my previous interview stand.

I was very grateful to her. However, it still didn't make it any easier to navigate the web of positioning and politics, while giving the proper loyalty to the division, all that would positively favor your promotional ascent. Still, it was my turn. Not really knowing what to expect, once I was able to really wrap my head around the promotion, I was brought to tears. It was finally happening, the moment I'd been striving for the last three years, captain.

Making a Way

As I was clearing out my office to transition to my new captain's assignment in Hayward, I felt simultaneously excited and petrified. Yes, petrified. I would be commuting back to the Bay area which was almost two hours away. I was going to be overseeing an entire command of other people as the boss, the captain. Additionally, my youngest child would be starting high school that fall and my oldest would be a senior in high school. It was becoming almost too real and that old familiar fear of failing was looming in my thoughts. What mother decides to take a promotion two hours from home when her daughter is starting high school? The thought of failing as a mother and as a new captain was truly overwhelming.

My ex-husband lived thirty minutes away even though he worked in town for the local police department. Unfortunately, we had become one of the dreadful statistics for couples in law enforcement whose marriage ends in divorce. Some of our last conversations hadn't been all that pleasant. He had made it clear that he was not a fan of me continuing to get promoted. We were both hurting and that type of situation can provoke some unkind conversations. It had been an emotionally charged moment when he spewed those thoughts at me and I must admit they stung. As time passed, I believe he became proud of me and my accomplishments, he became much more supportive after the divorce.

Sometimes women who are in both a relationship and a leadership position have to weigh and consider situations that men simply do not. Women need the same support that we give our men when they aspire to do new assignments, move up the corporate ladder and require them to balance more responsibility at work. However, many women have to make these exceedingly difficult decisions alone.

I faintly remember the going away party that was held for me with some close friends and staff at a local restaurant. What I do have are very strong memories of my African American female captain being so incredibly proud of me and making me feel like I was really ready for this promotion. I needed that. Sometimes we want to live our lives without ever letting anyone see us sweat or show any weakness. I worked daily at keeping on my game face. It is nice when there are those that know you, see you and give you the opportunity to un-armor. Having mentors and supporters that encourage and check on you and who will have real talk with you is absolutely vital to your growth both as a woman and a leader in your profession.

I was looking forward to this new assignment where I would be working directly for another strong woman. My new assistant chief was a high-energy female. She spoke in rapid fire fashion. I often found myself breathless while trying to take notes on all of the suggestions, directions and requests she would rattle off. I thrived on her enthusiasm for people and her desire for all of us to excel at whatever we were doing. I was thankful for her mentorship when I was sergeant. It provided the opportunity for her to see something in me that made her want to advocate for me in this new opportunity. Everyone needs these types of connections. These are the opportunities that open doors, which I believe, God has placed in our lives well in advance, so that He can make a way for us even when we don't see one for ourselves.

Speaking of connections and making a way, I was wrestling with how I would get my daughter to school every day. I would be commuting and the high school she would be attending was almost 20 minutes from our house. Previously I had requested an interschool district transfer so she could have access to more coursework which would place her in a more constructive school environment. She had blossomed in her Gifted and Talented Education (GATE) middle school and now, I didn't want to douse the flame of her enthusiasm for learning. But the question remained, how do I get her to school and back home each day?

My son was starting his senior year of high school at a different school. His school was 20 minutes away in the opposite direction. He had early and late hours due to basketball and track practice – such are the rigors of varsity. There were some days he could manage to squeeze his sister in for a drop off or a pickup but not on most days. An open mouth does not get fed. Ask not, receive not is what I'd always been told. So, I decided to share my distress with some of my co-workers from my old command, my church family and family. By the grace of God, some of them volunteered to create a schedule for getting her to and from school. Thus, my daughter had that much needed ride to and from high school every single day during her freshman year - every day. The village it takes to raise a child is real. I had that village growing up and thankfully, so did my children.

My First Captain Command

My new command in Hayward was considered a training office, as over two thirds of the officers there had less than five years on the job. They were hard working and eager, but they were also very green and prone to mistakes. Greeted with a warm welcome by most, the first question at one of the shift briefings was, "Captain, we hear you live all the way in Stockton. So, how long will you be here?" I wasn't surprised but I didn't think I'd be put on the spot so quickly. Carefully wanting to demonstrate leadership and commitment to the command I responded, "Well, that's an honest question. When I accepted the offer to come here, I knew that I would have to give 110% and be all in to the task that's in front of all of us. I will uphold that commitment. I will share that my hope is to get closer to home after my year commitment because I have two children still in school. With that, just know that I'm here and present." Perhaps I could have told them that I planned to be there for a long time. But honestly, I had no plans for that and I believed that being transparent would create more trust and reciprocity in our relationship moving forward. At least, that's what my inner voice was saying to me.

The commute was a grinding one, as the Bay Area commute corridor hosts a number of super commuters. According to an Apartment List study, 3.5 million Americans are super commuters. Super commuters are those who spend at least three hours per day getting to and from work. The Bay Area and surrounding regions lead the nation with more than 120,000 people super commuting each day with Stockton topping the list at 11.2 percent of the workforce being super commuters. Here I was back in the thick of it, a freaking super commuter. This certainly was not on my dream list growing up or in the promotional fine print. However, there are sacrifices you must make that come with promoting and it becomes a choice you have to make. Most days were just what I thought they would be, but if there was any rain, it was horrible. Even three hours would have been much appreciated.

Overriding the grind was this surreal space in my spirit about being back in the very command where I was an officer almost 20 years earlier. It was the same command where the misogynist, racist, male officer wouldn't ride with me, the relic captain would look through me, and where my 'narrow ass' was put in check. It was the same command where seeds of inspiration had been planted during that captain ride along. And in the long hallway, my picture as a captain was now hanging on the same wall as both of those captains. Pretty cool, wouldn't you say?

From my history files from those decades ago, I drew upon the good things and those not so good with the hope that I could derive a blended leadership style that would work for me, and still allow me to be my authentic self. Some of those positive resonating things were: how to make the time to get to know your people; how to ensure never to walk down the hallway without speaking and acknowledging someone like the old school disconnected captain had done to me and so many others. Instead, I wanted to ask my officers about their family, and to encourage the staff to have a family recognition board to pin up pictures of the new babies being born. I thought it was important to send cards to both an officer and their spouse at a time when they were facing significant illness or loss in their family. I wanted to re-implement the captain ride-along program that I had so enjoyed as an officer. I will say, there was not as much resistance to these programs as there had been when I was an officer. In fact, everyone hustled when we were on our calls and easily chatted with me in between. I tried to embrace generational differences. I found that it was a great way to shatter the barriers of real or perceived issues with the "them" versus "us" mentality that management had often been implementing before I arrived. My consistent message was, "We are a team. I just have the responsibility of being accountable for everyone." In this broadening of my capacity to lead, I was learning more and more that my journey was less about me and more about Him and serving others. I realized that the thoughts in my first speech regarding being transparent with my plans displayed a certain shallowness on my part. I came to know that spending the time in the field, showing up, walking the walk, doing the work, would be the places where trust would ultimately be built.

Being situated in a large metropolitan area, traffic in my new command was always heavy. Yet most of the incidents were relatively easy to navigate as a captain. It was odd to say, but I was becoming a bit complacent as the command seemed to run itself. I knew that I hadn't planned to stay there longer than my year commitment. What I didn't know was how all of it would be disrupted.

One night as I was just getting home, I received a call letting me know that one of my officers had been involved in a shooting. However, the shooting was not in my Hayward office over 70 miles away, it was in another command only 30 minutes from my home. How was my officer involved in a shooting not in his command? A couple of months earlier, this officer had asked to speak with me regarding a request for a hardship transfer. His wife was severely ill with extensive treatment anticipated and they had small children. Currently, he lived in the Sacramento Area, and as a new officer, his assignment directly out of the Academy was to the Hayward command more than 70 miles from his home. He would have to wait to see where his seniority would carry him through the normal transfer process which could take months, sometimes even years to get back close to home. Our policies and procedures are very stringent regarding the criteria for granting a hardship transfer. Following the process required, we were denied his request for a transfer. Frustrated and understanding the strain it was putting on him, I was able to negotiate loaning him to the command closer to his home and family. During this time was when he was involved in this shooting and as a result was significantly injured. How quickly my feelings of complacency turned to crisis.

Having been quickly briefed that he had been shot by a suspect during a traffic stop and had been transported to the local hospital in the area, I hurried to get up there. Responding from home, I went to the scene of the incident first and then to the hospital. The hospital was close by and as I arrived, I saw that there were several patrol cars outside the emergency room entrance. Because the officer's local male captain was already there, the situation felt a bit awkward. I somehow was not really feeling like his captain. I asked the captain how he was doing. He updated me on his condition and the incident which made me feel a bit more at ease. However, I was still feeling displaced as I was out of my own area. However, it seemed as though everything was being handled which I greatly appreciated. While he was being treated, I waited in the lobby hoping that I would be able to speak to him before I had to leave.

As I was sitting there, I heard a voice call, "Captain, Captain!" I looked up and it was a young woman who was coming toward me. I didn't have my glasses on but as she got closer, she started to look more familiar. She said, "Why are you out here? I saw you pass the room and so did he. He wanted me to come and get you." It was my injured officer's wife. I went into the room and you know when you you make eye contact that all is going to be okay, he had that look and so did I. He shared with me how much our time riding along and working in the area meant to him and what I had done for his family. I had no idea that would bring me to tears on my ride home later that morning.

Once again I was forgetting that my God is bigger than my own mental giants. He spoke to me through my officer to remind me that I have no control. God is in control. My role as captain was less about my position and providing oversight at a scene or an incident, but about how I was demonstrating His love through my consistent, relational leadership. Empathy, emotional intelligence, or whatever training moniker is being used at the time, is really about understanding how to connect with people and then how to respond as a result. We don't often think of this as being an important characteristic of law enforcement leadership; but for me, it was my essence. It is what has helped me to find the purpose in my calling. Emotional intelligence is not just a key phrase. It's how we need to engage with life and with people, both in and out of the uniform.

Over that next year, to avoid the complacency that would set in as a result of being blessed with days of easy commanding, I sought out ways to broaden my knowledge. Luckily, my sector assistant chief was full of ideas. Before I knew it, I was back in the spin cycle, on committees, promotional panels, developing promotional examinations, speaking at conferences, and sitting in our division office as an acting assistant chief. Yes, all of this in just my first year as a captain. Do not tell me what God can't do! It was surreal how the exponential changes and progression in my career, as well as my spiritual maturation and as a leader took place so quickly. One minute I am wallowing in a pity party and in the next, I'm basking in unmerited favor.

From Your Heart of Experience

These were the moments where my leadership capabilities were really being refined, sifted and tapped into place almost without my awareness. One of the phrases that I share with others when mentoring or helping them develop their leadership capacities is that they should try to become the "Go to person." Why? It builds and supports you when you're in a blind spot. It strengthens your resolve. It broadens your leadership horizon, and by its very nature, it exposes you to other leadersn in a positive way. But perhaps most importantly, it makes you uncomfortable.

For me, one of those uncomfortable moments came as I was speaking at a women's conference. Now I had attended many women's conferences, but to be one of the panel speakers was a big deal. My anxiety was ramping up as I was mulling over what I wanted to share with the over 800 women in attendance. My remarks were to be loosely framed around the salient points that the conference committee had sent to all of the panel speakers. What I hadn't thought about was how the 90 minute time frame would be shared between the four panelists that also included questions and responses. It sounded like a lot of time, but it wasn't, especially for a group of women.

On the plane ride to the event, I bounced my thoughts off of two of my previous female captains who were with me. They listened intently and gave me great feedback, "That's great! But remember, if you run out of time, just speak from your heart of experience." What was my heart of experience? That comment stayed with me and I carefully placed it in a small notation on my talking points, "Speak from your heart of experience."

The room was empty when I arrived, but quickly began to bustle as people started filing in. Several people came up to the other panelists to say hello and gush over how awesome they were. My humble self still felt honored to be amongst them but I was feeling like I must be out of place here. As we were nearing the time to start, I heard someone call my name. At that moment my back was turned toward the audience. The panelist tables were on a stage elevated above the audience floor. As a result, there was a blind spot where I couldn't see who was calling out to me. As I peered into the crowd, I realized that it was the deputy commissioner and assistant commissioner (the 2nd and 3rd in command of the organization) who were there to give me support and wish me well. I suddenly realized that I was representing not just my own thoughts but those of the organization as well. I began to get a little anxious.

Introductions were easy and luckily, the other panelists were sharing their stories and responding to questions before I had to speak. As my nerves settled down, I began to listen to the stories of these women. Once again, this time was not about me. It was about me being exposed to other amazing women that have blazed a trail for so many of us. It was about their resilience and perseverance through adversity. I felt proud to be able to sit on the same panel with them. Like those that came up to greet us before we started, I too was gushing over them.

My moment snuck up on me unexpectedly as we didn't have an arranged order for taking the microphone. All the copious notes I had taken to prepare for responses faded on the note card except for the words "Speak from your heart of experience." I was completely redirected and reshaped during the moment. What I shared with whoever was listening was not of me.

> *"Remember that each individual journey is both individual and collective. Choosing how you journey is often the difficulty, but it is not supposed to be easy. In order to navigate the nuances of your adversity, you have to champion and challenge yourself. Often, I ask myself this question: What would I do if I weren't afraid? If they were not afraid, what would they do? It's a short question but I know that very question to myself is what gave me the veracity to keep pushing, keep moving and keep striving. Sometimes it is not about the real barriers that are that are created to keep us from opportunities. It is often the self-imposed ones. Mine has always been fear. Fear of failing. Fear of my shame. Fear of my brokenness. Fear of my imperfections. Fear of not being good enough. I ask each of you, what would you do if you weren't afraid?"*

In that moment, it felt as though I was free to speak my truths. After the moment, I was just praying that it was what was needed - not too much, but just enough.

As we were gathering our belongings to leave the panelists' area, several attendees started to gather. I started down the stairs and realized several women were turning from the table where I was standing, and coming to meet me at the staircase as I descended. There were so many sharing how they appreciated my words, the stories and my journey. They told me how they had felt many of these same emotions and had been stuck in their ability to shake free from those feelings. But because of my words today, they felt emboldened. Chills were running up my arms as I was embracing this moment with them. Someone then tapped me lightly on my shoulder from behind. It was my deputy commissioner. He was only the second African American male to hold that position in our over 80 year history at that time. He quietly and simply said, *"Great job Jonni - very impressive."* His smile and demeanor said more than his words.

Sara Ann & Johnny Lee

After that conference, I spent time searching for the reason that I always have these floods of anxiety, insecurity, and unworthiness when at a table of importance, in the seat of command or in a room with important people. I desperately wanted to know where those feelings came from and why. My investigatory process led me to my mother, Sara Ann and my father, Johnny Lee.

Childhood isn't always easy; we all have our stories. My mother grew up dirt poor. There were many things I never knew about her life until after she had died. I hardly knew my father at all. All I knew about him was from the lens of my own limited experience with him.

I really knew so little of my mother - just fragments really. Sara Ann was a tall woman with red hair, hazel eyes, and freckles. She didn't take much from anyone unless she had to. She had a fiery spirit brighter than her hair. I smile because I am her. As I've said earlier, our life together, for the most part, was a rollercoaster. However, she was the center of all that mattered to me, even when she wasn't at her best. I knew her life had been hard when she was growing up, though she never talked about her previous life with me.

Sometimes I feel like I never really knew my mother. But after she passed away, my understanding of her changed. Both of my aunts, her sisters, filled in some of my gaps of knowledge about her life during a trip we took to visit my Aunt Betty in Idaho. She was getting up in years, but when she spoke of Sara it was if my mother was right in the room. On one of the days during the visit, she got on the topic of something from the past. Immersing myself in the conversation, I wanted to hear more of what Aunt Betty was saying about momma. Others wanted to chime in, but there was something pressing me to hear it from my Aunt Betty. She and momma were the closest and momma's death really took its toll on her. Sometimes, I feel like when she talks to me, she hears my mother's voice. I know she thinks I look so much like her, especially when she was younger and I do. I imagine it's a double-edged moment to see a ghost and a gift at the same time.

On that day she shared with me how this woman, my mother, had lived an entirely full life before she gave birth to me. Born in Seagraves, Texas, in 1933, during the Great Depression and growing up during WWII, she grew up poor with five other siblings. Their white family lived in sharecroppers' quarters growing up in Leon Junction, Texas, located on the Leon River and sometimes called "the Junction," a site settled in the early 1880s. Aunt Betty described their poverty and momma's pain. She told me how she was beaten by her mother's husband because, as the second oldest, she would stand up to him and try to protect her younger siblings. *"He would always call your mom a freckle-necked bastard."* Her life was hard. There were the long days of working in the fields and lumps of coal were a real thing for them growing up. When my grandmother remarried, my mother and Aunt Betty had to go stay with their grandmother briefly and then lived in an apartment by themselves in their early teens. It was safer and easier for them as most of the older women in their lives didn't have much tolerance other than to take care of their husbands. This is where some of the animosity comes in between my two aunts and my mother. I wasn't overly interested in those sidebar stories, which probably hurt a feeling or two, but I just wanted to know more about Sara.

Sara got married at 18 to get out and away from her childhood life. Unbeknownst to her at the time, the new life would be filled with its own pain and suffering. Her husband was in the military and would serve all over the world including Germany. She would be the wife of a military officer and live a more lavish lifestyle with a beautiful home and elegant dinner parties. She was a model wife and mother of two boys. Pictures of her during this time leave me with my mouth gaped open as they were of a woman I never knew. I got to know this fiery, red haired, hazel eyed woman in an alternate universe as my mother. However, my version was a working registered nurse who was both a heroine and yet, a broken soul. Seldom would we be in our own home, but someone else's. Sometimes we would go long stretches when she would display a certain heroism and stability. But then we would suddenly be spiraling into her darkness and be standing in the welfare line for cheese and food stamps.

It finally all started to make sense when my aunt shared with me how momma, after her lavish life, just left it. She was tired of her husband's escapades and nude beaches with family and friends. After her divorce, she traveled around to be with all of her sisters, including her identical twin, Mary who lived in California. My Aunt Mary was later brutally murdered at the age of 33 leaving behind 10 or 11 children, that is still being sorted out. My mother was around 6 months pregnant with me at the time of Aunt Mary's death. The crushing pain of her death left my mother in a deep depression. My Aunt Betty describes an unusual obsession my mother had with wanting to know who had killed her sister. There was a belief that it was an ex-boyfriend but there was never any proof. Yet almost unbelievably, my mother took on her sister's persona and dated the man. She went on to say, "Jonni, it was so strange. I didn't know what to do about it, but your mom was in such a weird head space. You know there were times I think she might have had this disorder her whole life. Perhaps she had been bipolar all along but was never diagnosed. As she got older, she seemed to get more into drugs. You know the heavy stuff like meth. She was so lost and sad all of the time. She even told me that she was living Mary's life and had seen herself in the coffin." She shared that over the years Sara was never really able to shake Aunt Mary's death. It fervently rattled her to her bones for many, many years.

Fascinated with her stories, I was in disbelief as to who she was even talking about. I knew this woman who would work off and on. When she wasn't working and we were on government assistance, she would stop caring about how she looked and wore those big dresses called moo-moos as she laid on the couch watching television. I would be so embarrassed. She would leave her dentures in a cup on a side table so she could easily slip them in when company would come by, but she never did. She would sleep long hours and read endless newspapers, books, and magazines while continuously watching the news. She was an extremely intelligent and sharp woman. But when the rug was pulled out from under her, she retreated to an "I don't give a shit" place where she stayed for long periods of time.

My aunt loved my mother so deeply, they were best friends. Her sharing with me this side of Sara wasn't easy but she knew it was something I need to know. It all made sense as Aunt Betty continued, "Yeah, your mother never got many jobs when she was living around me. She always wanted to live with me so she could leave you with me and just go. I knew her temperament pretty well and she would cuss me out if I didn't do it her way. She was like that with pretty much everyone at that time." Well, that's the person I knew most of my childhood and young adult life, the one who would cuss you out. It was a weird mother-daughter love-hate relationship that she and I had. I silently surrendered to this relationship until it would suddenly explode into horrible arguments between us.

When I was around 13 years old, she and I were arguing in the hallway of a house where we were staying with her friends. We had a room in their home - literally, a room. She was refusing to let me leave the house and I was going regardless. To make it worse, we were both screaming at each other literally just inches away from each other's faces. She suddenly picked up a big hairbrush nearby and struck the door frame right beside my left ear just missing me by a hair. Shaken, this quickly silenced me. All of my big bad toughness had been eviscerated. Cowering back to the room that we shared, I realized that she had snapped. I hadn't seen that in her before. And I didn't want to see it again, at least not as a child. She apparently was capable of something that I had never imagined, and it scared me. Yes, I was familiar with this side of her anger, but this particular darkness hadn't surfaced with me in that exact violent way.

As a child, my shame was complex for me. My biracial identity had been fractured as I spent my formative years in Texas, Idaho, Arizona, North Dakota, and California. My mother wanted me and then she didn't want me. I had friends and then I didn't have friends. I had a father, or did I? It was a constant ping pong match of disappointment and abandonment issues all wrapped up in my freckled faced mixed-ish persona. As a child, all I ever wanted was to have time with my mother and to know my father. It didn't matter how many times he didn't make time to see me. Or how many times I would wait for him for hours by the window until my mom would say it was time for bed. I felt like a cliché. PWT or poor white trash, but just not white enough. Black, but just not black enough. From the ghetto, but not ghetto enough.

I met my father only a handful of times as a child, but those instances are so vivid. I remember waiting and peering out of the window in hopes of seeing him, though he seldom showed up. Occasionally my mother would drive me down to see him in his usual spot, a rundown bar out along Cottonwood Road in Bakersfield. The bar had a dusty screen door that you couldn't see through until you opened it. Once you opened the screen, you could see that the room was slightly smoky and you could hear jazz playing out of the juke box. Men were scattered about either sitting at the tables or at the bar jawing about something. They always had a cigarette and a clear glass with brown liquid just covering the bottom of the glass. I was always eager to see him. So when Mom would pull up to the curb and tell me, "Go on in. He's in there. Don't be long," I didn't hesitate.

He'd always be in the same corner of the bar toward the back. He was tall and slender with a short afro full of soft curls. He was beginning to show a receding hairline. His skin was the color of a Hershey's kiss with bright eyes and a big smile. And then there was the jewelry. He always wore a gold link chain along with a gold nugget, gold bracelets and several gold rings. One ring was of smoothly polished gold with a tiger's eye blue sapphire. He would usually be wearing a linen button up shirt, opened at the upper part of his chest with slacks and business casual shoes. He always smelled of cologne. His fingers were long and thin with well-manicured fingernails. We always knew when he was inside as his sapphire blue Cadillac with a white top would be parked outside. It was always clean with white wall tires.

This reflection of both of them seems so real and alive: Mom and her anger with those beautiful hazel eyes, the very ones she bestowed upon me and my dad with his cool persona and me trying to hold on to a few fleeting moments of his presence. I still to this day miss my mom so much. She was, and is, such a large part of my essence, my spirit. I miss not getting to know and not spending more time with my dad before he passed. I am grateful that he did get to begin building a relationship with my children- his grandchildren. It was not until he was dying that his wife allowed me to visit him at their house. I know why. I looked too much like Sara, the one that was a reminder of his infidelity with a white woman. He also had another child out of wedlock, a son, but he looked like my father, not my mother so he was allowed to visit.

When I had the chance to be invited to their home as an adult, he was bed ridden. He had a hospital bed in his living room. He had become so frail. Yet he still had on his jewelry and his rings. The years of sipping that brown liquor in the clear glass had caught up to his liver. Those last times with him were good for all of us. When he died, his wife invited me and my family to join her in the family limousine for the funeral. When we parted that day, she gave me a small envelope and gave me a hug. In the envelope was the smooth gold ring with the tiger's eye sapphire stone. She herself died not long after.

As a child, it was a hard task to try and figure out the fragments of my life when neither of my parents had any real capacity for parenting. Yet, many of these memories are moments of unbridled love in ways most will never understand and that I came to embrace way too late. It was an interesting childhood. In part, because of all the places I had lived and all of the people I had known. The one thing that I realized as a result of my reflective research was something that I already knew. Sara, my mother, was my "why" and my "because" even if it wasn't always the best.

Interestingly in Brene Brown's book *Rising Strong*, she was researching the idea of "are people doing their best." There is a point where Ms. Brown is sharing a situation with her therapist while she was traveling. The gist of the story was she didn't appreciate how the person she was rooming with was behaving and it pissed her off, my summation. Her therapist asked her, "Do you think it's possible that your roommate was doing the best she could that weekend?" Brene, incensed, "What do I think? I think this conversation is total crap." She didn't want to hear the therapist rationalization or offer the "data" on the reasoning. Later that day, she shared the therapist experience with her husband and what she had asked her. She asked her husband what he thought. After he gave it considerable thought, he said "I don't know. I really don't. All I know is that my life is better when I assume that people are doing their best. It keeps me out of judgment and lets me focus on what is, and not what should or could be." It resonated, Sara was doing her best.

Bakersfield to Texas

There was one summer prior to my 7th grade year, when my mother told me that we were moving from Bakersfield, California to Lewisville, Texas. At this point, we had already lived in Idaho, North Dakota, Arizona, three different times in Los Angeles, and then back to Bakersfield, California. But Texas? I could not imagine why on earth we would be moving to Texas until I learned it was because of my maternal grandmother. Her name was Pauline.

Even from the few times I had seen her, I never got the feeling that I was welcome around her. It didn't seem like she and my mom were very close since we never really visited. I had always imagined grandmas having a big cherubic grin and smelling like apple pie and cinnamon. There was none of that with her. She was a frail elderly white woman who wore a hair net on the back of her bun and small framed glasses that sat low on the bridge of her nose. I remember her apartment so clearly. It was small and the furniture was covered in plastic. There was a metal TV tray next to her "sitting" chair that had a few pill bottles and tissues. By the sound of her, you might think she sounds like your grandmother, the apple pie baking type. She just seemed to pick at my mother, and me, always pressing the obvious differences between us. She was white and her granddaughter was half black. She never seemed to want to understand or embrace our differences. Let's face it, I don't think she was very proud of my racial makeup. You might be able to hide it if it's never around, but when you bring the child with you to visit in Texas in the 70s , well then it's all out there for the world to see. Actually, my biracial attributes were mostly chameleon because I was very fair. But when it came to my hair, it was another story. There was no hiding those pony puffs on my head. I remember her fussing with my mom about "taming" my hair. Telling her "Sara, you need to do something with that hair of hers before we leave outta' here."

After that first visit, we didn't visit as often. When we did, there were never any lingering fantasies of apple pies or traditional grandmother to granddaughter exchanges. As far as my mother was concerned, I understood it to a point. She was raising a biracial child and wanted to bring her to Texas to visit her mother. The fact that my grandmother was either racist or at the very least, not acquiescing to her feelings for me must have had its own challenges for my mom. Having matured a bit before this particular visit, I understood her disappointment. Still, it felt deeply painful and unkind, and quite frankly, totally unacceptable. The experience only helped to further disrupt my own tenuous and disjointed feelings regarding my racial identity. But even more importantly, this was not going to be just a visit. We were going to be living in Texas and I was going to be attending a junior high school where virtually all of the students were white – a totally new school environment for me. It was one that I was pretty sure would be difficult for me to navigate.

My fears turned out to be well founded. I saw prejudice and racial discrimination by white kids my own age. I witnessed their meanness and their total absorption in their whiteness. It was almost beyond disturbing. I struggled to fit in. At 12 years old, I was fair skinned. I had freckles, brownish red hair, hazel eyes, and stood 5 feet, 10 inches tall. My nose was wide and my lips were a bit fuller than most everyone else. My hair was coarse and thick, and I had a kitchen at the nape of my neck that I knew nothing about managing, nor my mother. My whole experience fits so poetically with the insights of Beverly Daniel Tatum's national bestseller, *Why Are All the Black Kids Sitting Together in the Cafeteria?* where she recalled, "When we begin to consider who we are, it involves integrating our past, present, and future into a cohesive, unified sense of self. It is a complex task that begins in adolescence and continues for a lifetime. Our awareness of the complexity of our own identity develops over time. The salience of particular aspects of our identity varies at different moments in our lives." As a result of all of this, the self realization of my own identity fluctuated throughout my life.

If having this overly complicated relationship with the matriarch of my mother's family wasn't burdensome enough for both me and my mother, we lived a life with very little or no money. We had lived in the extra bedrooms of people's homes, or in small travel trailers in their backyards, even at the Salvation Army. When we moved to Texas this time around, we lived in a trailer park. The trailer park was in a rural part of town outside of Lewisville, Texas. The school bus would pull up between our trailer park and an adjoining one to pick up students. The trailer park was not an unfamiliar living arrangement for me, but in this situation it was extremely embarrassing, as I was one of a very few students being picked up there. It would give me a pit in my stomach every morning to walk those few short steps to board that bus.

Although, I was not the only one getting on the bus, I was the only one that looked like me. I desperately tried to wear a scarf to cover my hair. This was not a scarf wearing era in time. But I thought I could use it as a kind of invisibility cloak, similar to Harry Potter, and that it would just meld into the rest of my attire. I can see it even now. It was a vivid, multi-colored, silk scarf. I would try to wrap and wear it in a fashionable style that hopefully would look nice. Most of my hair would be tucked under it with bushy bangs hanging on one side. Try as I may, it never quite worked out the way I saw it in magazines. It didn't matter. As I walked down the aisle on the bus to get a seat, the bullies would pull it off my head anyway. All the while calling me either a pickaninny, a mutt, a zebra, or just ugly. Every day I had to ride that bus. As a result, I came to hate most of my time at that junior high school in Texas.

Later my research, and many therapy sessions, would reveal that a number of my feelings of unworthiness, insecurity and not fitting in were derived from instances such as these. They were the culmination of environmental, maternal, and personal circumstances beyond my control. Collectively they could be traumatizing and overwhelming. But I also realize now, as I work through this careful reassessment of my life, that it fostered resiliency – both in me and my mother.

Chapter 5

Leadership Efficacy

Almost forgetting that I was being interviewed, I had to check back in with my interviewer to make sure I wasn't just babbling. She quickly responded, "Absolutely not. Your story is captivating and you're actually sharing more than I thought to ask about. Please, keep going." Picking up on the query of whether I felt that I had accomplished all that had I wanted and had aspired to, I had to ruminate on it for a moment before answering. Of course, tied to my career desires and aspirations were also how I felt my leadership may have influenced others throughout my career. Being a bit hesitant on some of what I'd like to say and not wanting to over-generalize, I thought of this quote from Reif Larsen, an American author who wrote the book, *The Selected Works of T.S. Spivet,* "A map does not just chart, it unlocks and formulates meaning; it forms bridges between here and there, between disparate ideas that we did not know were previously connected."

This was my journey of dreams, achievements, and influences in a nutshell. I never could have crafted a planned or unplanned life like the one that I have lived. This gave me such a deep sense of appreciation of how God has truly guided my footsteps and how my life had been transformed over the years. This was true even as far back as when I was a child growing up in my imaginary space and dreaming of all things that I wanted to be when I grew up. Do you remember when you were a child and you would sometimes list all the things you wanted to be once you became an adult? I wanted to be a princess, a ballerina, a journalist, a teacher, a model, and a mother. Well, I got to be all of those things as I pursued my career in policing. I was able to be a journalist of sorts for the organization. While it wasn't quite as exotic as I had imagined, I had modeled briefly before going into law enforcement and then ended up being in many departmental recruitment campaigns, in videos, posters, and other materials. My most important career choice, of course, was becoming a mother. It was the most profound and most priceless of all of my choices.

As I reflected on my career as a leader in the organization, I recalled my opportunities to be a statewide instructor, to oversee statewide programs and to eventually contribute as a subject matter expert on the organization's promotional processes. After having done all of that, I had come to realize that I had been not only broadening my own knowledge base but positively influencing future leadership within the organization. It was a profound realization of the span of influence that you can gain as you move up in an organization.

As an instructor for my department, I had not only cultivated a rich learning environment but had also developed the potential for wholehearted leadership. I had initially thought that the instructor's task was just about teaching policy and procedures, but it quickly became apparent that it could be so much more than that alone. It could be an opportunity for these students to express their disappointment in leaders which allowed them to experience a form of internal procedural justice. Quite simply, procedural justice is often consider externally relative to fairness and processes as police officer come in contact with citizens. What I was unknowingly cultivating was space to be heard, be treated with dignity and respect and helping them find new ways to harness the power of those experiences so they could be better leaders. I felt that my students wanted to be sure that their people would be treated better than they had been treated and perhaps to learn to be able to mimic the behavior of those they admired. I loved being a teacher, while at the same time, being a learner.

Once during my assistant chief assessment interview (yes, I went for another rank which I will share more about later), this question was asked of me, "I see on your resume that you are a facilitator for first line supervisor's academy. Tell us why this has anything to do with becoming an assistant chief?" For a moment, I thought, "Crap, why did I put that on my resume?" Ugh! Then, as I slowed my mind down, I did some four-square tactical breathing and paused for a moment to process the question. I responded, "Leadership is being a continual learner in many capacities, and I learned along with the supervisors. Facilitating the future leadership of the organization takes courage and humility. Difficult conversations take place, challenging questions are asked, and important contemporary issues are addressed. As an assistant chief, or for that matter, at every level of the organization, we should never be too far removed from those who are closest to the work of our mission. All of us have to authentically lean into these moments and help our people to rise strong." Mic drop, for me! Not a peep out of them. But I'm pretty sure I saw a few heads nod in agreement. It's such an important reminder that as we receive our blessings, we have to learn how to give back just as much, if not more. We should always have a heart of service within our leadership makeup, and we should never be focused on just getting promoted and on our own careers, our people are always the priority.

My heart's desire to give back to others in the organization started when I saw the disparities in how and which people had access to preparation resources for the examination processes. While I was at headquarters in Sacramento, I became aware that there was a lot of information that wasn't being shared with the field personnel who were preparing to take the tests across the state. For example, there were numerous private study groups available. Many of which you would have to have an invitation in order to participate or you would have to "know" about the group in some way. They were usually never advertised or made available for everyone. If you somehow found out about a group and tried to join, you were probably too late to the game or were often just not allowed to join. If you were able to join, you were really fortunate. None of this was in violation of policy, but definitely was not aligned with principles of equity. What I felt was most confounding was this obligatory need to set one group of folks above another even in these small, informal groupings.

As a sergeant, I decided to create a study framework that would assist in developing ways to help line officers and civilian staff be more successful in their promotional readiness. Eventually, I was able to build upon that framework by adding very structured study sessions and workshops for each component of the examination process.

Over time, as I was promoted, these innovations evolved with me eventually integrating and encouraging additional ranks to take on leadership roles in developing and preparing our staff for promotions. It became the impetus for me to develop the *"Survival Guide" to Law Enforcement Promotional Preparation* so that current and future staff could have a launching pad in their preparation for promotion. One of the finer points of good leadership is to build the capacity and capability of your associates and subordinates all while nurturing each of them as they prosper and mature to do the same. As a leader, it is paramount to remember that what is most important is the growth and maturity of the people that you are leading.

My first opportunity to provide training and insight to middle managers and commanders was by participating in a panel discussion on employee death. I wasn't sure if I wanted to participate in this panel initially because the incident which qualified me for the discussion was relatively recent and profoundly heartbreaking. Once I was able to rise above my own thoughts and feelings, I began to think of how I might say something that could really be helpful in coping with the death of an employee while still assisting them in their decision making and leadership development.

I remember sitting at a rectangular table at the front of the room. The table had four chairs facing a group of about 25 new commanders. I knew most of them and for those that I didn't know, I had heard of them in some fashion or the other over the years. They had all been recently promoted within the previous six months and were looking to us as the more experienced captains for guidance and assistance in developing their leadership skills. My fellow panelists were other captains that I had grown up alongside in the organization and with whom I had felt relatively comfortable, at least, until this moment.

As I sat facing them, I was lost in the awareness that out of the 25 faces peering back at me, most of them were white males. There were no women and only a few faces of color. I, like any other person of color, takes note of the variances in my surroundings. I found myself recalibrating how I wanted to approach the discussion. I wanted what I had to say not to come off sounding too sensitive because I was a female commander, or too weak, or too incompetent, or too... not enough. My old inner self talk was sabotaging me internally, while externally it looked as though nothing was wrong.

Calming my inner monologue, I heard one of the panelists begin by mentioning the circumstances that had lead them to want to share with the group. He choked up and then began to slowly relive the incident that occurred in the line of duty death (LODD). What I found so surprising was that what he was feeling was what I was feeling regarding my own LODD incident - the pain, the weight and the isolation. It had nothing to do with our gender, our race, our anything. It was our humanity that was enveloping the room. This was a moment that required honesty with ourselves. It required that we look beyond the imaginary challenges and boundaries we place in front of ourselves that keep us from meeting or surpassing our own expectations and potential.

That moment made me realize that I'd been carrying my grief silently inside. It made me understand how inexplicably hard it was for me to heal if I couldn't allow myself to grieve. Healing often takes forgiveness. For me, forgiveness of myself and of those who had been so unkind and undermining to me was very difficult. Harder still was forgiveness for those intangible things that words alone can never adequately describe or quantify making it almost impossible for the wound to ever heal. C.S. Lewis, the famous British writer and theologian wrote, *"No one ever told me that grief felt so like fear."* Throughout my life, hiding myself whenever I was afraid was my default.

By sharing this experience of pain and surrender with this group of mostly male colleagues, I found myself being able to invoke the darkest hour of my career, a line of duty death of one of my officers. Recalling that moment and the days that followed stirred these scars on my soul. However, I realized that reflection on a difficult situation that is done with honor and grace helps us to never forget there is much that can be learned from the incidents. It provides us with the opportunity to remind those future commanders that we never know when our mental toughness will be tested. But within the moment, it is a determination to conquer and master a difficult situation that calls forth a very special kind of perseverance. We must have that kind of strength – a strength that will enable us to face our calling to lead with confidence, courage, and compassion.

The beauty of surrendering to the true understanding of your calling, your leadership ability and your journey, is when you walk with Christ as your center. He will restore you. He created such a tidal wave of release for me and helped me to truly navigate the discussion in a way that made it thoughtful and powerfully informative for the commanders. Several of the new commanders then shared their own experiences of losing a colleague during their career and the good and bad of how their commanders handled it. Many of them recounted incidents from years ago like they were yesterday. In that open forum, these law enforcement leaders were healing and broadening their own leadership capacity to serve others better. Months, and even years later, I would hear from some of them in the hope that I could somehow reassure them of their decisions, reaffirm their feelings, or just to be available to listen to their problem(s). The giving of ourselves is the hardest and yet, easiest part of our leadership development process.

Barriers: Seen and Unseen

Surfacing from this deep reflective moment, I pondered the next question from my interviewer: What did the barriers look like for me as I was pursuing my promotional advancement? Some I had already discussed in the telling of my story. Interestingly enough, many of the barriers that I had experienced were self-inflicted. If you remember, I had been carrying around a childhood of shame and insecurity – a kind of fractured acceptance of myself in my biracial identity with so many, too many broken truths. I wasn't sure where to begin.

As you may recall, when I was promoted to Captain in Hayward, I shared that my intent was not to stay indefinitely if an opportunity became available that would get me closer to home. I needed to be closer, as my daughter was starting high school that year and my son would be finishing his senior year in a different high school across town. My divorce had been a couple of years prior, along with the passing of my mother and I was tired of commuting and ready to be at home.

However, this is where God stepped in, again. I was offered an opportunity to transfer to another command. It wasn't a promotion, and it wasn't closer to home. The words regarding the offer were coming through but every fiber of my being was resisting any acknowledgement of actually hearing the request. I had heard that this particular command had a toxic culture and many difficult officers ruling the roost. I had no interest in leaving the great environment of my current command to jump into a pool of quicksand. However, the sequence of events went something like this. The division chief asked me if I would be interested in putting in for the area command located in Martinez, California. The command had been without a captain for months and was in dire need of leadership. I only knew what I'd heard, nothing more and nothing less. Honestly, I didn't care to know. So, I respectfully declined. I truly felt that my own personal priorities were aligned and that I was in a comfortable place with them. Sometimes, even with our bosses, we have to create expectations and boundaries.

Shortly after I declined, my assistant chief approached me at an event and told me that she had heard that I had declined the chief's offer. She was a bit on the short side, so she had to look up at me when she smiled and said, "You may want to just think about it." She had been a mentor of mine for several years and I had high regard for her advice. But, at that moment in my life, all I could think about was how badly I wanted to get back home. I was truly tired of driving so many hours a day, getting so little sleep, and missing so many moments with my children. So, I decided to pray on it for a few days, maybe even a week or so.

I prayed often during my long commute. God and I found plenty to talk about, laugh about, cry about and discern. One morning, I woke up and it suddenly become clear to me what I should do. Calling the assistant chief, I said "Good morning, I just wanted to let you know that I'll go. I'd like to make one request if it would be considered." She was clearly excited about the first part of my comments and said, "Sure, go ahead."

"As you know, I want to go home at some point, and I would like to be able to put in for only one command no matter how long I've been in the new command. That command would be the one back home in Stockton." She agreed and the deal was done. I never told her that my spirit was deeply stirred. It was almost as though I was being directed to be there from God. It felt like whatever the command needed was how ever he planned to use me, but for what, I didn't know.

The transition to the new command was seamless. At around the 6-month mark as I was working to unravel various situations in the new command, the Stockton area command advertised for a new captain. It was the ideal one, it would be going home. I checked again with my assistant chief and chief to see if I could apply for it and was given the green light to submit my interest. I was hopeful. I was so excited and just knew God was working this thing out. Well He was, just not necessarily the way I thought it would happen.

While I was waiting, I was going about my business taking care of my command. One day my clerical staff buzzed me on my desk line to let me know that there was a call from the assistant chief in the division where the Stockton command was located. This was the call I'd been waiting for. It was late in the afternoon and I had the blinds slightly closed to keep the glare off my computer screen, so it was a little darker than normal in the room. My voice was upbeat as I had been waiting on the call to either get an interview or to get a job offer. Always wait expectantly - that's biblical. The assistant chief started off with the perfunctory comments that he had received my email and resume. Yeah, yeah, and…and then, it happened. It happened in a way that left me almost ready to cry and rip his head off through the phone all at the same time. With an almost indignant tone, he proceeded to explain to me that because I had not been in the new command for the "required" year, I would not be eligible to apply for the Stockton command position.

Miraculously, I was somehow able to contain the little explosions going off in my head and ask him where that particular policy was written. He stuttered in his response, talked around my questions, and ended up telling me the chief in his division had made the decision. Oh, I see, the division chief was saying this. Well OK, then that must be the gospel. Probably I should have just "sucked it up buttercup," but I didn't. It just didn't sit well with me at all. Responding to him with a bit of determination I remarked, "Per policy, the approval for me to transfer

101

only needs the approval from my current chief, in concurrence with executive management on your selection. She has already given that, so I don't understand."

Well, that didn't go over very well with him at all. His tone shifted quickly, and he loudly retorted by reiterating what he had already said. He told me, "Well, she doesn't know policy and neither do you. The bottom line is that you are not eligible." So, with a steady voice, I concluded the phone call without further comment. I mean, he was following his male chief's direction, right? But he had allowed his own male ego to flare up in his loud, belittling tone. Due to my subordinate position, I was not in a strong position to effectively challenge him with the facts supported by "his chief's" policy at this time. Nevertheless, I was really angry. My face was flushed red and as soon as I got off the phone, the tears began streaming down my cheeks. Luckily, the door was closed so my sobs were muted. But the fury inside me was a firenado.

The reflection of this moment took me back to a year in Lewisville, Texas, not unlike the other. My mother had been in nursing for many years, and at this particular time she was working through a nursing registry looking for temporary placements as they became available. There was no real place for her to have me with her as she lived in a rented a room and was gone a great deal because of all the hours she worked, or at least that was how it was explained to me. She had met a lady (let's call her Karen, you'll see why) at one of her assignments that had a young family and lived in a suburb outside of Dallas. She decided to move me in with them. I have to really strain to remember her face or her family's faces. To be honest, I simply can't remember what they looked like specifically other than Karen reminded me of a small Barbie doll-type blonde lady, maybe a little over five feet tall. She had a slim build, a slight tan and a big smile. Her husband worked somewhere in the city. She had two children, a daughter who was a few years younger than me, and a son who was a year older than me. From the outside looking in, it might have seemed like a nice family arrangement - a sort of *Blind Side* moment of them taking in this young biracial girl that has nowhere to stay because her mother is too busy to take care of her. They had dinner together every night as a family unit and there was homework and chores as well. It wasn't long before I started subtly noticing how I was being treated differently when compared to how her children were being treated. The smile on Karen's face that I had seen at work faded when we were at the house. She would become a tiny bossy woman and it seemed like I was the only one handling the chores while her children were doing homework or going to events. I had been struggling to fit in at the junior high school that I was attending. And now on top of that, I was having to deal with this weird dynamic at "home" at the end of the day. My mother didn't have much time to come around and I would see her only at random intervals. I wasn't really sure why, but I assumed it was because of work.

One day, after we had finished eating, Karen told me to clean the table and wash the dishes. For some reason her husband wasn't home at the time, so it had been just her, the kids and me having dinner. I asked her, "Is anyone else going to help me? I have a lot of homework to do." I asked because her kids weren't doing anything and they never seemed to help with much of anything. She told me to mind my own business and do as she had told me. It wasn't an unfamiliar tone or attitude, but I had just gotten fed up with the very essence of what we call a modern day "Karen." The very gall of this woman to feel entitled to subjugate me into a form of modern day servitude to her family. Of course at the time, I was just enraged. I recall that this feeling rising up inside of me was something foreign to my 5'10, 150-pound frame. I was almost unable to contain it at that moment.

As I started to wash the dishes, it was almost as though I was on autopilot. Then suddenly, I just stopped. I felt the fury rising up in my face, turning it beet red. I turned to her and asked her to call my mother. In a nasty and snappy tone she said, "I haven't talked to your mother in weeks." In that instant, something clicked inside me. I decided that I didn't want to wash the dishes. As I tried to walk out of the kitchen, she yanked at my arm and grabbed it. It all happened so fast, yet I felt like I saw it all happening in slow motion.

I jerked away and looked down at her and said, "You'd better never lay another hand on me again." She doubled down and told me she was going to get a belt and give me a "whooping." Now, I don't know if I was fully aware of what I was saying or doing as I was still in the fury of the moment. I'm sure I was looking a bit wild eyed when I told her, "I dare you to hit me with that belt." It was the first time she'd shut that face of hers all day. She became strangely quiet, almost shrinking in her space. She instead told me to calm down and go to the bedroom until her husband got home. I remember it all so vividly, like I was reliving the moment.

Sitting on that bedroom floor crying, I was scared of what her husband might do to me when he came home because there's no telling what Karen will say I did. I was scared that my mother had not cared enough to check on me for so long a time. I was scared that this is where I was going to be stuck for God knows how long. I don't know how much time passed, but it seemed like I had been sitting there for an eternity when her husband came into the bedroom.

He had always been the nicest person in the family but he was also gone a lot, so I really didn't know what to expect from him. From a distance, he said, "I talked to your mother and she's not here in Texas anymore. She's in California." The sobbing I was doing silently became a howl, with uncontrollable breathing mixing with rage and then slumping sadness. My mind was racing on what his words meant for me. He stepped closer to me but still cautiously kept his distance. As I started to pace the room, I was like an unleashed animal. I just couldn't understand. When I had calmed down a little bit, he told me that mother had told him that she couldn't afford to come and get me right away. But he then told me that sometime over the next few days, he would buy a plane ticket for me so that I could fly out to her. Some of the anger and fear released from my body. I didn't hear anything else other than I was going to get out of there.

I remember nothing about the days between the incident and the flight or even anything about the flight itself. I just remember landing at LAX and walking from the plane into the crowd of people waiting to board or those waiting for arrivals. My mother was standing among the people waiting for those arriving, some distance away from the area where you actually exit the plane. She was wearing an odd, brown, suede jacket with fringe pieces on the sleeve and she had on moccasins as well. Why was she dressed this way? There was a gray-haired white guy standing nearby with a similar look and it was easy to see that they were together. I wanted to be angry but I wasn't, at least not right then. At that moment on that night, I didn't care about why she was in Los Angeles. I didn't care why she was dressed like a hippie hillbilly with this guy or even why she left me. I was just really glad to see her and finally be able to be with her.

It's crazy how you can compartmentalize events from your childhood, even some of the trauma, but then have them manifest themselves in so many ways later in your life. Looking back on experiences like these, you can really begin to understand how they've impacted you. While I had been familiar with this transient lifestyle we had led for most of my youth, this time it had been different. I couldn't sweep this one under the emotional carpet. This time, she had left me alone. It quickly changed my attitude and it dramatically changed my persona - all during the summer before my 9th grade year as we headed back to Bakersfield, California.

That little girl who had fought back so many times was still fighting now as a Captain in the CHP. Throughout these experiences, there were moments that I could have easily created my own psychological barriers that could have blocked my blessings. And as importantly, there were those barriers that were being imposed by the department's culture "practices" that actually did block my way or at least were attempting to block it. I could have conformed to them and allowed them to block my way, or fight back as best I could. There always seemed to be a certain amount of mental gymnastics going on as to when to fight the demons on the outside, or to flail away at the ones you carried on the inside. I fought back on all fronts whenever, wherever and however I could.

Chapter 6

Darkest Hour

My interviewer softly interrupted my story to mention her appreciation for my willingness to share such vulnerability. In a low voice she said, "These moments in your life had to be so hard." Acknowledging her with an almost inaudible sound, I pressed on with my story.

Picking up from where I left off, I recounted the call that I had with the assistant chief and that my next call was to my own assistant chief to let her know about that conversation while advising her that I wouldn't be getting an opportunity to interview. She listened and shared her disappointment with me. It was one of those moments when you feel like things just aren't fair and you wonder how is it that folks can get away with what they do without apparent repercussions. Is it their white male privilege or the fact that they simply feel that they are somehow entitled and is that in some way synonymous?

Within the hour, a call was transferred into my office. When I picked it up, I was surprised to hear the chief's voice on the phone. Not my chief, but the other chief, the one that was seemingly making up his own rules. He was not unfamiliar to me as I had worked for him personally as a sergeant at various times during my career. With as much respect and control as I could muster, I greeted him and asked how I could help him. He started with an apology. It was an apology regarding the way the information had been conveyed to me by the assistant chief. It felt a little strained, but it was an apology. There actually was no policy that precluded me from putting in for the Stockton command. The assistant chief had either made an error or just made it up. He went on to say that they had chosen another captain to fill that position. The one chosen was a white male who had more seniority in the division. I listened silently and after a while all I really heard was "blah blah blah" until I could sense he was trying to wrap up the call.

After I got off the phone, I realized that my small epiphany was that had I created a ripple in their simple plan of moving that particular white male commander out to the field to give him a "change of scenery." He had seniority but he really wasn't all that interested in working at that particular command, nor was he the best choice for it. Instead of taking on the part of the work that was important, such as addressing performance or attitude issues, this senior commander would be pushed off onto an entire command of people who deserved better. He just wasn't the right person. We hear this concept from the author Jim Collins in his book, *Good to Great,* "Those who build great organizations make sure they have the right people on the bus and the right people in the key seats before they figure out where to drive the bus." This didn't happen and that command of people deserved an engaged, wholehearted leader. It's the politics of this pattern of misguided decision making that cripples our ability to become individually and organizationally better.

To Everything There is a Season, and a Time to Every Purpose

After that experience, I had no idea what was going to come next. I mulled around in my own feelings for a while in a valley of waiting, while continuing to work almost two hours from home. I was learning that I had to be patient and wait on God's timing versus relying on my own. I would later realize that if I would have pursued life on my own timing, I may have missed the alignment of God's will for my life. This experience had been a clear moment where God was in control and had slammed that door, locked that window, and basically redirected my footsteps. But towards where? I had no idea, but God did. I always marvel at the power of prayer and how very specific we should be when we pray. It's only when we get personal with our prayer, that God uses that time and space to help us grow in more ways than you could have ever expected or imagined.

As I was reflecting, the door closing felt bitter in the moment, but it also made me focus on where I was and where I was supposed to be. I knew that the command wouldn't be easy. It challenged my perseverance, patience, and my ability to lead on many days. In the 80 plus year history of the organization, I was the first female captain and one of color in the history of that command. It was a very proud moment, but there were no parades or fanfare by anyone other than me and my family. My new command had been wrecked by the previous commander who had been an unethical nightmare. He corroded a segment of the officer population with his toxic leadership. There were employee misconduct issues, internal investigations, citizen complaints and dysfunction within the command. As I was briefed by the assistant chief on the command, the biggest concern outside of those I've already mentioned was the exorbitant amount of overtime that was being paid out each month. The dollar amount was so compelling because it overshadowed the next largest command in our division substantially.

The lieutenant who was left as the acting commander had a tough time trying to straighten out the situation. You can only do so much when you have so little real authority. The whole situation had gotten very messy. He was a nice enough guy, but the web of relationships that he created in the command was complex and being an "acting" commander is so very different than being the captain. I know, I had experienced it in Stockton. Additionally, senior officers were undermining his leadership and supervisors had been disrespecting and manipulating his authority. It seemed as though his ability to hold people accountable, address immediate issues and separate himself from his "friendships" was overridden by his need to be liked. This happens to us all at some point in our leadership. We battle finding a balance between being friendly or being a leader. Leadership is not easy, it's just required.

In order to be sensitive to those still in the command who were not involved in the disruption of professionalism, I will carefully try to describe the complex web this ineffective and self-serving previous captain had left in the wake of his departure. For obvious reasons, leadership should always transcend you or your feelings even when you become disgruntled or unhappy in your role. Those you lead still need wisdom and guidance, not advice laced with cynicism, and the personnel in the command deserve wholehearted selfless leaders. This won't happen if you don't allow those under your direction to be free from the strongholds and barriers that are a consequence of your own personal journey. Several of his subordinates were drawn to the chains of the commander's dysfunction and were loyal supporters.

When I arrived, I was immediately tasked with finding answers and solutions to the overtime budget, reducing the number of internal investigation of misconduct and citizen's complaints, and bringing back those employees who had been off duty as a result of work related injuries or illnesses. In addition to these priorities, there were workflow inefficiencies, resource allocation challenges, unmet key stakeholder relationships, and a power struggle between management and supervision.

To give a bit of context, when a command is in transition between two captain commanders, one of the current lieutenants will be appointed to serve as an interim acting commander until the new captain arrives. This lieutenant is given authority to handle daily operations as a commander with limited ability to make big decisions or take complex disciplinary actions without the approval of division executive management. At this time, the command had been under the oversight of an acting commander for more than six months due to administrative issues surrounding the previous commander's vacancy. The lieutenant who had taken on this role had a tough time trying to balance all of the competing priorities of an extremely busy command environment. In all fairness to him, it had to be awfully difficult to have a good leadership perspective when you're mired in the day to day operations amongst peers and staff that are your friends and who had just experienced such a difficult leadership vacuum.

My approach coming into this new environment was to observe and handle the immediate issues based on sound risk assessment analysis, coupled with the urgency dictated by the need for professional policing. With regard to personnel issues, I felt the best strategy would be to take the time to become familiar with the employees, review their past performance and allow myself time to develop a rapport and a relationship with each of them. This approach looked a lot better in my notes and thoughts than it did once I had arrived at the office on my first day.

While I still believe that I could employ some of those initial approaches, I had to make a hard pivot to moving from relationship building to a much more authoritative approach after receiving pressure from those in command above me. The expectancy of a swift response to their demands took me off guard. However, I had to remind myself that although I wasn't newly promoted, I was new to this command.

After the typical pleasantries around the office to introduce myself, I met with the acting commander, the ranking lieutenant in the office. We needed to have a heart-to-heart conversation about the operational issues of the command. Something I'm sure that he knew was coming since we'd spoken on the phone a few times before my physical arrival. Not new to counseling, but still new to commanding, I said to him very directly, "Supervisors need to be working and not all on vacation at the same time. I need you to make sure they are monitoring overtime which is hard to do if they're not here. At the same time, absenteeism is high because no one is being held accountable. Much of this stems from a lack of leadership and being unwilling to hold peoples' feet to the fire - until now." He sat back in his chair and looked at me wide-eyed. He then said, "Excuse me, but you have no idea what I've had to deal with while there has been no captain for months in this office. You come in here and tell me what's not right and then want me to snap to attention and get all these things done. I know there's a lot messed up here right now, but you have no idea what's going on." Initially, due to his condescending tone, I wanted to slay him verbally right where he sat. I wasn't sure if it was his white male elitism that had rubbed me wrong, or if he had simply lost his mind. But after giving myself a moment to reconsider, a better response dawned on me as the firmness of my own tone echoed. "I know this is not something I want to have to talk with you about on my first day either. And, you're right. It will take me a while to know the command and all that's going on. That's why I need for you to work with me as we resolve these issues. This is what I need to get done, and it's our responsibility to work on them with urgency. Is this something you can do?" He was silent and then surrendered to the moment agreeing to help me with the work at hand.

I didn't have the time I would need to build a deeply connected relationship of trust with my lieutenant, but I was able to plant a fewseeds for a future harvest. My initial approach had been short-sighted and too direct. It wasn't until I took the time to actively listen to him and thus gain some measure of confidence with him that he was able to muster the courage to share what he was feeling. It was a moment where I could have chosen to slay him or hear him. Fortunately for all concerned, I chose empathy over apathy. And under further consideration, would this have been a worthy hill to falter on, or should we move forward unified for the larger battles, many of which were to come with one that would be almost beyond comprehension. It would be important moving forward to have unified command leadership.

This is extremely important for the success of executive leadership teams. As their leader you must ask them to work together, to set aside any personal differences and to work to build trusting relationships both internally and externally. As the captain, I had to take the first step and set the tone.

I've found that success in leadership is not just built internally within ourselves. It is developed through the collective rumbling and reckoning of the many involved. I knew that it was God directing my steps as He did when I had been thrust into a similar situation as a lieutenant a few years prior. Preparation for this type of position comes in ways that we don't immediately recognize, but that was how God had been sifting me in those previous years when I felt like I was being swallowed whole. All of those years when I was an acting commander had helped me to stretch my boundaries and refine, strengthen and accelerate my growth spiritually, personally and professionally for this moment. I empathized with this lieutenant's circumstances but nevertheless, we were both going to have to dig in together and with the other lieutenant in the command start to implement some of these much needed measures. It took some time for us to get in sync enough to create a unified approach but eventually we were able to start moving the needle slightly.

Accepting this assignment was what I felt was my response to being obedient to God's pull on where I was being directed. It was also a way for me to demonstrate my commitment to the division by being a team player. I felt as though I was contributing in a much broader way while moving out of my comfort zone. As we seek opportunities to foster and develop our leadership abilities and develop a broader capacity to be agents of change, we must be willing to stretch ourselves beyond our own boundaries - to be uncomfortable, over and over and over again.

The Call You Never Want to Get

There was no way that anyone could have ever known what would happen that year. It is the very line in our oath that we swear to and pray will never happen, *"to lay down my life for another..."* I don't want to delve too deeply into this moment or the details of it because I want to respectfully honor the fallen officer, his family, friends and colleagues. What I will share is that having one of your officers killed in the line of duty (LODD) is something you can never prepare for, understand, or forget. There is a physiological, psychological, and spiritual impact on your entire being that is indescribable. The weight of a loss such as this was crushing for everyone. There were so many people who were broken, angry, sad, and hurting as a result of this intentional and violent murder of one our heroes. A surreal level of chaos and craziness descended on the command.

I remember that I was shaken so badly at the time that I found myself trying to be everywhere for everybody all at once. Yet it somehow never seemed to be enough. It has been said that mental toughness is acquired over time. Quoting anecdotally it goes something like this, "To be mentally tough means that risk is your best friend, innovation comes as second nature and that you have grown accustomed to anticipating crisis and managing change." This moment was one that I was not prepared for emotionally. It went beyond my comprehension of "how" to lead during a time of brokenness and despair. I've since discovered that my vulnerability was not weakness, it was actually courageous. Even now, there is not a day that goes by that I don't remember that unthinkable day and all of the dark days that followed.

Each day was about finding a way to not only keep myself moving forward, but to keep my officers and staff from being swallowed up in their sorrow and grief. The initial days were filled with pain, chaos and commotion. The officer's death prompted a flurry of activities among so many people and an excruciating sense of tormenting loss for everyone. In the midst of it all, the generosity and power of the human spirit seem to rise from the fabric of our entire command, organization, allied partners and the community – all of which left an indelible mark of gratitude on everyone that carried us day to day.

As the days moved closer to the funeral, my life was filled with planning and coordinating. I needed to ensure that the critical incident stress debriefings were held for my employees – all while balancing my own personal family life and finding time in the gaps for sleep. A lot of this time was spent with my officer's family helping them to get through the coordinating and planning of the funeral and all that goes with it for law enforcement personnel (LODDs). The level of logistics needed is incredible and begins from the moment the 11-99 radio call is broadcast that an officer needs assistance. Funeral planning is something that takes on a life of its own. It is a delicately sensitive coordination designed to keep the focus on the family and not the department's expectations or that of the governor's office. It was hard sitting in meetings and methodically going over protocols, policy, and the minor details needed to accommodate uniformed and legislative VIPs. Traveling to the church, running the route, going to the cemetery, and back again, I had to do whatever was needed to ensure a solemn and respectful funeral for the slain officer. The family's wishes were really all that mattered. To get me to those important moments, my specially self-assigned peer commanders, would chauffeur me to all of the meetings. Our daily routine also included a small but significant stop, McDonald's. At the end of an emotionally hard day, we'd stop at a McDonald's and share French fries and they would have milkshakes. We'd just sit, exhale and see each other in our exhaustion, pain, and amazingly, in our strength. Those moments were priceless.

Allowing my armor to be momentarily set aside, both undergirded and unburdened me, or so I thought. I was grieving but yet didn't feel quite comfortable in it. I guess I felt this way because by being the face of leadership for the command I thought somehow I couldn't or shouldn't grieve - at least not so obviously.

During this time, I still had some members of the command attempting to undermine me which was making it even more difficult but all I could do was focus on pressing forward. Their arrows of hatefulness and blame were sticking, piercing and hitting my armor and trying their damndest to penetrate it. Even in the midst of all of this, I felt like God was drawing me closer to where He wanted me to be. I certainly didn't feel like I was anything special, and often my own staff challenged my leadership making me doubt my own worthiness to lead.

It was at that very quiet moment when the funeral and the reception were finally over that the weight and questions regarding the next steps I would need to take began to take shape in my mind. Whatever those next steps were, they would not be easy. Yet in the midst of literally cleaning up after the funeral reception, after the hundreds of uniformed officers that had come to honor our fallen officer, I observed a black male officer helping to pick up some trash from the tables. He had been in the office since the first day after the officer's death as a part of the employee safety and assistance team that responds to commands when there is a death or serious injury. This team is a great resource to help commanders navigate the overall response needed. I walked over and thanked him and asked how he was doing. He smiled and said, "Captain, I'm fine, but how are you doing?" I smiled back and really just silently let him know that I was okay. Changing the subject, I asked how long he'd been on the force and what his aspirations might be. He said he desired to promote. At this point, I felt that God gave me a wink to say remember your gifts and talents – here is someone who could use them and there are many others. So thankful for that small nudge and reminder to not worry about the next and the next whatever, but to be present in the moments. By being present, you can be a blessing, receive a blessing and it allows you to release the wheel a bit so God can take control. This officer is now a sergeant on the list to promote to lieutenant.

As the moments of the funeral had passed, disruption was still emanating from virtually everywhere in the command. Some of the officers were feeling broken. Some had resorted to just taking advantage of the moment to avoid work and unbelievably, some were getting into some type of misconduct. Underneath all of this was the insidious undercurrent of discontent toward my leadership fostered by the same loyal supporters of the previous commander.

Sitting in my office not too long after the funeral, one of the employee union representatives came to my office to speak with me. I was a bit guarded as these reps often come armed with attacks on either me personally or in response to the result or failure of what my lieutenants or supervisors may have done. Fatigued from the sting of the arrows I had been taking, I hesitantly allowed him to enter.

This particular rep was an officer I had known for over 20 years. He had been one of our new officers when I was working in Hayward as an officer. I hadn't been his field training officer (FTO) but he was still just a boot to me - even when he came to the office that day to speak with me. We always had a mutual respect for one another which is important in employee relations. He sat down and started off with asking me how I was doing. As we exchanged light banter back and forth, he got to the real reason he was there. As I already knew, he reminded me that many of the officers in the command were disenchanted with how I had been leading the command, my handling of the funeral, and a plethora of other miscellaneous complaints.

Looking over at him from behind my desk, I suddenly felt the weight of being completely worn out and exhausted from constantly having to deal with undermining people who simply spent more time creating drama than doing their jobs. He could see it on my face - I was fed up. It had been an uphill battle since the day I arrived, and now with the death of our officer, all the "ugly" was being laid out for full public view. One of the suggestions he tossed out was for me to allow a staff forum to come together so they could vent their concerns to me.

As he was explaining this, I was thinking to myself, how would this be different from any given training day commander's discussion? Or any better an opportunity for discussion than any briefing or staff meeting that I attended? With an inside cringe, I asked him, "What do you suggest?" He said, "How about an office barbeque?" At first it sounded too simple, but then, it seemed just simple enough. "It sounds fine with me. However, I have one disclaimer. This loss has been hard on all of us, not just the few that will team up to "vent." You need to convey to everyone that my expectation is that this will be done respectfully and with consideration for others and not just themselves. Understood?" "Understood." I trusted him. There was a caveat from the officers. They did not want anyone from division office management to attend. Now, usually, you always extend an invitation to your bosses to come by and maybe even address the troops. But in the interest of trying to heal the command and have more open dialogue, I asked management to give me this time with the staff alone, and they did.

The night before the barbeque, I had trouble sleeping. I wasn't sure of what I would say or what they would say. I was just trusting that God would steer me as I gave Him the wheel. However, I wasn't prepared emotionally for what happened. That morning they were gathering in the briefing room when I was summoned and told that everyone was ready. Accompanying me was one of my new lieutenants who brought along his note pad. I wanted to make sure that we captured each of their requests accurately so we could hopefully capture those things we needed to address that wouldn't be resolved in this meeting. I did not want to make this only a listening session as that would be just another reason for them to complain about not being heard. Thinking back, I'd wish that the notepad had been a shield.

As you enter the room from the hallway down from my office, the majority of folks are sitting with their backs to you. As I made my way to the front of the room, there was a feeling in the air that was palpable. I was dreading having to turn to face them. I did so without them knowing that inside I was already feeling beaten. As expected, the usual discontented culprits were in the room, towards the back, grouped together. Some of the area representatives and sergeants were present and everyone was dressed casually for the barbeque. There appeared to be about 25-30 employees in attendance out of the 130 that worked in the command. Many weren't in the room and were just milling about with the hope of remaining neutral – not really wanting to participate in this inquisition. I opened the discussion with how hard the last several weeks have been with the loss of our friend and co-worker. I reiterated the importance of balancing their mental health, family, and work. I encouraged them to seek help from the Employee Assistance Program (EAP) and to have conversations with their supervisors so everyone could work to implement those resources. I extended my gratitude for how well everyone came together to honor our hero and his family. At that point I began addressing the elephant in the room. I told those gathered, "This afternoon is an opportunity for all of you to share your concerns with me as brought forward by your area rep. It's important that we have this conversation so we can begin healing the command and moving forward - so that we might all get back to the work we need to be doing. I simply ask that you engage respectfully. With that, who would like to go first?"

If I was gambler, I would have raked in a lot of dough on who would have been the first to respond. The first respondent had been a thorn in my side from day one. He was very vocal about how I was changing things in the command and requiring more work of everyone. In truth, I was asking them to work a full day on training days and to be productive throughout their entire shift. It was an effort to hold them accountable and to get them to try and rise from their own mediocrity. I also very much wanted them to know that I would not be tolerating any "bad past practices" in the command. I was going to have to realign and adjust some of the beat staffing to create better coverage and reduce overtime. In actuality, this issue was truly at the heart of his and several others complaints.

Reflecting on my rearing as a young officer, I might have told them all to "suck it up buttercup," but I didn't. Instead, I gave him an unflinching look as he started off with, "I've been in this command for years (actually this officer barely had time on) and I've never had a captain come in and change so much so quickly. Basically, saying to all of us that we don't know what we're doing. You didn't even take time to ask us what we thought. Your leadership sucks and I can't believe you've been allowed to take away our beat structure and reduce our overtime. We've always been considered the black sheep of the division by management and we like it that way." He continued, "And how is it that two of our best officers have never been able to make the sergeant's list? Is it because division hates us that much? I know you've been cozying up to them - does that mean we'll always be the outcasts and never have a chance to promote? It's unfair how we're treated by division." The precision of how this white male officer conveyed his feelings that I basically sucked as a captain while juxtaposed as to how he was seemingly random with his other complaints left me a bit thrown off. The majority of the specific concerns were in place before I even arrived or they were ones that I had no control over. I had imagined that this discussion was going to be mostly about how the LODD was handled – all the way from the division involvement to the inner command issues. Some of that did come up, but it provided the undercurrent rather than the crux of the discussion.

I tried to respond as carefully as I could, acknowledging his concerns and harsh comments, but also asking the room for specifics on these feelings about division and the black sheep comment. I scanned the room and noticed one of the sergeants had on a tee shirt with a black sheep on it. That spoke volumes to me regarding a deeper supervisor and leadership issue that would need to be addressed at another time.

Many chimed in stating that they felt they had been overlooked for years by the division management. It was disconcerting to note the number of those that felt they hadn't received the proper recognition or consideration for promotions or assignments.

The "you're so lame" leadership arrows they were shooting at me pierced my inner armor, but not the outer. I responded as forthrightly as possible saying, "I'm sorry you feel that way. My intentions were not to come in and disrupt the command. However, I have spoken to each of you at briefings, on training days and in various meetings about the work we needed to do as a command. The lieutenants, sergeants and association representatives should have also been briefing you and working with you as we were making these changes. None of this has happened in a vacuum or overnight. It can be challenging when much of the disconnect comes from just basic resistance to change. Just because we don't want something to change, and do little or nothing to be a part of the process, doesn't mean that things won't change. I have been trying to make every effort over the last six months to be transparent, create communication and have a collaborative process with all of you but it takes engagement on both sides. Moving forward, know that I hear your concerns and recognize how you feel. I, along with all supervisors and managers, will work to improve our communication and engagement." Heads in the room were nodding as most in attendance seemed to be receptive to what I had said. My nemesis' head was hung a bit as though he'd lost some ground. I would not let him suck me into his miserable existence. Not today or moving forward.

More comments came up about things surrounding the LODD and the funeral. Now, in all honesty, planning a LODD funeral is a massive undertaking. There are many moving parts and an entire company of personnel working on the logistics of it. There will be hundreds and potentially even thousands in attendance. There are politics within the command, the division, in headquarters and at the governor's level to be considered. Inadvertently, things will take place or be overlooked that are not intended to happen or to harm or hurt anyone at any level. It's an incredibly raw and sensitive time. Much of this none of the rank and file officers ever see beyond what they personally experience. Many of the issues they brought forward seemed small, yet very real and specific for them, so I knew they were important. We worked through them one by one. I apologized for what I was sure was more about everyone's emotions being raw in the moment than any real slight or intended act of hurt or oversight by any of my peer commanders helping coordinate the funeral.

One officer then asked where the sergeants had been during the time between the incident and funeral. He stated that "I couldn't find any of my sergeants. We had other sergeants from other commands here helping out, which was great, but I never saw any of our own sergeants." Some of the sergeants that were sitting in the room wearing their black sheep t-shirts had felt that for this meeting they were just another group of the officers until they realized that the rank and file officers didn't see them that way. During these interactions, I could have easily found solace in seeing them engaged in what I had to experience daily. Instead, it glaringly brought to mind a couple of important points for me. The first point was that the intersection of the two ranks of officer and sergeant are intricately woven. As a result, it can be hard to delineate between them when you promote, especially if you're friends with some of them or have developed close relationships. It makes it difficult to create the level of professional and accountable leadership needed within your teams to keep them protected - not just from physical harm on the job, but also from the harm that comes from not keeping them ethically, morally and professionally above reproach. The second point was that the sergeants were exposed to their own vulnerabilities not only through the LODD incident but at that moment in the room. Some of them tried to defend themselves while others didn't have to because they were where they were supposed to be. Those initial days were so chaotic with allowing staff to take time off to be at the hospital, help or just to take a break. There was a peer captain helping at the command with my lieutenants but there was such a tsunami of community support, media tug, and executive level requests resulting from the incident on top of the daily command responsibilities of calls for service. Some officers got overlooked and sergeants were apologizing for not knowing they needed them. These sergeants would need time to heal, to restore themselves and to reset.

This exchange went on for over an hour - back and forth with arrows of attack toward me, toward the division, toward just about anyone in the room. Finally, as they seemed to have gotten it all out of their systems, I was able to close the meeting on a somewhat positive note by summarizing the good and constructive things that had been achieved that day. I felt, that after all was said and done, everything was out from the dark corners of the private conversations giving them life to the table of light where we could begin to bridge misunderstandings, own our individual and collective mistakes and work to be better than we were.

I was feeling exhausted as I walked to my car to head home. In route, one of the senior officers stopped me. He was one of those that hadn't been in the room during the discussion. We were out in the parking lot and there was no one else around. He simply said, "Captain, I don't know many that would sit there and do what you just did. Most of what was said was just mindless horseshit spewing from spineless turds. You've done more for this command than any commander that I've ever worked for, and I've been here for over 20 of my 30 years. You keep doing what you're doing, screw them." Saying thank you, he smiled and walked away.

Appreciating that at least someone felt that I was doing some good gave me just enough lift to get home. On the way home, one of my peers reached out to me. He knew that I was holding the "council" meeting that evening, and wanted to know how it went. As I regurgitated what had happened, it was like a tidal wave of emotion releasing from my body. While I didn't cry, I was certainly relieved that it was over. My peer told me, "Go home. Go to sleep. Don't think about that shit. Fuck those people! You've given them too much of your heart, your commitment, your all since you arrived, especially since the LODD. They wouldn't have any idea of what great leadership looks like if it bit them in the ass. Get some rest. Call me in the morning." As I normally don't use that type of language any more, I will say it felt good to hear someone else use it. Heeding the advice given, I went home to sleep. I won't lie, those next weeks and months were tough. To go in to the command everyday knowing how so many felt about me and my leadership abilities was difficult. But I showed up every day and stayed in the arena. I was certain that if I just kept doing the next right thing, God would do the rest. My son and daughter were the light in these dark moments. During this time, they seemed to understand the gravity of what I was dealing with and would find ways to be encouraging and helpful. Their support filled my spirit and gave me the proverbial wind beneath my wings that helped me to stay focused and remember my calling.

Divinely, because I really felt that it was due to God's timing, just a few days after the barbeque, I received a text from one of my officers:

"Thank you, Captain! I really appreciate your checking in on me. I hope you are doing okay and getting rest as well. If you start feeling low, here is a verse that's been helping me get through...

To everything there is a season, and a time to every purpose under heaven. As iron sharpens iron, so one man sharpens another.
Ecclesiastes 3:1-14"

The connectivity of that encouraging text bridged the gap of my uncertainty to focus on simply the next best ways to serve everyone.

As I mentioned earlier, leadership is a journey of mental toughness. Without that toughness, you can't effectively think, act or innovate. You cannot motivate or inspire the best in others, or yourself. At that particular moment, it was all about being able to find a way to motivate, inspire and still stand tall and remain steadfast. Above all, it was about going out each day and helping all of those under my command to hear and embrace the calling of our law enforcement profession, while helping them to heal. This included setting up a critical incident stress debriefing for my sergeants, lieutenants and me with our departmental clinician. These don't happen very often for the supervisors, and management teams, or at least they hadn't up to this point. After witnessing all that had taken place at the barbeque, this session was definitely needed for all of us. We had been so busy holding up the officers and staff that we hadn't been able to stop and connect except for a few, intermittent for a few, intermittent individual moments. The session started off with several of them defensively justifying why, why not, and how they were doing all that they were doing. Amongst themselves, they didn't really know what each other was doing, so this session created clarity and hopefully, a better understanding. When it was my turn, I kept it simple. I explained where I was and what I was doing. I included relating some things I thought that I should have done better. I was careful not to bring up any added disappointment that I had with some of them based on their undermining me from day one and throughout this incident.

Throughout the session, the clinician was able to draw out their emotions, create some connective understanding and begin to restore some momentum. As a result and after hearing how they were feeling, I realized that there was nothing more I needed to say. Experiencing the healing and being able to reframe our mindset to be better together as we move forward, I felt was a win.

The following days, weeks, months and following year became about building hope and recovery. With the help of my management and supervisory team, I refocused the staff on the mission of our work and the legacy we must represent for our fallen hero through our daily commitment of service. These efforts created tremendous opportunities for camaraderie and healing. We never know when our mental toughness will be tested. Within those moments, it is a determination to conquer any doubt or fear of failing and separate those emotions. We must have the strength and commitment to face the challenge of leading with confidence and courage. Having and maintaining that commitment will cost you something; it always does.

The entire experience left my soul deeply scarred. I didn't really realize how much until almost a year later. I was mentoring someone on a personal matter dealing with the loss of their family member. I was trying to commiserate with them on how they were feeling and to show them ways that they might use to cope, share their feelings and get assistance if they needed to talk with someone. As I was relaying all of this, I felt my own emotions rising up in me.

Over that past year, there had been so many activities, events, and memorials to attend and to attend to, as well as running a command, that I did not allow myself time to properly grieve or acquire the resources I needed to be able to persevere. In the first several days after the death of our officer, there were many retired and active commanders that sent cards, called, texted their support and even stopped by. Many of them had experienced the same things I had just gone through which made us uniquely connected, yet still broken.

During this horrible incident and in the weeks and months that followed, I had been a commander in crisis and hadn't even realized it. I felt as though all of these feelings were the price you had to pay when you get promoted and take on all of this responsibility, even more so as a woman commander. I was broken and I cried - a lot. But don't get me wrong, despite going through all of these emotions, I was still trying to maintain a pace that didn't allow me to get too emotional. I guess being almost numb would be the best way to describe myself during this time.

As a female captain, I kept telling myself that I had to be this different kind of person in order to demonstrate that I was strong enough, capable enough and woman enough to effectively do this job. These feelings were both real and valid at the same time. As a woman, especially one of color, everything I do in this environment would be monitored. Let's not forget, I was this command's first female commander, period. This creates an incredible responsibility-not to fail in any way, shape or form. Those old feelings of insecurity and inferiority were also there again ringing in my ears. I could hear them on the long commute home. I could hear them during the long days and the sleepless nights.

My spirit was fraying and it was affecting my mental state, which in turn was leaving me totally isolated by the time I got home each evening. I hadn't realized that so much had changed in my life and in my children's lives over the last few years. All of this change had happened at such a record pace that it was all finally catching up with me. My mother had died unexpectedly in the same year that my 18 year marriage was ending. To make things even more stressful, these very emotional events both took place not long before I was promoted. I was trying to balance motherhood with my professional aspirations – all while trying to rationalize the choices that I had made.

When I received my most recent promotion, I had no idea that all these other pieces would change and rearrange themselves and sneak up on me like the 25 pounds I had gained over that same period of time. The uniform pants that at one point had fit so nicely had begun to go from snug to constricting and that's just how I felt in my life and in my spirit - constricted. I rationalized that the loss of energy and fatigue was a result of having to do the long commute and the long hours. But in reality, I was starting to experience depression. I finally made a call to a therapist. After a few visits with her, I was able to begin to understand some of my feelings. What I was feeling was hopelessness. I just needed a chance to restore my soul through calming and regulating my mind. Therapy was helpful, it felt safe. No one knew me there and I could speak freely.

Sometimes the sessions would be no more than the therapist allowing me to feel as though I was solving my own problems. But, in retrospect, I believe it was what I needed at that particular moment -a little guidance and a little help. It was a place I could share my hurt, pain, anger, shame and disappointment that was resonating from so many places within me. I had felt such shame and embarrassment from allowing those officers in the command to bully me spiritually. It was so similar to my childhood memories of getting on that bus for school. I remember sharing with her how it made me feel versus just saying how it was. Those sessions were priceless though I wish it hadn't taken me over a year to realize that I needed them. It's not uncommon for officers to avoid therapists or deny they even need any help from cumulative trauma. The stigma of mental health is a real challenge in policing, even for those in leadership. However, God knew that I needed more than just therapy. He knew that I also needed a continual purpose.

God is always working well in advance of what we could ever hope or imagine. I had two lifelines in the wings, waiting for me to see them for what they were intended - His mercy and His grace. Once again while attending a church service, my pastor was giving a sermon on "How to Bloom in Babylon." His message spoke about how you are where you are because God wants you to be there. While you're there, it causes you to understand that God is sovereign and in order to survive, and thrive, you have to trust Him. It's a choice you have to make-either give up and give in or stand steadfast in such moments. In your own personal Babylon, you are called to make the most of your present circumstances. You are to build, increase and settle down in this place where you don't even want to be. You must learn to bloom where you've been planted and realize that you have been called to make the most of your present circumstances.

It sounded reasonable but there were still so many ghosts haunting me in my current environment that I wasn't sure how to really "bloom" where I had been planted. Daily, I came to work and tried to be actively engaged, but my spirit was yearning for something more.

One day my past mentor reached out to check on me. During our conversation, she asked me if I was going to take the upcoming assistant chief's exam. Having no real interest or time, I didn't give her a definitive answer. Our conversation was over the phone and I could hear the change in her tone after my lack of response. She has a certain way about her that always made me want to reconsider my initial responses to her. On this particular day, she simply said, "Just start studying and take the test. See what happens." I attribute this ability in her to her life experiences, her faith in God, and in her obvious gift of being able to read others' real thoughts. She had a great knack for coupling those abilities with her own strong desire to help others to meet their potential. If she was the lifeline that God was tossing out to me as I was crying out for help, well Okay. I thought it odd, but I didn't want to be a cliché and say I was still waiting on God when He had been right there with his plan all along. So I started studying.

In my home, we had a very large dining room table. Over the last 18 years I could count on one hand the number of times we actually ate a family meal there. During this time, it quickly went from table centerpieces to organized collections of study material. The routine began almost every night with arriving home after the long commute, making dinner or bringing dinner home for the kids, assisting them with their homework, a bit of horseplay with them, and then to my own studying to close out the evening. The dining room was painted a dark shade of blue with four large windows that looked out into the backyard. In the yard was a swimming pool that was hardly ever used, and beyond the pool was the fence line of the property. We were blessed to be able to afford this house with its expansive yard out in the country, which was more rural.

During the time I began studying, the days had become shorter due to the time change. It looked dark outback with just the faint lighting from the little elementary school next door. These would be my views for the next several months as I immersed myself into policy, procedure, laws, trends, and new concepts surrounding the department and the policing industry. It was my salvation of sorts. While I initially had a mindset of studying just to pass the exam, it gradually became more about the gaining of knowledge to become a better leader for those I would be serving. As a result, it would be better for me and better for the captains that I would someday oversee as their assistant chief. Perhaps I would then be better prepared to assist them in their darkest hour when I was needed.

Preparation is a process that helps acclimate you to a new position. Part of the examination process was preparing a resume. Words on a piece of paper really don't do any justice to you or your accomplishments if you don't craft them in a way that paints a very illustrative picture of who you are and what you can do. In this instance, for my preparation, it was going to be a verbal resume. You could say that the voice I had been finding along the way would be the same voice that I would be bringing to the examination table. In an examination interview like this, it is very important to be able to allow others to delve into your knowledge and experience. If I would have stayed closed off, I would have been limiting my future personal power and influence.

On this day, my mentor was running me through the drill of practicing my verbal resume with her over the phone. In preparation, I would send a written copy to her via email so she would know what I would be saying. She would then be able to provide more direct feedback. The first time I sent it to her, she just emailed me back and told me to throw it away and start over. I could say that my feelings were hurt, but in all honesty, it was a recycled piece of work with a few modifications. She was right - it wasn't my best effort. Truth can be blunt, but we need people in our circle that will keep it real. I will never forget how she helped me over the years. She showed me how to see myself in places I would have never thought to look to see me, or even have known to look to find me.

Her words still echo, "Don't just give me the crap that's already in your resume. Show me who you are and what you bring to the table. What are your skills? What are your experiences? Who are you as a leader?" She would have me rewrite this five-minute verbal resume over and over again. There were many times that I wanted to give in, but I felt that there was more to this exercise than again just preparing for an exam and a verbal resume. No, this was really about searching the depths of me and finding what it would reveal - hoping all of the time that it would reveal more than I was expecting. As I began to refine my verbal resume, I was discovering something intangible. It may be hard to truly define this epiphany. But I'll try.

When we get intentional with our focus, we are no longer distracted from what is all around us. I would almost get lost in a trance-like state while attempting to sew this resume together. It forced me to explore the depths of my own creativity in search of the real fabric of myself. I wanted all to know that my life and who I really was were not just words on a resume. Above all else, I wanted them to realize that this resume was giving energy and relevance to my life and it was being lived every day through my actions. When I called her and went over this new version of the resume, she was silent. It was as though I could see her smile through the phone as she simply said, "That is it."

Interestingly enough, I was never upset with her criticism and greatly appreciated the direct and very real conversations that we had about the process and how I was feeling as we worked through it. If you want to grow and mature, you have to be open to real talk and real constructive feedback. For me, I had to simply be open. It wasn't easy. It is so important that we don't shut people out. Recognizing that we need other people is not a weakness - it's actually a strength. We were created for community and the only way we can be part of a community, is to be open to others. At this moment, at this particular time and season, God was triggering in me the need to engage. It was a journey of restoring my confidence in who He created me to be. As I worked through the verbal resume exercise, He brought me back to me. My mentor was a big step in my being able to recognize my support system of friends and family - my village. In asking for help I was rebuking shame.

I'd always felt like I could do most things on my own, and perhaps that's what was expected of me. So, a part of me was always embarrassed to ask for too much from others. But from situations like this I discovered the real value of creating a community. A community or a village that we can build for ourselves is critical to our ability to function in a society that will gladly step over you to get to where it's going. I knew I had good people that loved me in my corner, I just didn't know how much and how important they were until all the things around me started to disintegrate. It was hard for me to be a trusting soul. While there might have been a lot of folks that were willing to help, there were probably just as many that simply couldn't be trusted. However, I began to pretty quickly be able to tell when someone was less than authentic, and by this time in my career, I had developed a very low threshold for BS.

My kids were often my best barometer when I would unknowingly say something in a particular tone. They would respond with, "Yes, Captain!" It's funny. They knew that I could see through their childlike shenanigans. However some adults still felt that they could pull one over on me. As a result, I found that I had become very guarded with my feelings, both professionally and personally. My guarded feelings were tightly wrapped around my guarded cynicism that had developed from my experiences in police leadership. I was now always suspicious of people's motives. I was very cautious with anyone who wanted to get too close. This is why it took so long for me to open up to anyone in an intimate, meaningful and personal way.

These years of my being a mother and a leader were a delicate balance that was sometimes hard to maintain. I don't know how good a mother I was at this time because I was still broken from all of the things that had just transpired in my life. My son was a little older now and was able to get around and help a little with his sister. He had grown into a young man so quickly - from the emergency room, a C-section, and being five week early baby to the self- sufficient handsome teenage son that he was then. He helped where he could, but I was so fortunate to have some awesome friends that helped me with those school pickup days for my daughter when I couldn't get home in time. I thank God for those blessings of favors and cover through loving kindness and good people. Gratefully, I was able to make many basketball games for my son, help them both with their homework, carve pumpkins and bake cookies...LOL. Yes, be their mother! My kids are really my best contribution to the world.

The Assistant Chief Examination Experience

Game day was here. The assistant chief's examination was awkward and nerve wracking. I walked into the headquarters' building and signed in. It's funny how people that you see every day can sometimes barely say hello or even acknowledge you. I suppose they felt there would be some big breach of ethics if they smiled or attempted to make you feel welcome to the test. Anyway, I took a seat at a table nearby and waited for the rest of the participants (other captains) that were taking the test to arrive. It was odd. As I sat there, I found myself not doubting myself, but wondering what the process would entail. I had studied relentlessly and felt as though there was so much information in my head that I was going to pop.

Two other captains shuffled in and sat down in seats on each side of me. One of them was someone that I used to work the graveyard shift with over 20 years ago and he had been a captain for almost seven or eight years. I had only been a captain for a little over 2 years. Hmm.... did I have a particular feeling about that as I wrote it out on paper? Nope. My spiritual maturity was fostering my professional maturity and my leadership growth. You see, there must be a dedication and desire, regardless of adversity, to press forward, to strive, and to advance to the next level. You have to be better regardless of what you have already accomplished in the continuous pursuit of excellence, despite if you've not been doing it for long. Who creates the "right" time to step into your moment? Not other people, you. God did not call me, or you, to be mediocre. And despite what it may look or sound like, we must press forward to break the chains of past strongholds and to free ourselves into our own potential. I was here to claim my victory!

The examination was an assessment center process that took nearly three hours. My exercises included making a presentation, working through an in-basket and the last one was an oral panel interview with the executive leadership of the department. All of the exercises seemed to be going well until I reached the oral panel interview portion. The beginning component of me giving my verbal resume barely squeaked through the buzzer, as all of the questions were timed. This rattled my cage a little, but I was not going to be shaken; I had been preparing. Preparation for this position was coursing through my veins. It was game day! The oral panel questions were not too grueling and outside of a few fumbles, not resulting in any loss of score, I was able to recover and cross the goal line. The test was over.

I walked out and got in my car feeling relatively calm until a colleague called and asked me how the test had gone for me. He had finished earlier in the day and was waiting for me to finish. No, we were not supposed to talk about the test. Yes, we had signed a little piece of paper. No, we did not get into details because they didn't really matter. It was his lack of confidence about how he felt he had responded and how the questions had been posed that started me to fear that maybe, just maybe, I hadn't done as well as I thought I had either. He kept going on and on and my mind was starting to shut down on his words. It sounded like "wah wah wah wah". Finally, as I got off the phone with him I noticed that somehow I had gotten from the parking lot of the building where I had taken the test to almost arriving at the off ramp to the exit for home, some 45 minutes away.

I began to replay every second of the examination process in my head so that I could hopefully assess the worthiness of my responses. Of course, it was fading quickly because my stress levels had started to rise. And now, after speaking with the other captain, I wasn't sure what the heck had just happened and that was freaking me out even more. It was anxiety - plain and simple.

This went on for a while before I could calm down and decompress. In retrospect two things rang very clear - be careful of whom you let speak into your psyche and never let the pressure we put on ourselves to be perfect override our common sense. We know darn well that we are far from being perfect, and that we just need to embrace our imperfections. I had gotten myself so flustered that I had forgotten to remember all that was good in my life. The blessings of waking up that morning, knowing that my kids were safe, feeling confident that my health was in order and that God had given me traveling grace to make it back home without incident. No more phone calls today from those who were not worthy.

Doing laundry is always therapy for me. No, it really is because it requires very little thought if you've been doing it awhile. Several days

131

after the exam, I was blissfully moving about at home doing laundry and other tasks when the phone rang. As soon as I picked it up and said hello, the voice at the other end said hello back. It was the sound of my mentor's voice that stopped me in my tracks. It was the call - the call that comes only after you have taken one of these anguishing examinations. You would have thought that I'd be better prepared for it, but I wasn't. "Hey, have you seen the list yet?" she quickly asked as I was still trying to process that it was she that was calling. "No, I've been busy here at the house," I replied. You know, doing that therapeutic laundry thing. "I haven't been on my computer or on the phone." She said that the promotional list was out, but it lists only by your competitor ID number. "What's your number?" she asked. It's funny, the competitor number is supposed to create anonymity so others won't know your score. But a list is recreated within hours of the exam with everyone's name on it located on an "unofficial" platform to which everyone can get access. Did I care right now? No.

Anyway, of course I knew my number. Well, I knew it but had to go find it on my letter that was provided to me through the process. So, after a few seconds of rifling through the stack of papers on the dining room table, I give her the numbers. "Oh, my God!" she exclaimed. That was it. That was all she said at first. I said, "Oh my God, good?" She again said, "Oh, my God! You're number two on the list!" Um, "What!?!?"

She repeated it, "You're number two on the list. Congratulations!" She rattled on about something and quickly got off the phone because she needed to call some other folks. I stood speechless in my bedroom with the clothes' drawers open waiting for me to put the clothes in them.   It didn't feel real. So, like most people receiving that type of news, I called the examinations unit at headquarters to confirm what she had said. Of course, I didn't believe her! I thought she must have made some kind of mistake. I called the exam unit and the female voice that answered sounded familiar. I went into my spiel about needing to check and verify my score on this most recent assistant chiefs' examination. I was waiting for her to ask me for my ID number when she said, "Hi there! And yes, you are number two! We are so excited for you, congratulations!"

Letting this new information sink in was so surreal. I immediately wanted to call my boyfriend. Wait just a minute, where has he been in this narrative until now? Well, actually he had been behind the scenes in these narratives for a good amount of time. He was the other lifeline that God had sent me. It was an interesting dynamic in my kaleidoscopic life. As I was battling myself on so many things, I was also fearful of opening up to someone in a real relationship. My emotional stability was always just a ripple away from creating a tidal wave of brokenness inside myself. The thought of having to explain that to someone was just beyond me. And quite frankly, I didn't have the energy. My 18 year marriage hadn't worked that well and the recovery from it was difficult for me and the whole family. I just didn't want to bring a man into the picture too soon and create a shift in the life I thought that I was balancing pretty well.

Facing My Fears

Reflecting on my fear of dating and being in relationship again was my misguided attempt to avoid what I had experienced as a child - my mother's entourage of gentlemen callers. There were several times when I could hear her and them in her room. It was less shocking as a child because I was completely unaware of what it really meant until I started to get older. I never knew their names or even recall their faces. The only incident I really remember still haunts me when I think of it.

One evening I had been playing over at my half-brother's house. I was so thankful my mother had kept the connection with his mother so that we could know each other. As an adult, I have a much better understanding of the difficult decision my mother had made to give him up for adoption. We had been born less than a year apart and neither of us had fathers to help her raise us. This part of my life is an entire book on its own. But my brother, he's my gift from Sara.

Anyway, it was time for me to go home and oddly enough, no one could take me, so they called a taxi. Yes, I rode in a taxi across town to my house. I remember it being nighttime, not too late, though the sun had gone down. The taxi driver seemed to be an acquaintance of my mother. He seemed familiar with my brother's mother and spoke to me about mine. My memory is that of an 8-year-old but to this day it seems so vivid. As we pulled up to the curb at my house, the dull porch light was on. You could see the shadows of light coming across the white porch fencing into the yard and lighting the concrete sidewalk to the white house from the street.

From outside, you could partially see through the screen door and that the inside door was open and the light in the bedroom to the right of the door was on. I jumped out of the taxi as he told me that he would wait there until I got inside. I hurried up the walkway to the screen door and went into the house. As I crested the doorway, I heard loud voices coming from that front bedroom where the light was on. I turned to go in but was stopped like I had run into a wall. The room was bright white with white sheets on the bed and the bright white light was on in the room. A man was sitting on top of my mother, straddling her and her legs were hanging off the bed. Blood was staining the sheets, the walls, and the floors. It was everywhere. To the left of the bed was a very big hole in the wall with blood stains trailing across the floor. It took me a few seconds to realize he was beating her in the face. All I could do was scream and run back outside. The driver of the taxi heard my scream and was coming toward me. He stopped me midway as he ran toward me. I tried to tell him what I saw, and he told me to go get in the taxi and stay there. He went in the house and I don't know what happened inside afterwards.

Time passed and my brother's mother pulled up and got out of her Cadillac with a long object in her hand. As she moved into the light, it was what I would later know as a machete. I don't remember seeing any police lights or ambulances. I was driven back to my brother's house where I stayed for a couple of days. I hadn't seen my mother or knew how she was doing. They just told me she was in the hospital. Finally the day arrived when it was time to go and pick her up. Excited and terrified is the only way I can describe how it felt to be on the way to see her and pick her up from the hospital. I saw her from behind and she was wearing a scarf on her head which she never did. As she turned my way, I didn't even recognize her face. It was a mass of purple, black, blue, and red and so swollen that I could barely see her hazel eyes. She sounded like my mom, but I wasn't sure. As I hugged her, she smelled medicinal and there was no scent of her. I cried because I wasn't sure of what completely had happened to her, but in my heart I knew it had been something terrible. We were dropped off back at that white house with the porch. I didn't want to be left there and it took me a long time to sleep there by myself again.

This man had been one of her many suitors. He had even lasted a bit longer than some of the others. It's still etched deep within my conscience. Actually, much of the shallow, reckless "gallivanting" around that she did has remained there as well. If you combine that experience with the fears of my past marriage, my own teenage and adult escapades, it is easy to understand the apprehensions I had regarding any future relationships. I kept most men at an arm's length away.

My comfort level was keeping him in the backdrop of my life. It felt safe. If I didn't let him all the way in my life somehow I would still have some control over the outcome. He was so patient with me and never once asked more of me than what I was able or willing to give. The absolute beauty of our divine connection was simply nothing but from God. I was in a place where my life felt like it was being ripped apart with loss and failed expectations both personally and professionally. Yet, somehow, he made me feel complete.

Some days I was in good shape and yet other days, I was running on autopilot, not realizing how I would get from this to that or that to this. It's as though God felt that I needed a tangible reminder of kindness, patience and unconditional love. And then one day, I saw him. Where you ask? Well, let's just say it was on one of the popular social media sites we use to stay connected to family and friends. He had posted on my sister's page, which I'm sure he had done many times before. However, this time, his smile and the twinkle in his eyes caught my attention. There was one problem - he was posing in the picture with a woman. As you can imagine, I was a bit cautious, but I requested he be my friend on the site. The status didn't indicate whether he was married or not and I didn't want to get into any drama if he was married. But how will you ever know if you don't step out of your comfort zone? Anyway, it was just a request to be his friend.

Well, he accepted my request. It took some time before we actually spoke on the phone. As it turned out, we had grown up in the same town of Bakersfield and he knew many of my personal friends and family. Oddly, we had only crossed paths once that we could really recall. He was a few years older than me and as you go through high school that can be an enormous gap. He was living in Santa Barbara and well, I was living in Northern California. Some may ask how in the world was this going to work? Well, God's plan is often not like we could ever think or imagine. Thank you, Jesus!

Our lives were forever changed the moment we first started talking on the phone. He was all that I had prayed and hoped for in a man – one that would give me his "rib" one day. LOL! We spoke every day building a friendship into a kinship which today is the love of my life. It took seven years before we got married but we both know God was working a lot out in each of us so that we would be prepared for the blessings He had for US. There is so much more that I could say about us. Perhaps I'll share some more about us later in this story. Or better yet, maybe I'll create an entire story just about our story.

Jonni in 1967

2 years old
1969

8-9 years old
1975-1976

6 years old
Bakersfield, California

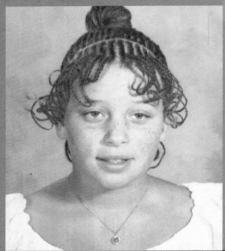

11 years old
Bakersfield, California

13 years old
Bakersfield, California
1980

Jonni's mother Sara (on left)
17-18 years old

Sara's official Nursing Photo

Sara in her late
20s - early 30s,

*Jonni and her father Johnny,
Bakersfield, California
1994*

*Jonni, Sean Jr. (1 years old),
and her father Johnny Lee*

*Jonni and mother Sara,
Stockton, California,
1993.*

A younger Sara

Pauline Echols Bazer, 1906-1998

*Jonni's Modeling Photos
(18/19 years old)
1985-1986.*

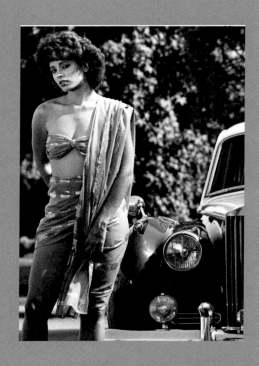

Jonni, 21 years old
CHP Cadet Picture
1988

CALLOWAY

Officer, Stockton. 1988 (right)

Jonni working graveyard shift in
Stockton, California. Stockton
Record, 1995 (below)

Region

The Record • Monday, December 11, 1995 B3

TRACY

Chemical leak capped

County emergency service officials said leaking chemical fumes that forced Saturday night's closure of Interstate 205 could have caused respiratory problems, burned skin and eyes or killed someone if inhaled or absorbed through the skin.

The chemical, hydrogen bromide, was reported leaking just after 10 p.m. Saturday from valves in a one-ton container inside a van at Yellow Freight Systems Inc., 1535 El Pescadero Ave., located 200 yards from the freeway, officials at the San Joaquin County Office of Emergency Services said.

Only a small amount of the chemical leaked out, and the leak was confined to the loading-dock area, officials said. Hazardous-material response officials capped the leaking valves about 1 a.m. Sunday, said Mike Parisi, OES duty officer.

OES and Tracy Fire Department officials evacuated Yellow Freight employees. No one was injured, Parisi said.

California Highway Patrol officials closed I-205 between Interstate 5 and Grant Line Road because wind was blowing toxic vapors from the chemical toward the freeway, officials said.

The highway reopened about 2:20 a.m. Sunday after being shut down for four hours. Traffic was diverted through city streets. No vehicle accidents occurred, officials said.

Krout in court today

Douglas Vernon Krout, accused of plying an 11-year-old girl with beer and marijuana in a motel room and then leading law enforcement authorities on a high-speed chase, is scheduled to be arraigned today in Tracy.

Krout, 50, is expected to appear in Tracy Municipal Court at 1 p.m. to discuss entering a plea and other matters concern-

TROUBLE AHEAD? — Officer Jonni Fanner directs traffic away from Interstate 205 at the southbound Interstate 5 junction after officials closed

Record photo by CRAIG SANDERS

I-205 from I-5 to Grant Line Road in Tracy because of a chemical leak at the Yellow Freight trucking facility. I-205 was closed for four hours.

ing his case.

Krout, a Tracy resident, was arrested Thursday after a round-trip chase from Tracy to Oakland. The chase began after Krout had dropped off the girl at her friend's apartment in Tracy on Thursday and was spotted by San Joaquin County deputies who were responding to a report of her return, authorities said.

Deputies said Krout, who had befriended the girl, picked her up from her friend's house Wednesday afternoon. The girl's sister reported her missing when she failed to come home

Wednesday evening.

Sheriff's officials alleged that Krout gave the girl beer and marijuana.

He is to be arraigned today on four felony charges: kidnapping the girl for lewd or lascivious acts, inducing her to use marijuana, evading police officers, and violating his parole. He also faces four misdemeanor charges: resisting arrest, delaying or obstructing a peace officer; annoying or molesting a child; failure to register as a sex offender; and reckless driving.

Krout is being held at the San

Joaquin County jail without bail. Authorities have not said if the girl was molested.

STOCKTON

Take it to City Hall

People with questions about junked cars, unsightly property or other possible city-code violations are invited to stop by Stockton's Satellite City Hall in Sherwood Mall on Tuesday.

Louis Valverde, code-enforcement supervisor for the city of Stockton, will be at the Satellite

City Hall from 4 to 7 p.m. Tuesday to discuss any code-enforcement issues.

On Wednesday, Vice Mayor Floyd Weaver will be available from 4 to 7 p.m. to talk to residents and answer any questions.

In addition, last-minute shoppers can find unique Christmas gifts at the Satellite City Hall, including fire hydrants, old signs, parking meters and golf course tee signs.

The Satellite City Hall is located in the mall near Montgomery Ward. Information: Cathy Sloan at 937-8096.

Alcohol sales seminar

The Stockton Police Department and the state Department of Alcoholic Beverage Control will host a training seminar today for business owners and employees who sell alcohol.

The seminar will provide information and training to assist local businesses in complying with state laws. In Stockton, there are 480 businesses licensed to sell alcohol. The training seminar, called Licensee Education on Alcohol and Drugs, will be held in South Hall of the Stockton Memorial Civic Auditorium, 525 N. Center St. Information: Officer Jim Tribble at 937-8422.

LODI/LOCKEFORD

Meet the superintendent

Del Alberti, acting superintendent of Lodi Unified School District, will hold an open office day Wednesday in Lockeford for community members who want to drop by and talk to him informally.

The open office will be held from 5 to 8:30 p.m. at Lockeford Elementary School, 19456 N. Tully Road.

Appointments are not necessary. Alberti will be available to discuss educational topics or to answer questions and clarify issues. Information: 331-7010.

THE DELTA

Reflections awards

The Marina West Yacht Club has announced the winners of its boat-decoration competition for last week's 16th annual Delta Reflections parade.

About 60 boats decked out in holiday lights and other decorations cruised along the San Joaquin River and the Stockton Deep Water Channel Dec. 4 for the annual event sponsored by Marina West.

Club officials said 42 boats registered for the competition, and 27 awards were given out following the parade. Here are some of the top winners.

■ **Judges Award:** Ken Flint, Stockton.

■ **Best Decorated:** Ed Kimball, Stockton.

■ **First overall:**

35 feet or longer — Frank Sumner, San Jose.

Under 35 feet long — Duke Wilkinson, Stockton.

■ **Best Lighted:**

35 feet or longer — Bernie Fritz, Stockton.

Under 35 feet long — Ken Lowe, Stockton.

■ **Crowd Pleaser Award, Best Animated Award:** Bob Moser, Santa Rosa.

COUNTYWIDE

Group seeks donations

The Imperial San Joaquin Delta Empire, a local nonprofit charity fund-raising organization, this month will hold its annual "From the Heart" project which raises money for children infected or affected by HIV or AIDS.

Families affected by AIDS often can't afford to buy Christmas gifts for their children, Delta Empire officials said. All of the money donated to "From the Heart" will go toward purchasing gifts children have requested.

Donations are tax deductible and should be sent to Imperial San Joaquin Delta Empire, P.O. Box 692262, Stockton, CA 95269.

Tahoe hit with 118 mph winds

PACIFIC AUDIO

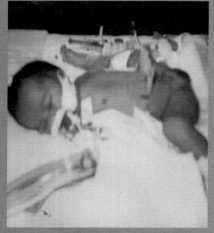

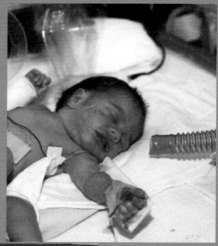

Sean Jr at Oakland Children's Hospital NICU, May 1992, (center) Jonni & Sean Jr. and below first time holding Sean Jr.

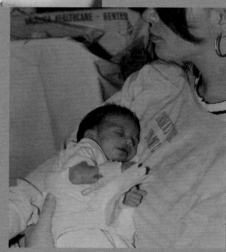

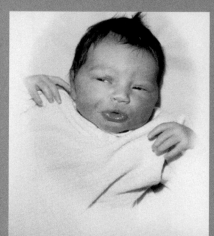

Jonni, Sean Jr., and Emily 1997. Emily Nicole Fenner, born in Stockton California, 1996. (center) Emily's High School Graduation 2015, and graduation day at William Jessup University, 2019. Finally baby Emily and Jonni sharing first days.

Sara, Sean Jr., and Emily.

Sean Jr. and Emily, 1997

Kevin and Jonni at graduation for her master's degree at University of San Diego,

Sean Jr. graduation from San Joaquin Delta Junior College

William Jessup University, 2016 (right)

Sean, Lauren, and Cannon (Grandson), 2021 (below)

Emily's art work

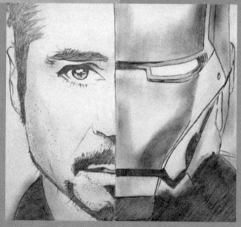

(Above) Wedding Day.

Kevin's marriage proposal to Jonni on her 50th birthday

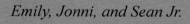

Emily, Jonni, and Sean Jr.

CHP Graduation May1989

Jonni working graveyard shift at Hayward CHP 1991

Jonni, CHP Academy, Physical Training Obstacle Course, 1988

CHP Graduation, my first time officially wearing CHP uniform, May 1989,

Sergeant Headquarters 2000

Sean Jr., Emily, and Jonni

CHP Academy Physical Training, 1988

*Jonni at CHP Academy
Range 1989*

*Jonni and Aunt Betty at CHP
Graduation May1989*

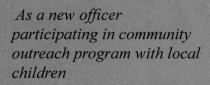

*As a new officer
participating in community
outreach program with local
children*

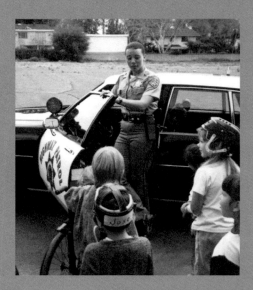

College Recruitment Event

Sergeant

Recruitment Event

Sergeant, Headquarters, Community Outreach and Marketing, coordinated the annual Tim Brown events. Pictured with Erik Estrada and Tim Brown (2001)

Lieutenant 2008

Assistant Chief Redick conducting a command officers open ranks inspection, 2013

Sergeant working a collision in Stockton, California

Captain Jonni Redick (Fenner) 2011-2013,

*Commission on POST Command
College, Class 56, Graduation*

*Assistant Chief
Redick, Dignitary
Protection
Detail, President
Motorcade*

*Captain, sitting on promotional
interview panels*

To Jonni Fenner
With best wishes,

44th President Obama and Assistant Chief Jonni Redick

Chapter 7

The 4th Promotion ~ Assistant Chief

Once I was able to calm myself down after receiving the news, I gave my boyfriend a call. He was just as elated as I had been. I can still hear and feel the comfort of his deep and loving voice as he told me how proud he was of me and how great I would be in this new position. We spoke for a while and then I got back to tackling the laundry. In the silence surrounding me at home, my inner voice began to awaken my insecurities. Prodding me by asking me silly questions like what happens now? What am I supposed to do with all of these new responsibilities? Where will my promotion be? Will I be able to do it? Why me? Really? Me? Those darn "ANTS." Then all of a sudden as if someone had silenced those voices in my head, I could hear God speaking to me, "Have patience and be still." In that moment, I did as I was told.

Trying to be obedient to God's request over the next few days was hard. My will wanted it my way and was looking for answers now. I needed to know what this path was going to look like and what I needed to do. As with most promotional processes, there are many phases to the entire experience. Each one comes with its own process and set of expectations and don't forget that beyond the promotional processes, there is the actual position and all of the new responsibilities that come with it.

As I'm waiting, an opportunity for an assistant chief position opened up right in my own division. Immediately, I feel both my ego and my insecurities begin to battle internally with my competitive confidence. One voice inside me was saying, "All that you have done for the department, the division and the sacrifices you've made, that position had better belong to you. You're certainly more capable and competent." I was more than competent and capable, but the other voice was telling me, "You don't really think you're going to get that position, do you? You aren't ready for something that important!" After doing the usual emotional rounds with myself, I decided to apply for the position. I was getting quicker at telling myself yes than no.

My interview was held with both the assistant commissioner who was commander of our field operations and the division chief. It was my first time experiencing the executive management selection process. Truly, I didn't feel that there was any discrimination in this process, at least not from the perspective of gender or race. Both of my interviewers were like me in both of those categories. What I was hoping that I wouldn't have to face again were the organizational culture politics.

Overall, I felt that the interview had gone well. One of the other candidates that interviewed was a white male who had worked in our division for most of his career. He and the division chief were very close friends. However, I was intent on keeping my thoughts positive and trying very hard not to think too much about their relationship but more about each of our work performance records and ethics. From my vantage point, I felt there was really no comparison between us and thus, no competition. He was a super nice guy, but the reality of it was that he did not have the capacity to handle all the responsibilities of being an assistant chief. Sometimes people promote beyond their threshold. This happens all of the time in our profession. Friends of friends, or tenured folks on the job are gifted with a promotion and those of us left in the wake of such actions can only shake our heads in disbelief and murmur amongst ourselves about how can this possibly be happening. Adding to that, he was two whole ranks below me on the promotional eligibility list.

Feeling pretty comfortable that things would lean in my favor, I tried to remain positive. In hindsight, I surely didn't see the train that came along and left me standing at the station. Yes, it's one thing to defeat yourself with your own thoughts but something totally different to be abruptly upended by someone that shouldn't have even been a consideration. This was quite a blow. When we talk about the obstacles that impact women, or anyone for that matter, these obstacles often never look the way that we think they should, or others might think we experience. Sometimes it ends up being simply the way the game is being played and how one gets caught up in it. Policing culture has an almost default mechanism that promotes many within the organization based on unspoken rules, relationships and reasons that have been standard practices for decades. The bottom line of it was that this other candidate got the job. I'm sure it was at least partly because he was her friend and he had worked with her for many years. There's often a loyalty and trust factor for selecting your leadership teams which has nothing to do with your competence. Was he a nice guy? Yeah. Sure. But the more important question - was he the best choice for the position? Apparently that didn't matter. She had loyalty to him and he had loyalty to her and that's what she wanted. She was the chief, so that's who she chose. I will say that it's not because she didn't think I was qualified as she was always very supportive of me and my work. Simply bad timing for me. I had to "suck it up, buttercup" and keep it moving.

I huffed and puffed for a while internally, but then decided to start the process of applying for the open positions in Sacramento, where headquarters was located and where I would be much closer to home. As you move up in rank, it gets more complex and a bit more difficult because there are far fewer opportunities available and the odds can be against you if you're not already in line for a promotion within your division. It's all about the loyalty connection. Just as I am working hard in my own division to be a team player and to excel in all of my undertakings, so are others in their respective divisions. The competition is a repetitive cycle of interviews that culminate in not only how well you do during the interview, but also how you compare with this one or that one who may be slightly better connected or who may know someone that you don't. It's all about how well you fit into the decision maker's scheme and basically who he or she wants on their team. This process can make you feel like a kid on the playground again waiting to be chosen for a ball game. There was always a captain for each team and they took turns picking their team members starting with the best players until they get to the last kid standing. This was the game and if I wanted to play, I had to abide by the rules. I had been through it all before as I had promoted through the ranks. I just had to embrace the process and find meaning and purpose during my valleys of waiting. Trust me, it wasn't easy having patience and being a good sport with all of the BS being tossed around in some of those rejection calls, but I did my best.

While I was still continuing to seek out opportunities for promotion, I was gradually starting to find some solace and beauty in the command where I had felt so constricted. The constant undermining by that small core of officers was continuing to be a problem even as I was trying to focus on bridging the despair from the loss of our fallen officer. It was a battle just to bring myself into the office every day having to face so many folks who were simply not very nice. That sounds kind of womanly soft, but it was true. It was hard to suck this one up like a good buttercup. Some of the people in that office were just mean spirited, hatefully self-serving and were abusing the privilege of being officers. What was so profound was that in the midst of these evil-doers, (yes that's a biblical term), were some amazing people. Folks who came to work every day whether in the office or outside of it, grinding away and striving to do the right thing - doing it with excellence, kindness and selfless service.

Within this "within," were a lovely heavenly group of people that saved my spirit daily with their smiles, their kind words, their hugs and their encouragement. This group of kind souls was actually a group of volunteers for our organization. They give of their time to help us and the community without a single dime ever being paid to them. All of them had previous careers and lives that we will never fully know, yet they chose to serve our organization freely and without compromise. It was simply amazing! These senior volunteers reminded me almost daily that they saw the good in me for all that I was trying to do. That helped me find my vision above and beyond all of the negative things that I was experiencing in those moments.

At this point I decided that I needed to stop having such a narrow focus on the negative and see the positive and be grateful. I was going to try to see the place that I was in for what it was. While understanding that I would need to look beyond my present to what the future may hold if I could just remain true to my purpose. A shabby analysis perhaps, but until you get locked into such an emotionally destitute place, you couldn't possibly understand the harmful and restrictive nature of its circumstances. It's so incredibly hard to stay positive and focused, but if we do, we can rise above the day-to-day battles and claim the victories that are in store for us. Believing and staying steadfast became my daily ritual. It kept me balanced and helped me to find peace during the other storms that would come while in that command.

Finding Purpose

Have you ever seen those comic strips where *Garfield* is just strolling along without a care in the world? Well, that certainly wasn't how my days were going at this juncture in my career. If it wasn't an officer involved in an incident, or a civil disturbance, it was a personnel matter. There was always something on this buffet table that was my command. Some days I would wonder where the time had gone because it was so doggone busy. As with any other day, basically because I don't remember the actual day, one day I heard a rumor that one of the other assistant chief, that had reported about 10 months ago from the southern division was thinking of retiring in the next year. Well, that was partially exciting, but it was still May of this year. Although I'd be brushing up to the expiration of the eligibility list which is only good for 24 months, it was something to look forward to but I would have to wait. Would I have the patience to wait? What good does it do to be in the top rank if it doesn't mean an actual promotion before those below you? Oh boy, what is God trying to work out in me?

The rumors began to shift as rumors often do. And the new rumor was that the retiring chief was leaving not next year, but this year - in July. What?!? That was only a couple of months away. Now this was a rumor I had to confirm! I immediately called up division and asked to speak to this potentially retiring assistant chief about something completely insignificant and unrelated. When she got on the phone, I could tell she was smiling because her voice was lighthearted, and she sounded happy. She told me she was transferring back down to southern California in July and her position would be opening. I listened but I don't know that I heard all of her words because my mind was blown. She was really leaving in two months. Shut the front door!! When I faded back in, I think she was saying something along the lines of that if I wanted to meet with her, she would help me prepare for the interview for her position. Wholly guacamole! You'd better believe I was going to jump on that.

The interview process was the same as it had been previously for this position; however, I was the only candidate interviewing from within our division, all of the others were from elsewhere. How did it feel having the shoe on my foot this time? Glad you asked. It felt GREAT!! Why not me this time? It had always been someone else. Let's not beat around the bush. Yes, I got the nod and was to be promoted to Assistant Chief. Finally! It was a win-win for both of us. The other assistant chief got to go home. I was able to rise to a position where I could increase my span of influence in the same division where I had experienced so much brokenness and dysfunction.

Still over two hours from home, I wasn't sure what God was calling me to do. Feeling again like God was moving and sifting me after the shattered moments of the year before, I just tried to be obedient to His whisper. I had gotten so lost trying to wade through the darkness and moral desolation of my previous command that I had almost forgotten how to lead effectively and who I was supposed to be for myself. I had forgotten who I was in Christ. In the captain command I was leaving for promotion, I had found myself trying to slide into my office hoping to go unnoticed – feeling ashamed that I had failed so many.

Think of it, the Captain trying to go unnoticed. That is practically impossible. But the reality of it was that I just didn't want to deal with hostile people anymore - with people that didn't or couldn't find any common ground where we might have a chance to turn the corner on all of the subterfuge and begin to focus on the mission. It had been a very difficult couple of years before the promotion to assistant chief.

My going away promotional luncheon was held in the back of the office in the parking overhang in order to be able to accommodate all those who came to celebrate and say farewell. As I looked out at those attending, a little face was looking my way with a big smile. She always saw me. I was her hero. I was glad my cousin had brought my daughter. It was so grounding to have her there. She looked a lot like me when I was a little girl, but far more beautiful. Seeing her anchored my spirit as amongst the faces were also those very glad to see me moving on.

After I had received the various resolutions, commendations, and acknowledgements, it was my turn to speak.

"As many of you know, I knew that at some point my time would be nearing in this season and I would be moving on to where I would be called to go. I've said it before, if I could put all of you, or at least some of you (wink), in my pocket and take you with me, I would. I'm looking out at all of you and beaming with pride at all of the greatness that I see. You are the reason that our organization has a great reputation. You are the cornerstone of our division, not the black sheep. I've gained more than you can ever imagine by being your commander.

Although I am leaving the command, I will be here in the division as one of the assistant chiefs. And I woke up this morning, thinking about the ride here in this division from being in Hayward, here and now in a larger role. This scripture stood out to me, Proverbs 27:17. "As iron sharpens iron, so one sharpens another." That is exactly how it has felt in my interactions with many of you. This scripture magnifies the mutual benefit in the rubbing of two irons together and it is with this that we are to sharpen one another- in times of counsel, fellowship, conflict and devastating loss. I will miss our shared moments in fellowship, the camaraderie and the way that everyone comes together to care for one another here in this command. Embrace it all and be grateful for every moment. They are not guaranteed.

To my daughter, I need everyone here to see you and know what sacrifices you made for me to be able to be here for all of them. I need you to know how much I appreciate your encouragement, prayers and belief in your mommy. You and your brother gave me the hope and faith I needed to keep striving every day to excel, never settling for mediocrity. Thank you for reminding me of what is important in this one life we live - family.

With that I leave you with something one of my favorite leaders shared with me... remember your ABCs: Attitude - always have a right one. Balance - make sure you balance your personal and professional lives well. Choices - strive to make the right choices every day, choosing to be positive over negative on any given day. It makes life better.

Again, thank you all for taking time to share this moment with me today, I'm deeply humbled. Many blessings."

The moment was somewhat surreal and I could feel myself internally exhale. This luncheon would be the last time I would see many of those here in the command. However, life does not pause, it keeps moving on.

Assistant Chief

Time sped up after the luncheon. While in my previous command, I had been in charge of a hundred or so people, I would now have six commands and several hundred people for whom I would be responsible. Finding my place and my voice in this new rank was going to be a great deal more work. Organizationally, I would now have a seat at the larger executive table for the statewide organization. This would include the commissioners, two star chiefs and the other assistant chiefs. In that top tier, there were only two African American women with one of us in a field division command and one in a headquarters (HQ) division command at the time.

Finding your voice as a woman in police leadership at any rank can be an uncomfortable tight rope when you first promote into the various ranks, yet this time it didn't feel at all unnatural, and actually - just about right.

Working with my peer chiefs could be interesting at times even though we were not always congruent or in complete agreement, we made it all work. Instead of being frustrated with the office politics between the chiefs and commissioner requests, I focused more on how to build better leadership in my commanders and their staff. This doesn't happen with me sitting in the office miles away. Having six commands within my sector in the Bay Area from San Francisco to San Jose, more than an hour away with traffic, I worked purposefully to get out to those commands frequently and meet with my commanders and their staff. Conducting operational meetings but also attending events, celebrations and just being present to acknowledge the good work by so many that often get overlooked. The organization is a huge machine, daily grinding out the mission. However, it would never get done without all the people that are both in front of and behind the scenes. I found this is what I loved the most about the rank of assistant chief, letting people be seen. Interestingly, I would hear how they didn't see any chiefs that often until I started visiting their offices. I get it, it's a grind in the division office too with all the politics, administrative responsibilities and tasks pulling you from every direction. Yet sometimes assistant chiefs can also get comfortable not being engaged like they should and before you know it, you haven't paid enough attention to a command and it's a wonder why things emerge that could have been addressed sooner. That's why intentionality was so key for me, for my commanders. Not perfection, but purposeful. What I was modeling was what I hoped they would model for their personnel.

At one point, I received a phone call from an African American assistant commissioner who I highly regarded, and we had mutual respect and admiration for one another. He mentioned after some light banter that he heard there was a concern that I might be micromanaging the commanders. I listened quietly waiting for the shoe to drop. Instead, he said, "You keep doing just what you're doing. Spending time with your commanders and demonstrating accountability is new for some of them. Stay the course, you're doing a good job." It was nice to know I was supported, but it also gave me pause on who was circulating this perception, or reality. Whichever, it was something I gauged and felt I should better communicate my intentions with my commanders in our monthly and quarterly meetings we held as a group. I discovered that some weren't used to the level of engagement and just needed to be reassured there wasn't something they were doing wrong versus it was my leadership style to be connected. After they learned more about me, my style and how we were a team together, we really came together as a sector. I enjoyed those days. You must have purpose. Rick Warren says it best from his book, *What On Earth Am I Here For?* And I quote, "Character is both developed and revealed by tests, and all of life is a test." All that was before and all that will come after is a test. My character had been shaped by the hue and cry of the trials and tribulations that I had just experienced. As a result, I felt more refined, comfortable, and confident. In Warren's book, he speaks about how everyone's life is driven by something. Within his book he quotes Thomas Carlyle,"The man without a purpose is like a ship without a rudder – a waif, a nothing, a no man." It was one of the first times that I saw and read my purpose clearly and consistently defined.

For me, a purpose driven life was about finding meaningful work that would serve others. I hoped that this, in turn, would give me the drive and hope I felt I needed for significance. Mr. Warren goes on to say, and I'm paraphrasing here, that purpose also simplifies and gives focus to your life. Through God's sifting process, we can become more effective by being selective on where we spend our time, talents, gifts, and energy. This is done to lessen distractions and increase our ability to be of better service. "Whoever wants to be great must become a servant" (Mark 10:43). Biblically, greatness is measured in terms of service, not status. It's measured by how many people you serve and/or help, not how many serve you. Leaning into my servant mindset allowed me to freely let go of the shadows of the past command. My relationships changed and improved, partially because of the new and dynamic folks that I was leading. As a result, we were able to create the kind of synergy needed to be transformational. One of my six new commands was Hayward, the same command where I once walked the halls as an officer almost twenty years prior. It is the same command where my picture as captain now hangs on the wall in the same hallway where the relic captain would look right past me without ever speaking a word. My picture hangs beside those who commanded before me, including the captain that I had admired so many years ago, as well as those who have had the command since me. Surreal is not a descriptive enough word to explain how this felt.

My span of influence had magnified exponentially. I was now one of about 35 other assistant chiefs in an organization of over 11,000. It was a small circle of individuals who had a platform for doing good things and perhaps, even great things and I was one of them.

For context on the infrastructure of the organization, the CHP covers the entire state of California with over 39 million in population. Within the CHP's responsibilities, they ensure safety and enforce traffic laws on approximately 100,000 miles of roadways which includes all state highways, as well as county roads in unincorporated areas. In addition, the department handles all responsibility for state security of personnel and infrastructures. In order to effectively provide that service, the department is divided into around nine field divisions throughout the state. Each division has an executive team of one two-star chief and two or three assistant chiefs that oversee 12-20 plus commands that have between 30-200 employees per command depending on geographic location. Administratively, the department has 4-5 headquarters divisions, often fluctuating to create efficiency, or inefficiency sometimes unfortunately. The entire organization is overseen by a commissioner and the executive organizational team of a deputy commissioner and two assistant commissioners. Due to our massive size, division field offices are given autonomy to operate within their respective jurisdiction to be responsive to their unique community and allied agency partner needs as they are very different from urban to rural location, coastal to valley demographics, and north to south state politics.

While for me in the Bay Area, our division had a total of 16 commands which included our communications center. My responsibility was overseeing six commands with approximately 600-700 people spanning from San Francisco to San Jose. When I went over to Sacramento, our division had 19 commands and I oversaw 8 of them, including our communications center, which covered Lake Tahoe to Tracy, over 100 miles. And as the interim division chief during an extended transition, I oversaw all of our over 2,000 personnel. Hopefully that painted picture gives you clarity on the vast dynamics. To provide even a bit more perspective, at the time that I was promoted to assistant chief, I became one of only two black female assistant chiefs – the only two out of over 7,000 sworn personnel at that time. There had been two before us but had retired. Not long after I was promoted the "other" black female chief retired, and while I may not have been the first black female assistant chief, for that moment, I was the only one. It wasn't too long before another black female was promoted. She has done exceptionally well since that promotion and it makes you feel proud. But one or two at a time, that's not enough. It's hard to create succession that includes diversity, equity and inclusion when there is no one in the pipeline. During this time, we only had around 23-25 African American women on the entire department and there was a big gap in middle management to executive management, meaning one or two again. It's still the same today.

One day, I and the other new, black assistant chief had been asked to attend a Bay Area nonprofit event for young girls in a STEM (science, technology, engineering, & math) program. As we stood in front of the group with our PowerPoint slides scrolling behind us, each of us taking our turn to address these young ladies, I was humbled. Whenever one can influence the life choices of a young person, it's a moving experience. At that moment, I felt like I was living my purpose. I and my CHP comrades were a little intimidated as we were talking with them about the STEM program. After all, we were in the company of aerospace engineers who had just spoken before us. After hearing them, I couldn't imagine what we would have to talk about. But as I was walking toward the podium to say a few words that would hopefully inspire this future generation of young ladies, one of the pictures on my PowerPoint came on the screen. I heard some "ooohs" and "ahhhs." As I looked up, it was a picture of me and the 44th president of the United States, Barack Obama, our country's first African American president.

Feeling the chills running down my arms, the memory of that moment when I met him became so palpable. The picture was taken during a one in a million opportunity which had provided me the chance to meet him in San Francisco at an event he was attending. I will never ever forget that moment. His words were so kind, his eyes were genuinely thoughtful, and he was warm and personable. He asked me my name and we exchanged a few other pleasantries. Afterwards, all I could remember was smiling so big because I couldn't believe that I, that broken little girl in the mirror, was standing with the Commander and Chief of the United States of America. Wow!!! Pinch me, is this really happening?! Okay, that was my inside voice at the time because outside I had to be calm, reserved and professional. Checking my composure every second was hard, but I realized it was okay when I saw Herbie Hancock, a legendary jazz musician, appear to be just as star struck as I was. It was a moment that will forever be imprinted as one of my most powerful memories.

As I drifted back to the present, it came to me what I would share with them. It isn't about what people say you can't do or shouldn't do. It's not even about your own self-doubt. It's all about what you can and will do. It's about being passionate about something that's important to you and finding ways to be of service to others. Working hard today in your chosen field will hopefully provide you a wealth of opportunity for the rest of your life. It won't be easy, but it will be well worth it. They had a number of questions about that presidential moment. I'm not going to lie, I loved talking about it as well! It was, and still is, just as exciting to me as the moment it happened.

These types of moments were the fun part of the job. Modeling something positive for young girls and especially those of color. However, being part of a small group of executives within the organization that is even smaller within your division, the politics of being a chief was not fun. Within our executive leadership team for the entire Bay Area, I shared responsibility with my two peer assistant chiefs and the chief. Together, we covered 20 plus commands spanning nine Bay Area counties with over 100 allied agency partners serving a population of an estimated 10 million people. Our communications center answered over three million 911 service calls annually. Talk about God enlarging your territory!

Day-to-day operations assured you that each day would always be busy coupled with numerous other high-profile incidents as well. "Occupy" and "Black Lives Matter" protests were growing nationally and found themselves local in many of our Bay Area commands. Standing up an Emergency Operations Center (EOC) for coordination and planning for the protests was becoming a standard daily operation. Within this swirl of chaos, I was inspired by the grit and determination of our field staff who day in and day out met the moment by providing safety and security while protecting the rights of peaceful protestors. Until the voices of dissent against the police work a shift in the boots of those police men and women, they shouldn't speak to an experience that they've never lived.

Are there police who abuse their authority and power? Yes. Are there some of them in our organization? Yes. But it is not fair to paint all police officers, us, and/or me, with that broad-brush stroke. Not many folks choose to don a police officer's uniform every day to go out and face uncertainty veiled within the lines of humanity. We are people just like those we encounter. There is no perfection in policing. There is only the space between discernment and discretion - individually and collectively in any given moment. That's why leadership is crucial in transforming policing paradigms and enriching the training available to those on the front lines. This training will help these officers to better understand aspects of trauma informed care, mental health crisis response, implicit bias and help them to expand their emotional intelligence quotient as well.

In addition to the high wire acrobatics of dealing with those incidents, we had large scale projects sitting in the bureaucratic fishbowl. Additionally the last phase of the historic re-construction project on the Bay Bridge was drawing to a close. The bridge would have a new self-anchored suspension bridge added to it and thus become one of the most expensive public works projects in California history with a price tag of $6.5 billion. The bridge carries over 260,000 vehicles across it each day and has one of the longest spans in the United States. Although this project took nearly six years, my captain and I inherited the last phase and all that came with it. The level of public scrutiny we were exposed to was exponential, and it would provide new lessons for me as an assistant chief in both leadership and politics.

The bridge interest was like something going viral in social media every day. I was becoming keenly aware of the insane cycle of "notifications" to the commissioners on this particular project. Not unfamiliar with notification of unusual occurrences, this level of keeping people informed increased my hypervigilance, similar to as an officer working the road from threats of dangerous contacts with suspects only it was surfacing in this environment. The perpetual scanning to stay on top of anything that needed to be reported, kept me on high alert and created increased anxiety leaving me exhausted. Trying to stay ahead of the narrative and keep everyone notified so they could notify the governor 24/7 was impossible. I was not a precog.

It wasn't that they necessarily needed to know right away or like the old saying goes, "yesterday." And it was never just to get the information promulgated to those who were expecting it because that just wasn't enough. It was all about being able to report it up the food chain before anyone else.

As I learned in the following incident, and so many more over the coming years, my work as an assistant chief was a marathon filled with sprint intervals that keeps your heart rate rising. I'll share a funny story about the Bay Bridge. It's funny now, but wasn't so at the time that it took place. The media -you've heard of it, right? I thought I knew what it was about, but I didn't really know...or maybe I really did. As I recall early one morning, a large commercial truck, a big rig for those who are used to that term, caught fire on the west span fo the Bay Bridge. This happened shortly after the construction had ended and the bridge had been completely opened. This truck fire impacted commuter traffic into San Francisco for the entire day. (A point to remember is that the bridge is one of the San Francisco Bay's crown jewels – one of many architectural and engineering gems adorning the world-renowned San Francisco Bay.) The volume of traffic that flows across the bridge during normal business hours on Monday through Friday causes the city's population to surge by at least 20 percent.

The media had pictures of this commercial truck on the span with smoke coming from it being broadcast on all the local TV channels. They didn't have much information, but they were running a continuing narrative that entices the viewers, including the Governor.

I was in my office, having just returned from another incident, when I got a call from the commissioner's office directing me to provide updates every 30 minutes to both the executive offices and the media until the scene was clear. At this point, I was a little frustrated but I completely understood the need to provide updates, just perhaps not so frequently. But being familiar with the process, I fell in line with the directive and made sure the commander and his staff would adhere to it. Within 10 minutes of that phone call, I get another one. This one is from the same executive office, though a different person, directing me to provide them updates every 15 minutes so they could beat the other notification. At this point, I had to try to figure out what in the world was going on. Remember, I'm still a "newbie" Assistant Chief. Momentarily, I forgot that you don't really have any autonomy for making good sound decisions and using professional judgment on your own. I mean, what was I thinking when you have a paramilitary hierarchy to do it for you?

As I would find out later in the day, the reason for the 15 minute interval updates was that the Governor wanted them before the media. One of the reasons he began requesting this information more quickly was that he had seen on the news that the truck was not only smoking, but on fire. Since it was carrying very hazardous material, he was afraid there could be more explosions. More explosions? I was scratching my head. My commander was still at the scene and constantly updating me. Yes, the truck was on fire and was causing a traffic nightmare. But there had been no explosions. None – period It was a large commercial vehicle and cleanup was going to take forever. But Geez!!! Let's not make it worse with a whole lot of incorrect information and just downright misinformation. All day, until that truck was out of the roadway, it was like pushing repeat on the worst music on your playlist. To me, both media and politics sucked. And I didn't want to embrace either of them. Learning where you fit in and what your role is within any new position is a growing period.

As I moved past that incident and got my first lesson in Media and Politics 101, I began to get a clearer understanding of the set of expectations that my bosses had for me. But I was also back to unraveling the real purpose for my placement in this new position. I came to realize that it was to remember the people that actually do the workday in and day out. It's the support staff and administrative personnel that grind it out daily to make sure that the organization is efficient, credentialed, trained, financially prudent and in compliance with the rules of the CHP. All of them working hard to maintain the highest standards of excellence in trying to sustain our always vulnerable information technology infrastructure, saving lives through 911 calls, ensuring the safety of our fleet, and even more importantly, representing our organization with pride and professionalism every day with every incident. Whew! I wrote that without taking a breath...really! For anyone in a leadership role, we must always remember that our people are the most important part of anything we do. When we don't see everyone, we don't see anyone. When we lose sight of that, we lose sight of our purpose. Our "why" as Simon Sinek, the bestselling author, world renowned motivational speaker, would say.

My first assignment as assistant chief was a great experience. When compared to some of the other divisions across the state, it was similar to doing what we call "dog" years. Every year was like seven, in a command that's incredibly busy with the type of critical incidents and high-profile interactions that you could expect to have.

About a year and a half later, one of the senior assistant chiefs in the Sacramento area was preparing for retirement. This division was the closest that I would ever get to being home and it was one of only a couple of opportunities that I would ever have at getting it, and this was one of them. I immediately began to consider how I should approach the chief in charge of that division about the opportunity.

We had met several times and even worked on a project or two over the years. However, one of the things I remembered most was that whenever I saw him, I would always mention getting back home. So important when manifesting our dreams. Talk about it as if it is or has already happened. Now my opportunity had arrived. I called him to express my interest and let him know that I would be sending a follow-up email with my resume, while, of course, working through the proper chain of command. It was a great call...I had it with his answering machine!

It had been a couple of years or so since the Stockton command debacle and I was going to try not to get caught up on a technicality again. Yes, I knew it would be a similar process of a senior assistant chief potentially being interested, or that I would have to interview. I was emotionally ready for this round and had already completed some practice sparring rounds inside my mental arena. Not long after I left the voice message, I had a return call to my work cell phone from the chief. I was nervous when I saw the name on the cell phone and my heartbeat picked up its pace pretty significantly. Darn anxiety. You know that odd feeling you get in your stomach right before you speak to a large group of people? Or the one you get when your nerves get a hold of you and you're not sure of what's about to happen. I picked up the phone and since he is such a normally upbeat person, he was typically jovial and almost bouncy over the phone. Before there was time for me to find any ease in the tone of his voice, he got right to it. He simply said, "We'll see you on June 1st. Well, wait a minute, it's May 20th and it usually it takes 30 days. The sooner the better for us but whatever will work best for you before the 30 days. I know how bad you want to get back close to home. Welcome back!"

After the call, I seemed to be in an alternate universe for the moment. I faintly heard him explaining that there was no interview necessary as I was the senior assistant chief and my reputation and performance in the Golden Gate Division, Bay area, was excellent. He felt my experience in community engagement would be pivotal to the work we needed to do in his division. I muttered with what I believed to be comprehensible language, "Thank you! Thank you so much. I cannot wait to get to work!"

This is a critical reminder on navigating your organizational network your entire career if you have aspirations to promote or to simply be considered for an assignment. Networking is not butt kissing, it's building relationships and bringing value in your contributions to the greater organization. You never know who will be in a room making a decision about your future when you're not in it, so always work to make a good impression authentically every time you get a chance. You may get the chance to go home, I did.

As my heart was singing, my mind was spinning. There was some really great work being done by some amazing people that I would be leaving in my current division. I felt good about the leadership development that had taken place with my commanders - through the promotional preparation study groups and promotions. There had been some great losses, some great gains, and more than anything, so many memorable and influential moments. All of which I would carry with me and hope that all of those that I had worked alongside would feel the same. But my time here was done. It was time to go home.

The transition to the Valley Division command in Sacramento felt seamless. I was welcomed with open arms and in the same breath thrown into the thrashing of daily operations of my direct responsibilities. Eight commands from South Lake Tahoe to Tracy California, the third largest communications center, community outreach, recruitment, media relations, backgrounds and hiring. It felt like a good fit.

It was now moving into late fall and the beginning of early winter in Sacramento. The incidences of protests were subsiding as the weather began to get cold and wet. I was sitting at my desk in my new office looking out of one of the long vertical windows from the third floor watching the storm clouds roll in. As I sat there I penned this blog:

"Stormy weather blew in slowly with big, billowy clouds changing from milky white to ominous grey. As it seemed like the clouds expanded from inhaling deeply, as there was a dramatic pause, to prepare to blow out all of their energy, the skies opened up with torrential rain and sheets of hail. The energy was electrifying as the sky lit up and the clashing of the clouds sounded thunderously. It was a brief, but extraordinarily powerful display of nature that was unrestricted and free to dance across the sky as it chose. Almost as quickly as the storm had blown in, the skies returned to the clearest and most vibrant blue with cotton ball clouds. As I watched from my tiny office window, I was amazed at the glory of God's power and authority. It was so seamless how the weather can change in a moment's notice from blue sky to stormy weather...and in that same moment, back to blue sky. I smiled as God spoke with that very simplistic reminder that our circumstances will blow through and all we have to do is wait out the stormy weather."

That moment was important. Just as I was getting comfortable in my new division, there was a rumble emerging around the next promotional examination for two star chief. At the same time, my daughter was only a few months away from her high school graduation.

Regarding the promotional examination, my chief encouraged me to take the exam as he was going to be retiring soon and he was thinking about succession in the division leadership-a very kind consideration, but at the same time not possible. It rarely ever works out in the CHP that you actually assume a command that you've been working in as the next whatever the rank may be. People are shuffled around and put in positions miles from their home. They are sometimes made to flip their life upside down to meet the random checkerboard of so-called "good fit" placements throughout the state. Basically, tenured chiefs, anywhere in the state, have the inside edge regardless of competency, capability, or capacity. I really wasn't sure if I was ready to fight another one of those battles either externally or internally. I told my chief that I appreciated the encouragement and would think about it.

Emily's Sand Trays

My daughter Emily's graduation from high school was quickly approaching. I couldn't believe that she was going to be finished with high school - my baby girl. We had completed numerous applications for college admission that fall. It was a trying time as it was like pulling teeth to get her to sit down and get this done. But, somehow we did it. She had finals coming up shortly and I know that she was distracted. But she seemed very anxious and overly stressed. I had only a sliver of access to her personal life, only whatever she chose to share with me, you know how teenagers can be. Every now and then I might come across her talking with her friends when they stopped by. One night, I was sitting in the living room watching TV when she came down the hallway from her room. She stood over the back of the couch and looked down at me. I could see her sadness and worry. Emily has such beautiful brown eyes with wildly curly long hair. Her little nose sits so cutely on her face. She's a beauty-God's creation for sure.

Now I know that mothers are intuitive, but as a police officer as well, I am hypervigilant on all things. Because of all the incidents of death, injury, and broken lives that I had seen or been involved in with young people drinking and driving, trafficking, and the one that always kept me on my toes - suicides; I stopped and paused the TV to fully acknowledge her. I asked her what was wrong, and she began to unload all that was on her mind and heart. What I hadn't realized was that she was having relationship challenges with her boyfriend on top of the pressure she, and I'm sure we as parents, placed on her to get all As was becoming overwhelming.

As she continued to shower me with this rain of fears, insecurities, anxiety, I heard words that struck a very specific chord with me. Somehow, my own insecurities regarding how I saw myself and whether I was ever good or being perfect enough, had rubbed off onto her. Yes, our children are just like sponges. Yet somehow we want them to only absorb the good things and certainly not those things that will hamper their emotional, spiritual, and mental growth. She was only 11 when the divorced proceedings had begun and when my mom, her grandma, had died. Those had been exceedingly difficult times for her and for all of us.

My ex-husband and I had both thought about taking them to counseling, but we didn't. My son was 16 and didn't want to go and my daughter had been before. That was then. She was now 18 and as we navigated her conversation, she was sharing with me very intimate details of her relationship with her boyfriend. It took everything I had to remain neutral while another part of me was fuming over the things she was describing about the dynamics of their relationship. I decided to offer a mother's ear and only occasionally mention some considerations I thought she might want to do or think about. I've learned, through trial and error, that active listening is so much more valuable to her than trying to solve her problems or overly agree with her. I think she felt better as she talked through it but it was apparent that she was going to need more than her mother. She was always in my prayers and now they would be a lot more specific after this conversation.

I suggested that she could go to the therapist that she had seen when she was younger. At that time she had been having some anxiety issues. Her expression acknowledged that she remembered Dr. Velma. She said that she had really liked her. She had seen her when she was five and again when she was around ten years old. The first time she met with her, she had stopped eating. We could barely get her to eat or drink anything. After a couple of days of that, I became very afraid and took her to the pediatrician. At that point, I was open to anything, but she just wouldn't eat. Other suggestions included taking her to a therapist - one that works specifically with children. Desperately seeking help, that is what I did.

Dr. Velma was a small Jewish woman who was maybe all of 5'1" and had a very soft voice. She first met with me and my husband. I suppose to get the details, but also I think to assess our family dynamic and our relationship as parents. These inquiries were subtle but I know they were intended to help our daughter. Even back then, my husband and I had a jagged marriage. There were many sharp edges and eggshell moments. It was definitely a "suck it up and keep it moving" marriage. After she spoke with us a bit, she invited Emily to join us. I didn't think Dr. Velma's soft voice could get any softer, but when she spoke to Emily it was like she was the most precious child she had ever met. It disarmed Emily's fears and within no time she was freely talking with Dr. Velma.

Interestingly, she used sand trays when she worked with children. How does it work? Glad you asked, because I had been curious too. Well, it's literally a tray filled with sand and it is used to allow patients an opportunity to express their thoughts and feelings when words alone are not enough. She gave Emily no real instructions other than to go play with the sand trays. She could use any of the toys, figures or anything in the room to put in her sand tray. Throughout the session, she would check in on her from time to time but she pretty much let her move about on her own.

When we were wrapping up the first session, Dr. Velma had Emily bring the sand tray over and explain what she had placed in it. In the tray was a TV with her dad sitting on the couch watching it. There was a figure representing me in the kitchen, along with another that represented her brother playing in front of the TV and finally one representing her sitting with her brother. At the dining table was a figure that was supposed to be her grandmother. She was sitting all by herself far away from all of the other figures. This was all explained by my daughter through the questions Dr. Velma was asking her at the time. She then asked her, "Why is Grandma sitting way over here by herself?" My daughter told her because she moved and now lives far away from all of us.

As Dr. Velma explored all of this with my daughter, it was like a light came on for all of us. She missed her grandmother, my mother who had raised her for the first 5 years of her life. My mother had, without any notice to anyone, decided to move to southern California and live with her niece who was very ill. However, a few times she had alluded to her feelings being hurt after I had created some boundaries to give me, all of us, some healthy space.

She had said that she felt she wasn't needed that much once Emily had started school. During the first five years of Emily's life, she had literally lived with us for a time and then had moved right down the street from us. If my mother had been able to have her way, she would have lived with us for the rest of her life. However, that wouldn't have worked at all. It had been a difficult decision for me as a young wife. Trying to find the proper balance was hard. It was like on the TV show *Everybody Loves Raymond* where his parents, the Barones, are always walking over to Raymond's house. Sometimes it worked, and other times, it made it difficult for everyone.

When my mother moved down the street, she came by our house frequently. I felt that was a fair compromise. I was trying to establish my own family, to be a wife, to be a mother and still go to work everyday. We needed some boundaries. However, as I look back on this situation now, I realize that I could have been more compassionate, empathetic, and perhaps more patient with my mother. After she had a significant injury when she was in her early 60s, she had to retire permanently. In addition, she was dealing with her own long history of depression and loneliness while still battling a nagging prescription medication addiction even then.

In retrospect, I forgot to lean into her with love. So when she shared the news that she was suddenly moving 400 miles away, and that she had sold her home for a fraction of its worth, on top of trading in her brand new car for a used car just so she could get enough cash to facilitate this move, I was not at all empathetic. She was always so compulsive and never communicating so I could understand. To me, it looked like she was reverting to how she had been when I was a child, careless and inconsiderate. I was angry with her for again being so irresponsible. Acting the way she had off and on for my entire life - throwing away the only things she owned, withdrawing all of her small retirement settlement, and just packing a few bags and moving away. Her way of living was nonchalant and flippant and I struggled to understand why she was this way.

As a child growing up, she never owned a home, a new or newer car, or ever had much of a bank account. We lived in pieces, or fractions of a living space. Sometimes I'll have a moment where I cringe remembering that we had stayed in a Salvation Army (SA) facility and had slept on cots with other homeless people because we didn't have anywhere to stay. But in those same moments, if I stay with them a little while longer, I remember the chicken fried steak with mashed potatoes that the cook at that same SA facility would make for dinner. How it was one of my favorite dishes and would think about it often in the moments after we had left there. I guess that just as quickly as I am to be embarrassed and ashamed of my mother, I am also ashamed and embarrassed of myself. Shame is a shadow that has followed me for years.

Recently I was reading Brene Brown's book, *Daring Greatly*, where she shares her research on shame, vulnerability, and fear. "Shame derives its power from being unspeakable. That's why it loves perfectionists..." I had been ashamed of myself, my mother, and my childhood for so long that it was not until my mother had passed away that I finally realized how much I really loved her and how very intense my sense of loss was in her passing. Not just her physical death but in all that I had missed out on because of my own veil of shame - the same veil of shame that had kept me from seeing beyond her imperfections - that had kept me from being able to love her fully.

CHAPTER 8
Time to be a Mother and Sugga

As Dr. Velma concluded the session, she suggested we let her talk with her grandma more often and it worked. She gradually started to eat again. She began with some pudding, then a little ice cream and over time she was again able to eat regular food. But in reality she has never been able to overcome her love-hate relationship with food. She is still shy when eating out and with other people.

As she was now reaching this teenage crossroads, seeking out Dr. Velma seemed like the right thing to do and something that we should do right away. Her anxiety was more worrisome to me now because she was a young adult, and she was dealing with things that only she really knew the depth of their importance. Young people often only use their limited network of friends to help them navigate these very serrated issues. In reality, most teenagers have the same limited life experience and sometimes they can plant thoughts and ideas among themselves which can be even more dangerous than the original problem.

We were able to get an appointment pretty quickly, and I was so thankful that my health insurance covered the sessions. Since she was now an adult, I only drove her to and from the appointments. I explained to her that she didn't need to share anything that she and Dr. Velma had discussed unless she wanted to.

The conversations between them were intended to be confidential and she could share anything that she wanted to in that safe space. For the most part she didn't discuss the sessions but on one occasion she asked me bluntly, "Mom, how did you learn to get back up and move on after the divorce?" I was taken by surprise with her question as she was very young when the separation and divorce took place. I wanted to be careful not to make this about her father or her father and me, but about what she needed from me by asking that question.

What I shared with her was how important it is for us to be able to forgive others and ourselves-it's how we regain our peace. From that place of peace, we can restore our capacity to love and commit to relationships, knowing that they will not be perfect. In all of this, it's important to remember that we are all different. We should start each encounter with a small level of trust and until that person begins to demonstrate behaviors that either encourage or erode that trust, we can't assume or create concerns or worry about what might happen. They'll be trustworthy, or they won't. You will either choose to forgive and move forward with them, or forgive and move on without them. It is important for you to find your peace through your own lens of vulnerability, openness, and forgiveness. It will set you free and you can finally exhale.

The sessions with Dr. Velma were helpful and she began to find some coping strategies through working in her creative space of sketching and painting. She is amazingly gifted in both the left and right sides of her brain. One minute she can solve the most complex math equations and then take 20 minutes to detail the most beautiful sketch of anything she desires with just one look at it. My favorite sketches are the ones she does of the "Marvel" comics' characters. Through all of this, she was able to ease into the final steps of transitioning from high school to college.

Emily's Graduation

With the graduation approaching, there would be some family dynamics that would require all of us to put on our big boy and girl pants and get it done. Thankfully we were able to do just that. Her grandmother and aunts on her father's side came all the way from the east coast. I hadn't seen them in years. I had felt a bit hurt that none of them ever reached out to me during the separation and divorce, but through it all we had remained cordial. I have had more connection with an aunt and some of his cousins over the years which has been nice.

There was no animosity or resentment - what had happened was just a fact of life. After the divorce, one thing that I had tried to do was to make sure that her father and I always worked together as parents for both Emily and Sean, our son. I was a little nervous about seeing all of them since I was hosting a graduation celebration for Emily at my house the next day and they were all invited.

The graduation and the graduation party went well. I had tremendous support and help from my beloved boyfriend. He worked tirelessly behind the scenes to avoid any distractions. He didn't attend and my heart was broken that I didn't have the courage to have him by my side. It was just too overwhelming to consider how it might make my daughter and son feel with both their father and my boyfriend there. Wanting to refrain from drama, he made the decision for me. He is so kind and is always willing to take a step back so that I can maintain balance in my world. I think he feels confident knowing that we are connected in a way that left us no doubt of who we are or where we belonged.

That night was both wonderful and defining for me. It was a time that needed me to put on my own big girl pants. It was so challenging for me to find separation form past "family" to the present reality and to allow myself, yes me, the chance to be free to live my life for me too. Wasn't I entitled to more than just my duties and responsibilities as a mother, to the department, or as an assistant chief? It was time for me too, right? It was time for me to have a personal, private, and loving relationship with someone who adores me. I cried at the end of the evening, conflicted with trying to be considerate of everyone else, while trying to rationalize that I wasn't very considerate of Kevin. But he came back over later and helped me to clean up and we cuddled the rest of the night. If he had been hurt by any of it, he never said a word. He has never really expressed to me any problem that he may have had in accommodating whatever either of us needed to do to make it all work. He always just did whatever was necessary and to this day, he still does. Either way, my heart was bursting with my adoration for him because of his selflessness. I was truly in love with this man. It felt good.

Miscarriage to Miracle

After the divorce, the other man in my life had really been my son. Helping him to navigate high school, junior college and finish his education at a four-year university was my focus. There is no way you could have told me after my destructive teenaged years that I would still be blessed with being able to give birth to him first and Emily later. I should probably hide myself from those promiscuous days, but I've already given this area of my life over to God. Beginning at the age of 13, boys my own age and young adult men were having sex with me. With my first one, I didn't know what I didn't know. With my second one, he knew better, but I didn't know that I had a choice. This was my shameful battle for many years.

Shortly after I got married, I found out that I was pregnant with my son. I was scared because just a few months before I had miscarried. It was a tough time emotionally as I was still trying to navigate work. At that time, I had only been on the force a few years and didn't have much sick leave or vacation time. But as Sean grew inside me and I seemed to be getting past those more worrisome milestones, I exhaled. However, I started having complications with blood pressure and toxemia and was placed on bed rest. Toxemia is a dangerous condition and can cause low birth weights, breathing problems for the baby, premature delivery, stress on the mother's organs and high blood pressure with swelling occurs. I was experiencing it all.

187

This was difficult financially, as I could no longer go to work even in a limited capacity. As a result, the benefits that I had at this time (1992) were literally less than a quarter of my regular pay. We could no longer live in our apartment and had to move in with my mother who lived nearby. I was thankful for her willingness to help but also felt a little awkward. After all I was newly married, having a baby and wanting to be self-sufficient.

My son was born roughly five weeks before his due date and he arrived on Mother's Day, 1992. I had gotten up early that day feeling some pain in my lower back. I felt a little stiff. But having been on bed rest for the previous four months due to the toxemia, I didn't think much of it. However, as the pain intensified over the next few hours, I let my husband know that I thought we should get checked at the hospital. After a few scans and tests, the doctor felt an emergency cesarean section was needed. The baby was breech, and the doctors were having trouble confirming a regular heartbeat. I was just 24 years old.

Not knowing what all of that really meant, my husband and I agreed to do whatever was needed for the baby. After the epidural and whatever other meds they give you in such an instance, everything for me seemed to slow down and get blurry. I remember that there was a sheet covering me so that I couldn't see the actual procedure. Off to the left side of me my husband was watching all that was going on, keeping me apprised of the events as they unfolded. All that I could feel was an intense tugging in my lower abdomen. After they got my son out, I was able to briefly get a glimpse of him. He seemed blue or purple, but I couldn't be sure because I was so groggy.

He was whisked out to the NICU because one of his lungs wasn't fully inflated. Being sedated, I couldn't really comprehend what was happening. It wasn't until I started coming out of it, that I was told and became aware of the problems he was having. He had been transferred to the NICU at the Children's Hospital in Oakland. I couldn't go with him because of the surgery, which would keep me in the hospital three days for recovery. While there were no video calls or instant messaging in those days, there were "Polaroid" pictures. My mother and husband brought some photos back to me and he looked worse now than what I thought I saw when I was sedated. Scared that I had done this to him, I was devastated until I was actually able to see him.

On the day of my release from the hospital, we went right over to see him. It was a moment that left my heart in my throat. For safety's sake, we had to put on gowns to go into the room where these itty bitty babies were hooked up to ventilators and oxygen tents. As they led me to him, I immediately began crying with relief and uncertainty. He was of good size, 5lbs. 3oz., but he had been intubated with an oxygen tent over him. I wasn't able to hold him, but I could touch him. I could see him breathe and see his little fingers and toes. It was a long 3 weeks of spending every waking moment at the hospital, pumping breast milk and sitting in the rocking chair next to my son's spot in the NICU. His father and I rotated when possible, but he still had to work. Hard to believe that little miracle has now grown into a 6'6" 240 lb. athlete and is now the father of his own little miracle. God works in full circles in our lives.

God's Plan is the Plan

The summer had since faded away and the blazing 100 degree plus temperatures were starting to slip into the low 90s and upper 80s as we moved closer to October. Emily was all moved into her dorm room at her university an hour or so away. She would be there in her first year with her brother who was a senior at the same school. That gave me a great amount of comfort. The last time they had been in school together was grade school. He was a 6th grader and she was in kindergarten. God's timing is so perfect. My son's transition to the university was a path that could have only been orchestrated by God. For you see, he had been an all 'A' student for most of his school life. He excelled at academics and he had enjoyed learning, especially reading and even the overall structure of school itself. Sometimes, even when he was still in elementary school, he would surprise me with his wisdom. I often thought of him as an "old soul."

During his junior year of high school, he suddenly lost his grandmother and almost simultaneously his father moved out of our house. As a result, his grades began to take a steep decline and if it wasn't for maintaining the required GPA for playing basketball, he might have simply just stopped trying all together. Or at least that's how it seemed. I'm not sure that I will ever really know what he was experiencing. He rarely expressed any interest in talking about such things. I noticed my young son was turning into a young man and, along the way he had become very particular in his ways. He had grown from looking up to me, to looking directly into my eyes, to now towering over me at 6'4" by the age of 16. He had a girlfriend, Lauren, who he had been dating for quite a while. She was good for his spirit and still is to this day. Although at that time, I was still getting to know her and I felt their relationship was going to give him the support he needed during these difficult times.

As we worked through the divorce and the new realities of our family dynamics, Sean began to regain some of his academic equilibrium especially as he moved into his senior year. In spite of that, I couldn't shake the fact that the problems of his junior year had placed some barriers in the road to some of his college opportunities. Yes, I, like most parents, have these high expectations of where we want our children to be in life and how they should get there. What I forgot again was that I'm not in control. God is.

In November of his senior year in high school, we began applying to various colleges on Sean's behalf. There weren't many university options available, at least not without literally having to pay the proverbial "arm and a leg." What I also noticed was something that I really didn't want to accept. He wasn't ready to go to a four-year college. He was still dealing with some of the residual emotions from all that had happened over the last couple of years. Also, he was very much in love with his high school sweetheart.

As a result of all of this, I began to explore some opportunities for him to play basketball at the local junior college. This would allow him to finish with his AA degree in two years. He could then transfer to a four year university and get his BS or BA degree in just two additional years. He would be the first in our immediate family to have finished high school and have gone straight to college. Emily would be the next. Although, I obtained my Bachelor of Science in management and then my master's degree in Law Enforcement and Public Safety Leadership at the University of San Diego, I had done it over the next 30 years of my life after high school. I wanted to change that legacy in our family to placing a priority on education. It's not the only thing you need to get ahead in this world, but it gives my young black adults a very significant step up. It helps and bolsters them as they seek employment, contribute to the greater good, and build their relationship with Christ. My pastor always says, "When you know better, you do better." Now as a parent, I know better and so do they, so my expectations are higher.

For some of his last few high school basketball games, he was playing in an out of town tournament. He was having a great game. I noticed an old friend of mine who had played ball overseas sitting in the stands. I went over to say hello and catch up a bit. As we were standing near the hallway to the locker rooms, I saw one of the coaches from the junior college near our home watching the game. Suddenly, I heard someone say, "Go over and speak to him." I had heard it, but I wasn't sure if my friend had heard it too. I paused and let it sink in. I excused myself from the conversation that I was having with my friend and proceeded to walk toward this coach. I had only seen him a few times when my son had been playing tournament games that were being held at the junior college. As I approached him, I said, "Hello. You may not remember me, but…" and before I could finish he said, "Yeah, you're Sean's mom, right? You're a police officer!" A little surprised by my notoriety, I smiled, and we began to chat. He mentioned that my son was having a good game and had really improved since he had seen him last year. This was my moment, so I decided to take advantage of it. I asked him if he thought my son could play on his team at the junior college. He smiled and said he was only the assistant coach, but he thought he would have a good chance. I finished the conversation by asking him if he wouldn't mind speaking with my son after the game if he got a chance. I thanked him for his time and went back to my seat to watch the rest of the game.

Later that evening when my son got home, he had a big smile on his face as he mentioned that the coach I had spoken to had acknowledged his great game. He also said that they had talked about future opportunities for him to play. Check. One seed planted. The next step on my list was to reach out to his current high school basketball coach and see if he could help by giving him a good recommendation to the head coach over at the junior college. His high school basketball coach was a gruff guy and didn't like to deal with parents during the season. He believed the players were becoming men and could speak for themselves if they had something to say or had any concerns with his coaching. Well, let's just say that during my son's first year of high school basketball, I had to learn a few lessons about staying in my lane! It was the coach's world and I had to learn fast how to work within it. So, shortly after basketball season was over, I approached him at the awards banquet. I simply made my request and without hesitation he agreed to speak with the junior college coach. He also shared with me that he thought very highly of my son both for his work ethic and his commitment to the program over the last four years. He never missed a game, or practice and whether he started or came in off the bench, he played hard. As a

191

parent that moment was pretty profound. I had watched how hard it was for my son after all he had gone through, to give so much to the team. It was so nice to hear it from the coach.

Let's fast forward a bit, Sean Jr. is now in his second year of junior college while playing on the basketball team as well. He's not a starter, but he gets to play, which for me is plenty. You see, my overall goal had been to keep my son's interest in basketball alive while ensuring he got an education. Being on the team allowed him to have priority registration so he was able to sign up for classes before the general student population. And you'd better believe we were registered early and with the right classes to ensure a two-year completion. It was around the fall of his second year that the assistant coach left to become the assistant coach at a university. My son had developed a great friendship with him since their conversation after his game during his senior year in high school. His departure would be a big loss for the team and for my son. You know how often it is said that it takes a village to raise a child. Well, this coach had been a part of our village.

Unbeknownst to me, he had been talking to my son about following him to the university and had shared with him some basketball scholarship opportunities that might be available. Well, as all of this had been happening, I was working to see where he could finish his final two years. At that point it looked like he was going to finish at the California State University of Sacramento which I was hoping would be affordable. In the spring of my son's last year at the junior college, he came to me and asked if he could attend the university where his former coach was working and if we could check it out. I agreed.

We drove up to the school that was about an hour or so away and sat down with the financial folks in the administration office to work on the dollars and cents of his attending there. You must remember that he was supposed to be able to get some basketball scholarship money to help with the cost. Once the university financial representative had asked all of her questions and finalized the numbers, including any estimated FAFSA (Free Application for Federal Student Aid) assistance, she gave us the form with the final numbers. I looked at the numbers, looked at my son, and then looked at the lady. My question to her was, "Is this the final number? It doesn't appear to include any scholarship money that my son said he would be able to receive for playing basketball." She let me know that she did not have any information regarding scholarships from the coaches or anyone else at that time or she would have included that information in my son's FAFSA portal. As calmly as I could, I told her we would need a minute. My son already knew what I was going to say as his head was hanging low. He had completely lost the anticipation and excitement that he had when we arrived.

We left that afternoon feeling deflated. He was heartbroken and I was distraught because there was no way his father and I would be able to pay such a large amount of money for one semester, let alone for four. We were going to finish junior college without having to take out any loans. It would be paid in full. As we drove the hour and a half back home, I kept mulling over how I could finance such a large amount and make it work. The years after the divorce had been hard for me - balancing the first and second mortgages on our family home, along with car payments, household bills and expenses for the kids. I never told anyone that during those years we almost lost the house to foreclosure. It had only been recently that we were doing okay. As we got closer to home, he relaxed a little and began to talk with me. He explained that he understood and didn't know what had happened regarding the scholarship. He told me how much he appreciated me taking the time to go and see if it was even possible. We later found out that the head coach didn't have it in his budget to offer him a scholarship starting that spring, but that he might be able to offer him something in the fall. Sean Jr. was hopeful again.

As he was completing his second year at the junior college, he began putting his information together to send to the university to apply for the fall semester. Unfortunately, as they were assessing his transferable units from the junior college, it became apparent that he needed to have a higher grade in one of his math classes in order for that credit to be transferable. Without it, he would have to take an additional class and as result be at the university for almost three years as opposed to two.

I quickly did the math and realized that this would not be an option at all. So, it became imperative that I find a way for him to pass this class with a higher grade that would be acceptable for transfer. The only class available was a summer class. He signed up and took the course, but unfortunately was not able to raise the grade. He had to appeal to the junior college to be able to take the class again in the fall. Yes, time was passing and the fall semester at the university was no longer an option.

During all of this, my son's optimism had been drained. He became sullen and I felt that he seemed to be in a very dark place. I wanted this for him so badly, but I couldn't do it for him. We signed up for the fall math class and waited to see if he was going to be able to improve his grade.

Have you ever wondered how God is able to work out all of the things in your life that you absolutely have no way of seeing or believing? That next year, after my son had completed the math class, he was able to enroll in the university and make the basketball team as a starting player. And wait...when we sat down with the financial advisor at the university and she placed the final numbers in front of us, I looked at Sean Jr. and he looked at me.

God had taken $24,000 a semester down to $8,000 a semester with the ability to pay in three installments. Let's do this! Don't tell me what God can't do! Sean's father and I could easily afford that together and there would only be a small college loan debt for my son after his final two years. Oh, let me not forget to tie this all together in a slight recap of how God is always working. The junior college coach, who God had directed me to talk to and who then took the time to speak with my son while he was still in high school, ended up helping him get on the junior college team. He kept him focused on his grades, encouraged him to continue his education at the university level, and helped him get on the university basketball team. This man was a blessing to my son and our family in ways I'm not sure he will ever understand. My son graduated with a degree in psychology and a minor in child development. He maintained a 3.5 GPA and even ended up coaching for awhile as the junior varsity head coach. There are no coincidences with God. His plan is the plan.

Empty Nesting

Summer was gone. Both kiddos were basking in the new school year in college. Sean was handling it pretty well but Emily was going through some separation anxiety and homesickness. According to a survey by the UCLA Higher Education Institute, 69 percent of first year college students report feeling homesick. I missed her as much as she missed me, but I would not buckle in to her wanting to come home. I couldn't help remembering all the times that I had called my mom from the pay phone at the police academy crying that I wanted to come home and telling her that I couldn't do it anymore. She would listen to all my whining and complaining and simply tell me, "You're not coming home. Get some sleep. Tomorrow is a new day." Despite all I had been through with my mother, she wouldn't let me give up on myself and I certainly wasn't going to let Emily give up on herself either. She was ready to leave college and she also had a high school boyfriend who apparently wanted her to come home as well. However, I didn't think he was good for her spirit. I really thought that their relationship was unhealthy. Immaturity can create those dysfunctional high school paradigms.

I felt the distance would be good for her. It would give her an opportunity to mature and learn to navigate an environment at a Christian school which I hoped would give her room to bump her head yet hopefully not suffer a concussion. Let's just say that she got through it without injury but I'm not sure I can say the same for those she may have bumped heads with… LOL. She never really bumped heads with anyone physically, but she found her voice in college. She began to stand up against the things that she didn't agree with amongst her peers which with the fear of being ostracized can be tough to do. She would share with me how she felt "judged" by some of the students who were overly "religious." She felt something similar even from the few students of color because she didn't talk like them or by some of the other students who wanted to go out drinking and just hang out all of the time when she really didn't want to. She wasn't perfect, but she was doing her best.

Although outwardly with her I was firm in my stance that she stay in school, I missed her terribly. The same separation anxiety that happens for our children during this time happens for us as parents. Empty nest syndrome is real and we can experience grief, fear, loss, sadness, and anxiety. I don't know how many times when I'd walk past her room, all kept ready for her visits, was absolutely empty and silent. Sometimes I would just go take a nap in her room to feel close to her. But I felt grounded in the spirit that her education, this experience of maturation and personal growth, was pivotal for her to be able to launch into her adulthood with an advantage. It was hard, so hard but we both did it.

While balancing the calls from both of my children and work, I began to allow myself to openly date my boyfriend. I loved how he called me his "Sugga" and simply, but sweetly, "J". We took a big step and moved in together. Initially, I didn't feel that I was ready to move to where he he was 400 miles away, but if he was willing to take the leap, then so was I. Why not? It was an adjustment in many ways as I had been on my own for several years with the kids. I really didn't know how to be in a relationship with him without the distance between us, as that's what we had done for the first four years. But it was nice having him around. He helped me with everything you could think of and one of my very favorite things was that he loved taking walks with me. I could remember so clearly all of the times that I prayed to have someone to walk with me and talk with me - someone that would be my best friend and soul mate. He would pull my blanket back on my side of the bed and cuddle me as we fell off to sleep. He would sit on the couch with me and laugh. We would share the happenings of our day, and all while he'd massage my tired feet without skipping a beat. Yes, ladies, he rubbed my feet.

We'd have our two-person book club and he'd write me beautiful love letters that would speak to my soul:

Baby J,

Your eyes cut with a shyness which speaks aloud that voice alone cannot say. The quiet stillness of your spirit has moved many a mountain but has remained steadfast. Simplicity is sought but not without strength and wisdom for the present requires steadiness and resolve. Ah, the Spirit which has upheld when the shadows, have at times, overwhelmed, yet you move forward. All is true beauty beyond the eye.

It's as beautiful as any love story I had ever read or seen and it's mine–it's for both of us with our broken and baggage filled lives. We were creating our own synergy and God was easing my fears of the "what ifs." With him, I felt like I was enough. We were enough together. And he stills rubs my feet.

CHAPTER 9

One Last Promotional Examination ~ Chief

Study? Ugh! Who has time? I remember studying when I could, but I was so busy being a yes person to all the things executive management asked me to do, I really didn't have time to study. I was on so many internal and external committees, sitting on promotional panels, developing curriculum, being loaned out for other agency hiring panels, working on EEO and internal investigations, all while overseeing my eight commands and sometimes the entire division. The very epitome of the twelve habits that keep you from rising in a healthy way as you ascend in leadership. Just in this list alone of things I was doing it's evident the level of people pleasing, perfectionism and overvaluing expertise imbalance that I was allowing to envelope me. I knew better, but it was easy to fall back into those default patterns of behavior.

The community smoke was billowing once again with the scourge of injustice. It felt as though we were in a daily marathon without hydrating stations or an apparent finish line. Often, finding time alone to anchor my spirit and my thoughts on anything other than the daily grind was impossible. Toward the end of one particular day, my chief and I were the only ones still in the building. He was at his desk, which was through the outdated wood paneled wall to the right of my office, and I was in mine. Needing to finalize some verbiage on one of my assignments, I wandered over to his office to get his approval before submitting the package.

As I was cresting the doorway, I overheard him on the phone finishing up a conversation. "Absolutely, we will have no problem making sure we have a chief over there first thing in the morning to represent the department. Ok, sounds good sir. I will update you after the event." Internally, or at least I thought it was internal, I cringed at the thought of what one of us was going to have to do this time. You know, when I was first promoted to assistant chief, I was all in for whatever was ask of me. I was eager and passionate about transformative change and doing great things. You know, "With great power comes great responsibility." Either you're a "Spider-Man" fan or for me, you're based in biblical principles. Actually, I enjoy a good "Spider-Man" movie as much as the next person. However, what I had discovered over the last few years was that the needle hadn't moved very much. At times I was able to see small winkles of change, but for the most part, it was just a continuing cyclical conversation on never changing issues.

He looked up with his best "boy do I have an opportunity for you" grin on his face. I appreciated him championing me for the next promotion because everyone needs support at each juncture of their career. But to be honest, by this time, I had reached a point where my desire to keep promoting was waning. So many discouraging and disappointing moments had occurred stemming from vicissitudes, insufficiencies, to sycophancy, that I began to shrink away from wanting to promote into his position. Politicking is tiresome and I was certainly getting tired. Luckily, all of this was how I felt inside. Outwardly, I just smiled and asked him how I could help.

Almost before I knew it, the Chief's exam was happening, and then it was over. During the rotation of panels, I just hemorrhaged information. Riding home afterwards, I felt relieved that it was over. I also felt like I was stuck in some sort of weird slow-motion reflection on what I didn't say versus the really dumb things I felt that I said. I think I really wanted to cry, but I didn't. I couldn't. I was just trying to breathe. After a few heart flutters more, I was able to exhale enought to drive myself home for the day. Once I got home and walked through the door, it was like the weight of my professional self fell to the floor. I went to my room and took off my business suit of armor and sat on the edge of the bed.

The inner voice telling me that I still was not good enough was raging in my mind. This feeling was so strong I couldn't even understand my mumbling as I was repeating what I thought was words. It went on for what seemed like an eternity of metacognition. I was searching for a heuristic moment to try to navigate the chaos of my thoughts. Ugh! Why do I want to continue to put myself through this gauntlet of promotions when afterwards, this is how I treat myself.

Trying to eradicate my inner voices is an overwhelming chore that can sometimes be handled by simply taking a nap. So, on this day, that is what I did. Mom had always been right about getting some sleep.

When I woke up, it was still early enough to get myself together and prepare dinner fo rmy daughter who was home from school. Somehow, moving through the rest of the evening dulled my thoughts and desires about trying to replay or ruminate over the exam. The space quickly became filled with buoyancy of my daughter's day. She had a good day and that really mattered. I leaned into her and the rest of our night gave way to slumber a few hours later. The next morning, I woke up to a small epiphany of sorts. It was a total deviation from my normal routine of continuing to mull over my successes and failures with an examination and the never ending desire to kick the dead horse that was my worthiness.

This time, I was filled with a sense of peace. It is hard to describe without sounding overly dramatic. My heart was beating normally, my mind was calm, and my emotions were singing praises to the Lord. "I will bless the Lord at all times..." was chorusing in my head as my REM sleep gave way to consciousness. What had been missing was my need to acknowledge the blessings of my life and simply having gratitude for all my provisions. As I looked around, I realized that my feet were on solid ground. My home, that had almost been lost because of foreclosure due to divorce, was still mine. My son was in a four year university and my daughter was in her first year at a university as well. My relationship with my sweetheart was strong. My God was still in control. The old feelings of not being good enough were silenced.

The results of the exam hadn't posted yet, and I was traveling on one of my special assignments. We were down in southern California taking part in some lieutenant promotional examination panels. I really did enjoy being a part of the team that was selecting future leadership for the organization. It's a tough reality that, due to the way the process is designed, often those who are really good test takers can slip through the cracks and make the list when they might otherwise not be truly qualified. Instead, my hope was always that those who were strong leaders would be able to rise to the top in the process and as a result be able to get their promotion to the next rank.

Several of my peers, most of whom had just taken the chief's examination with me, were selected to sit on the panels as well. We were going to grab a bite to eat in between the interviews. The lunch spot we chose was crowded and there were no regular tables available. We ended up eating at the high top tables near the bar. It must have been kind of funny seeing the five or six of us crowded around a small high table in suits trying to juggle our food and respond to our cell phones. The need for constant phone access was ridiculous at our rank and above. Most of us didn't juggle just one phone, but two. Scanning our cell phones to make sure we hadn't missed that all important email, text or phone call on anything that may be happening in our divisions, or the results from our chief's exam, someone blurted out, "The list posted!" All of us had taken the chief's test so our lunch was no longer important.

Phone calls were being made to see if they were on the list and one by one their smiles broadened. I didn't want to know and yet I did want to know. Before there was an opportunity for me to check, one of them let me know I was sixth on the list in rank one. Numbingly, I responded with a smile. Faintly, their voices were in the backdrop as they went from their placement on the list to when they thought we'd promote and what was available. We rode back together to finish the interviews for the day. However, I must admit that I can't remember any specific words we may have shared other than the droning of the same question that I read to the candidates for them to respond to in the interviews. We see so many on those panels throughout this process, at least 5-8 a day sometimes for 3-4 weeks depending on how many are competing.

I was very excited for all my friends who made the list, and for myself, I guess. It was another physical validation of my ability to perform and compete. Perhaps even another mark of success in my "not good enough's" face. Yet, inside, I was not sure of how to feel.

Remember, my enthusiasm was waning, my flame was a flicker. I was tired of politicking and tired of being subjugated to the pursuit of proving my worthiness to men – yes, men. Law enforcement is a male dominated industry. Women are doing some incredible work, achieving great heights, but the reality is, men dominate the industry. A side note, bravo to us women who do make it and keep making it, but it does get tiresome.

Now let me clarify. I did not say bad men, simply men. It's a fact, so men reading this, don't get offended. Men in executive leadership look around, isn't it time for more inclusivity? When reading any relevant leadership book, we know that the systemic organizational culture that breeds the theory of "like likes like" stymies growth, innovation, and change. So why can't we break these chains and strongholds? The subcultures that create the micro silos of "like likes like" throughout an organization perpetuate themselves. Take a look at any picture board in most executive offices and definitely in most law enforcement agencies. As a bonus, add the academy graduation pictures of your most recent graduates and remove all the men. How many women and women of color are in your photos?

I was feeling compelled along with my other female peers to keep promoting in order to energize and provide sustainability in the executive leadership that would make up the tone, culture, and vision of the organization for the future. We were trying to break down those silos of similar leadership in the hope of providing a succession plan that would create better gender equity within the organization.

On top of not wanting to be "like" anyone but myself, my heart, mind, and spirit were out of alignment and reaching an eclipse for which

I was unprepared, or had I been being prepared all along. Around this time, I happened to be cleaning out a couple of file folders in my office. They unintentionally provided me with a reflective moment to review my career development plan. It was an unreal moment. The year by year dates on the folders literally lined up on the plan according to the dates that I accomplished each of those goals - all except for this chief promotion date and the date for finishing my college education.

Becoming a Life-Long Learner

As some of you may know, or maybe you don't, many law enforcement agencies don't require a college degree. My organization only required a high school diploma. I had that along with a few junior college units. After high school, I had planned to go to college. However, it didn't work out because I didn't know what I wanted to do. And my mom, well she didn't really push me one way or the other. She was still dealing with her own stuff liked she'd done most of my life.

Not wanting to feel completely left out of the loop that most of my friends were in, I took a few classes at the local junior college. The classes were things like accounting, typing and business. I figured I would be able to, at least, get a clerical job after high school. I was not having much of a vision for myself. Doing just that, I was able to pick up a county job with the Department of Human Resources. It was for many of us like getting hired on with the US Postal Service. It was one the holy grails of employment. You had benefits, retirement, an opportunity for upward mobility and a minimum wage of $3.75 an hour. How naive was I? But in reality, being a clerical typist for a unit of social workers at the age of 18 wasn't that bad. I had spending money and I felt accomplished at the time. I didn't take another college class for over a decade.

I've mentioned earlier a bit about the experience with my English teacher and my introduction to the book, *The Bluest Eye,* by Toni Robinson. It was such a gateway experience into growing my intellect and my creativity. Looking back even more into that moment of returning to school to finish my education, it's hard to believe I stayed the literal course. My kids were young, my son was eight and my daughter wasfour. I was a sergeant working the graveyard shift in Stockton when I decided to go back to school. I decided that I wanted to finish my Associate of Arts (AA) degree. What was I thinking? I didn't have enough to do being a supervisor and raising two kids? Obviously not. Walking into an actual, physical classroom, as now many classes are able to be completed online, was as if I was entering the *Twilight Zone.*

My fellow students looked like babies and yet, here I was. I wasn't sure why I was there, but there was something about completing this goal for myself and modeling this for my kids was my driving force. The classes were Speech and English. They were classes that were easy to transition back into the learning environment, or at least it seemed that way in my mind.

My English teacher, was maybe five to seven years older than me. He was an eclectic and easygoing educator that believed in seeing all of us versus just speaking through to us. Over time, I found myself enjoying the class and was working hard to excel and not just pass. The writing assignments were the most enjoyable part of the class. I was able to escape the realities of my life and all that it included for that hour. One of the assignments was writing about spending time with someone in your family. It sounded easy enough. I chose to write about spending time with my mother when she'd ask me to go to bingo with her. Those experiences were quite a hoot. They also reminded me about better times since she and I have both gotten older. This was a time that we had spent together, not fussing or fighting, but just being together. This excerpt of my paper makes me smile.

"One time in particular, I accompanied her to bingo. The aura of bingo begins the moment you enter the parking lot to catch the bingo bus. The evening was hot and muggy and the cool air on the bus would be inviting. Standing in the line to get on the bus was an elderly woman with blue-gray hair, swooped up in a chignon of sorts, which went well with her ensemble. She wore a canary yellow sweater, polyester baby blue pants slightly above the ankle, with plain white sneakers with nylons. Slung over her forearm, was a vibrant floral bingo bag, erupting from the top or a barrage of multicolored bingo daubers. Under her other arm was a green seat cushion and a neck bone pillow. She was smiling from ear to ear as she slowly ascended the steps into the bus. Once on the bus, a coterie of predominantly early 1900s baby boomers sat bantering amongst themselves.

The interior of the bus was gray and blue striped with television monitors hovering over the seats every third or fourth row. The seating on the bus was segregated by placing smokers in the rear of the bus and nonsmokers to the front. Staking a seat on the bus is a strategic maneuver in order to avoid as little contact as possible with the poisons floating from the rear of the bus. Sitting in the very first seat, behind the driver, was the oldest looking man on the bus. His name was Ed, and he always sat in the same seat for luck. He was noticeable write-off, because he did not sit alone. Alongside of him sat a female in her late 40s with straw blonde hair, and a "Tammy Faye" makeover. I took a seat located mid-range between the front and the rear of the bus, next to a sleepy looking lady with a low raspy voice, Mattie.

As the bus pulled out of the parking lot around 5:30pm, the driver, Maria, placed "Sling Blade" into the video player, but the movie didn't start. I asked Mattie if the video player was broken. She told me how the bus has to make several more stops before actually heading to the Chicken Ranch Bingo Hall in Jamestown. The movie would be started after picking up players in Manteca and then the last stop would be Escalon before going out to the Indian reservation for bingo.

Mattie only appeared to be sleepy. Once she had warmed up to having a conversation, she made many unfavorable comments about old Ed up front every time he said a word. She unfolded his past life prior to his obsession with bingo as the pavement moved quickly beneath the bus. Before long we were at the bingo hall. There had to be over 150 people with a sea of metal cafeteria tables with plastic chairs. The sea of seating parted at the bingo callers booth, located in the center of the room. The ladies sitting at my table with me and my mother were a jovial bunch. It was quite a sight to see all the lucky objects, there was even lucky salt sprinkled on he cards by the waitress. Everything on the table was logistical on how their bingo packets and daubers would be situated. When the game started, the room grew strangely quiet, carrying a respectful tension. Every breath waiting for the numbers to be called, their number."

As you can see, I really enjoyed being lifted away while writing but also I saw through this writing exercise how my mother and I had grown closer over the years. I reflect on this paper even today with gratitude for those moments. My AA degree was completed over the next four years, a class or two at a time. Over the following five years, I completed my Bachelor of Science (BS) in Business Management online. During this time my son was finishing his senior year of high school and my daughter was entering high school.

Acquiring my BS degree was just in time to provide a guidepost for my son continuing his education. If I did it, he could easily do it, and as I've already written, he did do it.

To Promote or Not to Promote

During the wait for the two-star chief promotional offers, our division suffered so much death, loss, and destruction. Our teams were fraying and becoming broken. It was becoming clearer with each new tragedy what God's purpose for me was by delaying what I thought I wanted for my plans.

By the time I was able to interview for my first opportunity for promotion to two-star chief, I was 49 years old. Maybe that doesn't sound like a significant number, but it is in a law enforcement career. I had almost 29 years invested in the department and at 50 would be eligible to retire. However, I had convinced myself that if I promoted, it would all work out. I just needed to keep pushing myself forward. It was a pattern and practice that was stitched so tightly into my neural pathways, a habit so hard to break even knowing all that I knew. But to create new neural pathways, I hadn't repeated the pattern consistently for long enough. In full transparency, my unarmored leadership growth revealed to me that I was caught in this loop and had not done well at changing long-term behaviors for healthier boundaries for me, not the organization, me.

An opportunity came up close to home, but I was hesitant to apply because "rumors" had it going to another person on the list. This person was someone who had been on the previous list and did not get a promotion before the list expired. They had retested and were now viable on the new list. The problem that I created for myself was listening to others voices and listening to the whisper inside my head. Those voices around me were saying that there was no one specified in the ranks above me along with things like, "They really like your work ethic and character - this could be the one for you." I was being enticed and lured into believing it when in reality politics, the "right fit" and gifting promotions before retirements was a very real thing.

The interview wasn't overly complicated. However, I should have realized the outcome before I ever got the "after the interview" phone call. The commissioner sitting in on the interview was on his cell phone most of the time, so that made me feel like we were just going through the motions to get the interview over with as quickly as possible. It wasn't exactly like that old captain that used to look past me in the hallway, but it was close. Basically, I was just going through the motions. The call afterward was just as perfunctory with the usual, "You had a great interview. Your time will be coming soon." As many of us do, we tend to flow with the downriver current whenever possible as it is easier that way. And that's exactly what I did.

However, in the process of preparing and interviewing, I began to consider my options regarding retirement versus continuing to work. I was also thinking about how many times I felt God had spoken to me about discerning His purpose and not my own, or others. Most of those times had not been completely clear to me. I don't think I was being still enough in my quiet moments or even listening for His whisper on this matter, at least, not very well.

There were a couple of more opportunities that ended with the same result – door closed with no promotion. Now, I had several ways I could have handled these experiences. Every day I could have been "hot as fish grease" and bucked each of the decisions. There were so many other people, including me, that would have been a better fit in each instance, but maybe that's just how we all feel when we don't get the job. Moreover, that would have been the anger of the flesh rebelling at the very idea that I couldn't control God's plan for my life. I opted for what I felt was His Plan B. In these very strange and awkward moments of fighting the flesh, I discovered that my obedience to what was stirring in my spirit was critical to what He was going to bring me through and to what He was planning for me. I had to work on my patience. It was my active waiting in this valley that helped me to refocus on serving others.

The work was nonstop, but everyone had begun to work with a certain synergy. It wasn't perfection, we're human too. During that particular year and a half, we had lost too many officers as a result of LODDs, illness, and suicides. If you added in all of those who had been traumatically injured and were facing complex and extensive recovery processes, this time period had been beyond any articulable words. The weight of those losses and injuries had left broken families, friends, commands, commanders, and chiefs in their wake. Amid all of this, we endured some of the most atrocious and maleficent personnel matters that only served to further scar the delicate veil of our leadership armor. The fact that we came together as an executive team in our division was such a blessing. Each sector supported the other as we all needed each other to persevere through the fragility of these catastrophic moments.

Planning law enforcement funerals should not become a familiar task for any of us, but it had in our division. Our commanders were inspiring as they came together to provide the support for their fellow commanders who had lost officers. There were more than enough planning meetings that were filled with staff trying to hold back tears as they worked to finalize logistics.

The second LODD compared to the first, (even that sounds awful to have to say), was more refined due to the experience of the one that had happened such a short time before. The inner will to press forward was emanating from everyone in the room, wanting to be of excellence for their fallen hero. It's in the moments after it is all over, when each of us were leaving to go home, that we were finally able to exhale and feel the pain, sadness, grief and loss. Those moments were some of the most unbearable for all of us.

There Really Are Angels

It was several months later before I started to have more complicated issues with my health when I was on a walk with my fiancée one late summer morning. As we came around a corner on one of the long county roads we were on, he pointed to his right. I usually just ignore him when I'm in a funk. I looked over and through the trees I could see a faded yellow house with a dusty old Mercedes in the front yard and the little elderly lady I that would usually see out walking each day. Her slight figure was visible from our distance, but it was hard to see clearly as the trees still had some leaves on them and the limbs were hanging a little low across the front of the house. The house was a small 1,500 square foot home with fading mustard yellow paint. The shingles on the roof seemed out of place compared with the other homes in the area that were sporting composite roofing. The little lady was wearing a gray sweater with loose fitting pants and dark brown shoes with socks pushed down to the tops of her shoes. Her silver hair was wafting in the slight breeze as she slowly walked in her yard with a cane providing her balance.

She yelled over good morning and I just instinctively stopped and went over to her to say hello. I wanted to let her know that I hadn't seen her lately and that we missed her on our outings each day. We would always think of her as we'd pass her house and wonder if she was ok but not wanting to seem like a stalker by going to her door to check on her. My memories of her over the years were always of her walking - in the heat, in the light rain, walking early, walking late, always walking. She has an inner sense of strength and amazement that couldn't be bought, borrowed or broken. I was, and still am, so inspired by her will and that slight smile she would always give you when you'd just say, "How are you doing today?"

As we chatted, she shared that she gets out earlier when it's warm. She went on to say, "I have to have my cane more these days. It weighs only three lbs. but feels more like ten when I'm finished my walk." Before we knew it she was talking about her family history and about her aunt, "My aunt lived to be 105 years old, but my some of my brothers died in the wars." She told us that her family has genealogy that went back to the settlers that came over from Europe on the Mayflower. She said, "I attended Cal Berkeley when tuition was $27 a semester and an all-female school at Harvard. They didn't have a campus but a yard back then. I majored in English, History, and Economics." The whole time we were talking she was looking at my grey, bright pink and yellow running shoes. She moved closer so she could see them and finally asked, "Where do you get those kinds of shoes?" We told her at the local shopping center. She then told us that she hadn't been there since she had stopped driving. She said that she use to pay six dollars for shoes and we mentioned that now running shoes can cost up to $206. With a stunned look, she asked, "How can people even live?" As we ended our discussion, I just thanked her for giving me some perspective. "I was supposed to see you today," I told her. She smiled and chuckled with her eyes shining brightly. Before we headed back up the road, I mentioned to her, "By the way, I never got your name, Ma'am." She replied very slowly and with great pride, "Lenore Van Dyke."

As Kevin and I finished our walk, we talked briefly about our chance meeting with Lenore. He was surprised at how easily she rattled off so much history with such clarity and detail in so short an amount of time. I smiled and said to him, "There is something about her that always makes me feel warm inside. She has such an unassuming manner, and now I know why." She had lived a full 93 years and what we experienced was a small snapshot of her life–it was so priceless. It's in those moments of opportunity that we can choose to lean in or pass by. We truly have it all wrong if we think that when we are younger, we have everything together and we will need to take care of and worry about our seniors. Most of them have an abounding effervescent peace. So much so that when we get a glimpse of it ...we would give anything for that tranquility. They know their days on this earth are growing fewer, but they live each day, with gratitude, humility, and grace. At least that's the way it was for Lenore. I was beyond grateful for that moment of her on that day. There was even a message in her name, Lenore - it means "light." Once again God had spoken and I was listening this time.

Discernment On My Decision

Unfortunately, in policing, there are far more uncertain and difficult times than I'd care to even remember. However, what is profoundly important is remembering that no matter what the crisis may be, you and your personnel are always the common denominators. Just before in 2015 and 2016, I'd been working tirelessly with my staff across the entire division as we navigated some of the state's largest fires that year.

California has a history of having incredibly devastating wildfires. During 2015, we had experienced one of the largest wildfires in Calaveras and Amador Counties in our region of California and my responsibility as incident commander involved multilayers of uncertainty. To give context, the fire grew quickly to over 70,000 acres, threatening 6,500 structures and over 10,000 residents had to be evacuated, including some of our personnel who lived in the fire zone. The level of resource management and operational incident management was extensive involving multiple jurisdictions and allied partners.

The fire was ravishing the landscape at a record's pace and the fire behavior was erratic at best. As we know, fires are not put out overnight, so the days and weeks were exhausting for everyone. There was no certainty I could provide about what I could not control or foresee, but what I could provide was consistent, competent, authentic servant leadership. During this time, what I found essential during the chaos, was how I showed up every day. Showing up is important, but how I up spoke volumes to my personnel. Also, permitting myself to absorb the magnitude of the incident, but not lingering in how overwhelming it was so I could lead with confidence.

My daily focus was making sure to engage authentically with my staff daily, checking in on their well-being, and allowing flexibility where possible for them to experience their own emotions and tend to their families was a game-changer. Not only ensuring their safety as much as possible while they had appropriate resources for the mission of the work daily but also access to assistance for their emotional and personal needs. Despite any crisis, or difficult time, giving so much daily can take its toll on you physically, and it did, on me.

The previous several months had been heavy baggage on my spirit led by the uncompromising pressure to promote. Not feeling well physically only added to the spiritual unsettledness within me. My body, mind, and spirit were overwhelmed from years of the long days of the continuous onslaught of cumulative incidents, and especially with the exponential challenges of the last few years.

During the previous couple of years leading up to this time, I had several health issues that had caused me to briefly pause, but after the fires, they had become far more pronounced. My blood pressure was high and I had vertigo and heart palpitations. Stomach discomfort and pain that I had off and on for years began to intensify. I was experiencing sciatica with lower back and neck pain to the point of, at times, finding it very difficult to move or stand up. I found myself steadily feeding my body OTC (over the counter) pain relievers and getting chiropractic treatment. They seemed to ease the pain or at least, used to ease the pain. Always trying very hard to never let anyone see me vulnerable, I worked through the discomfort and pain more often than not.

During this particular summer, the summer that I came across Lenore, I got extremely sick. I was running a high fever. I had diarrhea and was so weak and disoriented that I had to take some time off from work. Honestly, I'd never taken off a long amount of time for an illness in over 28 years, other than child birthing and one surgery. I initially thought it might have been food poisoning, but it didn't pass for over 72 hours. By then I had lost 8 lbs. and was still not feeling right, I was becoming worried that I wouldn't be able to get back to work. There was so much to do at the office, in the field and my son's wedding was coming up soon. Finally, I decided to make an appointment to see the doctor since I wasn't feeling much better. As with most doctor experiences, at least mine, they often don't know what they don't know until they think they know. With that perspective, she ordered a barrage of labs and scans and medication to manage the discomfort. That's always an unsettling experience when you don't know and they don't know either. I found myself worrying a lot. I wanted to scream out loud, "Not at the end of my career, Lord! Why???" Because I had been so sleep deprived and uncomfortable, fatigue was winning instead of faith. Fear, worry and anxiety, all were my enemies.

A couple of days later , the doctor called and ordered some antibiotics for me. Over the next several days the fever went down some, but I was still having pain in my lower right pelvis area. She felt that I should take a few additional scans, so I did. As a result, she told me that they had found a mass on my ovaries and that she was referring me to my gynecologist. During the appointment with my gynecologist, he did a physical exam as well and confirmed that he felt something. The polar bear on the ceiling that had comforted me all of those years during the annual physical exams seemed distant. He felt that we needed to schedule a procedure to remove the one ovary that I had left and get a biopsy of it. The procedure would be conducted with robotics and would be an outpatient procedure. It all seemed reasonable.

It was scheduled relatively quickly, within a week. The surgery seemed quick also, or at least it did for me as I was heavily sedated. When I began to wake up from the anesthesia, I remember hearing mumbling about some aspects of what took place but nothing I could string together in a thought or a sentence. Apparently, the surgery went well, the ovary was removed and was sent off to pathology. It was explained to me that during the surgery, the doctor discovered a pocket or a cyst behind the abdominal wall that felt soft to the touch and was possibly filled with fluid. He told me that it was beyond his expertise but that he had consulted with another physician while we were in the operating room. It was recommended that I have the cyst drained and the fluid tested. Of course, I agreed and a few days later the cyst was drained.

The emotions I was experiencing were like a shotgun blast to my spirit. Physically, I was tired, had little or no energy, was unable to eat well, and still no one had any definitive answers on what was happening. I was still losing weight and unable to really eat. Through all the examinations, labs, results and uncertainty, I was slowing finding this time to be still. Not perfectly still but growing more still as the days passed. Those work priorities and busyness were no longer important. Days later, the pathological report on my ovary returned with negative results for any cancer and the fluid from the cyst that had been drained showed an infection. I was told the course of antibiotics that I was on should clear up the infection. Yet, I spiked a fever and was sent to the emergency room. I was diagnosed with sepsis, a life-threatening complication of my infection. The symptoms cause fever, difficulty breathing, low blood pressure, fast heart rate and mental confusion. I was treated in the hospital for a few days on heavy antibiotics and intravenous fluids.

Although it was a relief that I didn't have cancer I still discovered I had a digestive illness and needed to recover from this most recent bought of infection. While I still wasn't well enough to go back to work just yet, I was well enough to answer emails, take phone calls and be engaged remotely. Or at least, I tried. Before I realized it, I had been off from work for almost a month while going through all of the tests and recovery. I had lost over 25lbs and even more importantly, I had been disconnected from the thing that I thought was so important the thing for which I had always felt so needed. While I may have been feeling better, I still wasn't well. It was just better than when it was worse.

During this time, it was the self-realization of those quiet moments of prayer that God was re-crystallizing his message to me. This intentional timeout is where I was be required to be completely still. At one point, I couldn't even work remotely so there were no phone calls, emails, or multitasking. No responding to another critical incident or to someone else's worst catastrophic moment...just quiet. It was as though the quietness was enveloping me, keeping me in a tight, soundproof cocoon. I wasn't shielded from the sounds of my family or friends, but just from the noise of being busy – work busy. The quiet pulled me close, requiring me to be present with it.

It became a defining time for me. It gave me the opportunity to finally be able to decide what I wanted, needed, and, most importantly, what I would do about my future. I'd been saying yes to people, to others, for so long. I had always felt like commitment, dedication and a good work ethic would translate into my value to the organization and ultimately, to my success. The idea of slowing down had recently entered my mind several times, but I would always set it aside, saying to myself, "I'll get to it soon. I'll slow down, I will." Well, God got to it before I did. My illness appeared to happen out of the blue. But in looking back, I realize it had been percolating for quite a while, if I had only remained still long enough to see it. After all that I had gone through, my flesh was still stubborn. I was feeling that doing a little here and a little there couldn't

213

hurt anything.

One day, as I was sitting on the couch with the intent of relaxing, I thought I'd just catch up on a few work emails. The silence in the room was broken by a clear whisper - I heard him say, "It is time, well done." It is time. I looked around to see if there was anyone else in the room who heard it, but the doggies were sound asleep in their dog beds and Kevin was in the office. Sitting in the experience, it slowly rippled through my body. I started smiling. Almost giddy, I felt a spirit of peace overcome me and my load was immediately lightened. I surrendered completely and wholeheartedly in that moment. I didn't fight it or rationalize it or defend a position. It felt right. It didn't feel scary or seem foreign. It was as though God had been waiting for me to listen, hear and obey. If you're not familiar with these type of experiences from a biblical perspective, I'm sure you've simply just felt it in your spirit. It's a distinct knowing that is deeply personal and an intimate connectedness to your circumstance and situation.

The first people I shared it with were my fiancé and my children. Kevin was all in and couldn't agree more, as he'd been by my side through all of the doctor visits and emergency room escapades. He had seen the toll that work had taken on me physically, emotionally and spiritually, day in and day out for the last several years. The most piercing response was from my 19-year-old daughter. I shared how it was time for me to retire and she simply said, "Mom, I'm so glad. You have given way too much for way too long. You should be proud of all that you have done, of who you are, how you lead and for what you've done for so many. I'm more than proud of you and always have been. It hurts me to see how sick you've been the last few years, and how tired you've been since as far back as I can remember. I think it's going to be a great thing!" I tried to muffle my tears as my youngest spoke with such wisdom. They gave me comfort and confidence.

The next notification was to my division chief. I called and calmly told him, "Chief, I just wanted to call and let you know I won't be putting in for the upcoming chief's vacancy, or any position for that matter. I'm going to retire later this year in December." He was silent on the phone. I continued, "In this time away, I've had a chance to spend time really considering all that I've accomplished and all of the things that I'm going through now. I've prayed over it quite a bit and I feel good and comfortable with my decision. I really appreciate all of your support and encouragement." When I was done, it felt like the weight of the world had lifted from my shoulders. He, being a Christian also, didn't try to talk me out of it. He simply said, "Who am I to stand in the way of what God has whispered to you? I'm just so glad you're at peace with it. Know that I will always support your decisions. Your leadership will be missed as there are not many like you." If felt right and oh so good to say it out loud, "I am retiring!"

A Big Birthday and a Beautiful Surprise

A couple of months passed and my 50th birthday was fast approaching in September. To me, that would be a major milestone both in policing and in life. By this time, the retirement party planning was in full swing with ladies from the office, my girlfriends and family all taking part. Personally, I was still recovering from all of the medical procedures and infection, and I was still not feeling 100 percent healthy. Office work was still busy, but a bit lighter since the staff knew that I was retiring and that made it nice. On the day of my birthday, in late September, my girlfriends planned to take me to San Jose for a day of shopping and massages. I loved the idea and my honey had to work that day so it worked out well. They came by and scooped me up early and off we went to San Jose, about an hour and half away. It was so cute as we had a driver take us over to the city while we sat in the back of the SUV enjoying snacks, drinks, and laughter.

Relaxed and enjoying this timeout was something I very much needed. We had a wonderful Italian dinner after our massages. Who doesn't love to shop at the outlets? As it was getting time to head back home, I was so relaxed that I fell asleep and woke up as we were pulling into the driveway of my girlfriend's house. Curiously, I asked why we didn't go back to my place. She told me Kevin was going to pick me up at her place and take me to dinner since it was already so late. Thinking nothing of it, I waited for him to pick me up. I had actually missed him all day and was so glad to see him. He suggested we drop my shopping haul at the house before we headed out to dinner. A part of me was thinking that the family must be gathering at the restaurant to surprise me for dinner. I thought that it would probably be a good idea to go in the house and freshen up before we head over to the restaurant. After all I had been literally face down for over an hour during my massage.

He unlocked the door for me and as I crested the doorway,

"Surprise!!! Happy Birthday!!!" I nearly peed in my pants! Literally! The light was low so I couldn't see who was yelling "Happy Birthday," but like ants, the "good ants", they all came from the darkness of the room and huddled into the light. I was so overwhelmed when I saw all of their faces. I was paralyzed in the doorway. My brother, my cousins, my children, friends from southern California, friends from Northern California, friends from high school, friends from 30 years ago, friends from…well, you get the idea. I was crying and smiling at the same time and then I cried some more. This went on for several minutes until I was finally able to calm down. How in the world did they manage to pull this off? I had just had lunch with or seen several of the guests a few days before and not a peep. I was blown away.

My Kevin had coordinated every bit of this surprise. I was beyond elated. I can still hear the laughter, the conversations, and the love. As the night moved along, he suggested that I go out in the backyard by the pool where most of the folks were sitting at the tables and say a few words to thank everyone for coming. Not sure, at first, of what I would say, I started off with my favorite - it takes a village. As I shared how much it meant to me, and how much they meant to me, I was filled with admiration for Kevin.

After I spoke, both my children came up to add their love and humor to the moment. Thinking that they would be the last to speak, Kevin came up to say a few words. Slightly overwhelmed with 65 faces looking at us, I heard him begin to tell a story about a boy and a girl. Not sure where he was going with it, as some of his stories have strayed off the path a time or two, I began listening carefully. Before I had truly heard all of the story, he began to bend down on one knee in front of me and everyone. Now I know that we had planned to get married. We had talked about it, and basically had just called it a done deal. I didn't know that he was going to formally propose or that he even wanted to, especially in front of all of these people. "Jonni, J, will you marry me?" Slightly shocked, and feeling a bit like a silly girl, I covered my face with my hand, smiling, "Yes…yes!" He stood up and we kissed with the background chirping, "Yasss girl!" "That's what I'm talking about!" "Mic drop!" whistles and applause. It was magical. The birthday party was such a special day. I was floating on cloud nine for days afterward. Everyone should have a Cinderella moment, or Hallmark moment! I surely had mine and it felt good, so good.

We were now into October and things were wrapping up as the holidays were growing near. I used much of this time to have lunch with those I wouldn't see again, or at least not for a long time. I found time to get out in the field a bit and visit commands on my farewell tour. I still wasn't feeling all that great but I just attributed it to fatigue and all of the changes that were taking place.

The Thursday before the week of Thanksgiving, I began to run a high fever. I was worried so I called the doctor's office. I didn't get a call back that day, so I tried again on Friday, with still no response. Finally, on Sunday evening, the doctor called to apologize that she had never received my call message from her staff. She asked me if I was still experiencing a high fever. I told her that I was and that even with taking a pain reliever the fever was still 103 degrees. She told me to go immediately to the emergency room. Without hesitation, we gathered up what we could and headed down to the hospital.

Sitting in the triage area of the emergency room was grueling, but they had almost immediately started giving me an intravenous solution that contained medications that would take the edge off the flurry of activity going on around me. It was a sea of dark blue, light blue, grey, maroon, green and occasionally a white coat. There was only a thin curtain between you and the patient next to you, which didn't provide much privacy. Kevin was sweet, patient and kind with everyone. On this particular day, he was definitely the better half.

As the meds dripped into my veins, I began to get sleepy. But each time that I would begin to drift off to sleep, there would be a jarring sound from the flurry of activity going on around me. Within a couple of hours, I was booked into my room for my stay. "My stay? Can someone explain what I will be having done?" The nurse, not the doctor, since I had not seen one yet anyway, explained that I would have to have the cyst in my ovary drained, and the fluid being sent to pathology. I would then be put on a regimen of antibiotics. Feeling a bit overwhelmed, I didn't fight it. I thought to myself, "Haven't we had done this already?"

After a series of check in procedures for the hospital, I was finally in a bed in my room. The procedure would take place in a couple of hours. The room was like most, but I did have a window that looked out over the rest of the roof and the back side of the hospital buildings. Sunlight could come in and you could see a few trees. Hospitals can be depressing. It was the holidays and here I was back in the hospital. Ugh! The doctor finally came in to see me and explained that the blood draws that they took confirmed that I had a bacterial infection again and it was septic again. It was very serious, could be deadly if not treated rapidly. I was a little scared now, and nervous. He assured me that this time the procedure will completely eradicate the issue and resolve the infection.

The procedure was once again was not overly invasive and didn't take very long, at least I don't remember it taking very long. The anesthesia was so good. Once I was back in my room, the nurses were busy hooking up my leads to the machines and getting my vitals. Weary from the adrenaline pump of emotions, I was ready to get settled. Kevin was there the entire time, quietly and lovingly watching over all of the work and me.

The end of visiting hours was growing near and he would be heading back home, without me. I suddenly felt scared and just wanted to go with him. He kissed my cheek and told me to get some rest; it will be much better tomorrow. After he left, I tried to sleep but the antibiotics they gave me created a raging, churning feeling inside my gut. It felt like there was a battle going on inside my body, to the point that I felt my throat constricting and felt as though I couldn't breathe. I tried to get up, but I was too loopy and had to sit back down. Ringing the buzzer for the nurse, I asked what I was being given in my IV. She told me I was getting antibiotics and morphine. I don't usually take more than an Advil or Tylenol for pain, so the morphine was sending me through quite an experience. Asking her to reduce the morphine, and to eventually stop it completely, worked wonders on my paranoia and out of body experience. I was in the hospital for three days. Just a day or so before Thanksgiving, I was released to go home - infection and sepsis free.

Although I couldn't eat much at Thanksgiving, I was able to muster enough energy to make all of my family's favorite dishes, which were macaroni and cheese, peach cobbler, candied yams, and sweet potato pie. It was the best Thanksgiving we had enjoyed in many years, and I was very grateful. It felt good to smell the sensory aroma of delightful food as opposed to the medicinal smells of a hospital. For those three days in the hospital, it was at times strangely quiet. During that time, I was a little nervous and afraid that my future days would be filled with more of the view of the hospital than of the view at home.

The Retirement Celebration

The day of the retirement party came upon me quickly. I was still trying to recover and regain my energy. All the while I had lost another 20 lbs. Several people had come up to me over the preceding several weeks asking with that worried look in their eye if I was okay. I reassured them that I would be fine and that I didn't have cancer. I let them know that it was just an illness that I was slowly recovering from though it didn't always convince some of them. What I failed to do was give serious attention to how ill I had gotten. Cancer is not the only killer in our world. The cumulative burden of work can cultivate and manifest itself in a litany of health issues from heart and gastrointestinal problems to all of those issues that can rob us of our mobility and mental health.

I tried not to worry anyone too much as the time for the retirement party was upon us. The party would be a luncheon at a country club. I knew it was going to be beautiful and special. We were dressed and ready to head over to the event when I suddenly felt flush, became a bit lightheaded, and started to feel a shortness of breath. I was becoming anxious, and my preparations started melting. My hair was losing its fullness and my makeup started to slide down my face. I tried to get myself together but I could hear my heart racing in my chest as I literally felt like I needed to sit down. We were running right on time, or rather on CPT (colored people time) which is usually called late for most everyone else. I wanted to be there early enough to greet people and thank them because by the end of most events many folks just slip out and I wouldn't get to see them. At last, we were finally able to get out the door.

A lot of folks were already there - the family, my girlfriends, my church family, friends, colleagues, my sisters and the Odoms. There were so many people from all over that it felt like my 50th birthday party on steroids. As I made my way over to give my love and hugs to June and Cecil Odom, I almost lost it. My life collided with the Odoms' in only what I can describe as a divine way. My mother and I were living in Bakersfield at the time. When we first met, Cecily, their daughter, was in my fourth-grade class. Both of us were around eight years old. We both had a quiet thirst for knowledge and were well above grade level in reading and other subjects along with another girl whose name I can't remember. We spent a lot of time working together separate from

219

the rest of the class.

One day on my street, everyone was gathering to play baseball. I was relatively new to the neighborhood. As you may recall, my mother and I would move quite often. Though I must admit, Bakersfield always seemed to be in the rotation, however we never made it back into the same neighborhoods very often. With smashed soda cans serving as bases, and the teams being made up of literally whoever was allowed to come out and play, the game was about to begin. I arrived with an aluminum bat which made me a bit special. As I looked around to see who was playing, I saw that Cecily had joined us. We played and ran the bases barefoot until the streetlights began to come on. It was then that she waved goodbye and started to head home. "Hey, where do you even live?" I asked her. She pointed back behind my house, "I live on the street behind you, just on the other side of the alley a few houses down from you." Having no idea that she lived so close, I was excited to have a new friend.

Over time, I would go over to her house to play. But before she could play she had to do her chores. Chores? I didn't have any chores. On one of my first visits, her mom, June, answered the door. She had a beautiful smile that lit up the room and a spirit of peace and joy about her. She told me, "Come on in here. Cecily is finishing her piano lessons. Are you hungry?" As I came in, there was Cecily playing the piano. I had never seen a real piano, or one being played, especially not by someone my own age. My instrument was the flute. Cecily's other instrument was also the violin. It was all so mesmerizing to me - the piano and the feeling of home within her home.   Back in my house, my mom was working double shifts which meant that she would either sleep all day or all night depending on the shifts she was working. We rarely had a home cooked meal or anyone visiting other than her suitors. Her sleep was aided by prescription drugs. So even when she was off from work, she was usually sleeping. After school, I would just stay outside until dark. I tried to stay out of the way by being immersed in either comic books, playing make believe in the backyard or playing baseball out front.

That year Cecily and I really bonded. I grew to know all of her immediate family. I would venture to say that I spent more than half of my fourth-grade year at her house, until we moved. Right near the end of fourth grade, we moved to Idaho, near my mother's sister. It wasn't that bad. It was just so abrupt and it disrupted a really good friendship.

However, fate would have us move again. In time for my sixth-grade year, we moved back to Bakersfield. I was a couple of years older and much taller, but I was back. We didn't move back to the same neighborhood however, but it wasn't too far away from where I had met Cecily. I ended up going to the junior high school that was next to my old elementary school. It meant that I would surely run into Cecily again, and I did. It was a whirlwind school year with a lot of new interests that didn't always have to do with homework, baseball or chores. You guessed it – boys! It was the funniest thing to have boys chase after you at this age. For me, since I had no guardrails in my life, it was my introduction to the attention I would be getting from boys and later men.

Once again, it was moving time. For my seventh-grade year, we moved to Texas. I've shared earlier that this particular move was a spear to the heart of what little inner stability I had been able to muster. After the 8th grade and the harrowing experience in Texas, we returned once again to Bakersfield. This time it was the summer before entering high school. Initially we moved in with a family member, another aunt, in the south area of Bakersfield. My brother stilled lived in the northeast part of town, so I would go over there and spend a lot of time with him, almost living between two places. My mom wasn't around much so it didn't really matter where I was as long as I was somewhere.

The summer that we moved back to Bakersfield, I wanted to see if I could connect again with Cecily and her family. It had been two years, but I thought, why not give it a try? Looking them up in the Yellow Pages (for those of you who've never used one in this digital era, it was a book that contained the names, telephone numbers and addresses of people within the town) and to my surprise, there were pages and pages of listings for Odoms. If you have ever used the Yellow Pages, you know the listings are done alphabetically. So, like any good student, I started with the first one in the alphabet. I wasn't completely certain of her father's name until I came across "Cecil Odom." Cecily, Cecil. I felt pretty sure that this was their listing. I dialed the number and her sister, Rowena answered. I was a little nervous and afraid that she might not remember me. She was a few years older. I said hello and asked if Cecily was home. Rowena laughed loudly and said, "Shoot, we wondered what happened to you! Welcome back home! I'll go get Cecily."

That summer I spent all my time with the Odoms. I started going to church with them, singing in the choir and I got baptized. It was the first time I acknowledged Christ as my Lord and Savior. I was 13 years old.

At the time I wasn't sure what that even meant, but I know that it felt good to be in the company of others who were kind and loving. We played in the church league softball games at the local park where it was always bustling with activity. So many young people our own age some from the church, and some not. It was my introduction into really being preyed upon by boys and men. Even though I was baptized, I wasn't prepared for how easily I could be drawn into places and things not meant for someone my age.

It was getting close to moving season again. And while my mother didn't yet know exactly where she wanted to move, she said that she just, "Needed to be the hell out of Bakersfield." But this time I was older and I didn't want to go. I wasn't going to go. In fact, the Odom's said I could stay with them if Sara needed some place for me to stay. Something about that discussion shook my mother and she didn't move us, we stayed. It was the first time my mother hadn't moved when she wanted to. She said she couldn't leave without me. Honestly, at the time, I didn't know if she was being sincere or not as she had done that several times before. Why would this time be any different? Looking back on it now, I imagine that she was getting older and the fun of the dance she was doing with herself wasn't as fulfilling as it once had been. Perhaps life looked a little lonely without me. I always felt that during all of those years she seemed to be seeking something that she could never find in earthly places. The search for whatever it was haunted her. With the death of her marriage, her family, and her twin sister, it was as though she daily walked among the dead. In the wake of all of it, her grief and sorrow left footprints on me as well.

By the time I reached my senior year in high school, we had moved several times within the town of Bakersfield. We had lived in the country or the south part of town where I had to be bused into a more upper class neighborhood and school. We moved to a half address that was a small trailer in the backyard of a friend. Finally we were living in a new low-income apartment that wasn't that bad. We each had our own bedrooms and it was finally nice to be much closer to school and not have to ride a bus.

Cecily had brought me into her life and home over 45 years before. During that time I had gained an extended family, and though while at times it seemed imperfect, I began to build a relationship with God. June was the grace that God was extending to me. She could have told her daughter she couldn't hang out with me because I was a wild and lost teenager in those high school years. Yet, she didn't. Instead she loved on me, included me and held me accountable like her daughters when I was with them. She treated me like I belonged, they all did. We are family. With them, I was able to survive and deal with life better than I ever could have done without them.

Often when I think about this part of my journey, I know that God made a way for me through Cecily and her family. My mother never said much to me but after she died, June did let me know that she and my mother had spoken several times about me. Sara thanked June for loving me when I needed more than she could give. My mother, Sara, had needed a village, and while she may not have known where the village would be coming from, God certainly did.

Back at the retirement party, the room was beautiful with all of the peach flowers and décor. So many hands had played a role in pulling all of it together, it was truly a blessing. I was able to greet people as they came through the doors. My heart was bursting with emotion to see all of those who had taken the time to come from far and wide in order to give me a beautiful send off.

With all of the hugs and handshakes, thank goodness it was before pandemic. Among those in attendance were my past mentors and role models. There was my fiery sergeant who had threatened to whip my narrow officer's ass into shape. There were my female captains who were so boss that I couldn't help but learn so much from them as a lieutenant. There were so many "first" in the room that was filled with people of all cultures, races and gender. Absolutely a sight to see! There were so many other people both personally and professionally who were integral pieces of my life and village in attendance as well.

After greeting the flow at the door, I began to walk around and mingle. Quietly sitting at a back table, without me truly seeing her, was a wonderful woman who had been my supervisor when I worked for the human resources department as a clerk typist making $3.75 an hour That had been over 32 years ago. Wow! A flood of warmth went through my body remembering how she had mentored me, watched over me, had me over to dinner with her family, and encouraged me so many years ago. With the beauty of social media, we had stayed in contact over the years. When I extended an invitation to her for the retirement luncheon, I really wasn't sure if she would be able to make it, but here she was. Gushing like I was still that 18-year-old from years before, I went over and gave her the biggest hug. Her grin ear to ear and she simply said,

"I'm so proud of you. Well done, well done!" It again reaffirmed my whisper from God.

Everyone had mingled, lunch had been served and the slide show was playing. The rites of passage in our lives are always interesting. In some ways, I felt this was similar, only in some form of reverse. As the photos streamed across the screen, I was reminded of events that spanned almost the past 30 years - events and times that included my children, my family, my friends, my colleagues, my special moments, and me. In this moment of pause and reflection, I was proud of myself. I believe Sara would have been proud of me. I missed her not being able to see so much more of her legacy, her story. But as I tell my kids, we are her story.

The slideshow wound down and it was time for presentations. It's customary at an event such as this to receive citations and awards acknowledging achievement from different points in your career. These were nice to receive at my retirement celebration and important for my children to witness and experience. For me, this luncheon was shaped in a way that would minimize those type of presentations and instead magnify all of those in attendance the fellowship, friendship, kinship and what God's love looks like when we take off the masks of perfection, the armor of policing, and meet in the middle with grace.

The formal presentations were first to the podium. It was important to have my young adults see their mother receive recognition from legislators, other chiefs, and commissioners and know the level of accomplishment for those 29 years she was away from home. For me, it was always humbling but also important the official element of my policing service acknowledgements. The next speakers were colleagues, friends and family that had been hand selected by me to further reflect the essence of the luncheon. Their words were kind, special and personal as we had been through many things together over the years. With all of the moving as I was growing up, having friends and maintaining friendships had always been difficult for me. But in this profession, within this organization, I had been able to create some of the best, strongest and longest of all of my friendships.

Before I closed the afternoon, the last couple of speakers were my children and stepdaughter, Sean, Emily, and Lauren. Knowing that they all adore me is moving enough, but their words swept over my physical, emotional, and spiritual being like an ocean wave at high tide. My tears were a streaming release of my self-control that many in the room had never seen from me. Today, they saw me not only as their chief, but as a mother, a wife, a daughter, a sister, a cousin and a woman.

During this moment of vulnerability, it felt like there had been a fresh anointing over my life-an anointing that would allow me to be free of the burden that the title and responsibility of being a chief demands. All of the expectations, whether real or unreal, whether they were mine or someone else's, could finally be released.

As a part of the program for the luncheon, I included one of my church choir members to sing an opening song after the prayer. Before I went up to give my closing comments, the lyrics from the song resonated in my spirit:

"You made a way.
I don't know how You did it but You made a way.
When our backs were against the wall and it looked as if it was
over...
You made a way
And we're standing here only because
You made a way. You made a way..
And now we're here looking back on where we come from
because of You and nothing we've done
To deserve the love and mercy You've shown but Your grace
was strong enough to pick us up
And You made a way..."

The version is by Travis Greene and leaves an indelible impression on how God is always providing, working on our behalf, and making a way.

Walking to the podium while trying to gather my composure to speak was difficult. My inner voice was telling me, "you've done this so many times, holding back your emotion - you can do it one last time." Considering what my final words would be to an organization that I had grown up in from the tender age of 21 and still be able to also reach those who knew me as simply Jonni, J, or Mom would have to be a delicately woven speech anointed by God. As the words had made their way to the page, some of it had come from me, but much of it He had spoken in and through me for that moment. I wanted not just to say thank you, but I wanted to demonstrate discipleship to those in the room.

It was important for me that my words would be able to show that a life lived with purpose, centered on service to others and guided by

Christ, can foster and manifest itself into your greatest contribution.
My Retirement Speech:

Jeremiah 29:11 NIV
  "For I know the plans I have for you," declares the LORD, "plans to prosper you and not to harm you, plans to give you hope and a future."
  First giving honor to God the one who had brought me all the way. I am grateful and humbled by this all. There are so many wonderful great people in our organization and in my personal life that have been inspiring, supportive, and opened doors. God? It had felt off centered for quite some time but like most of us, I press forward to meet the mission. Along the way I believe people were speaking into my life on balance, perspective, priorities and saying to me very specifically, to give myself permission to end one season and start a new one. I feel I've always been dutiful, loyal and given my best to the department and always saying yes. This time I'm saying yes to me and to my family who has watched me spend too many long days working and always on that cell phone. (Laughter)
  Yet, there is one who fills my spirit and orders my steps. Taking me in and through and over all things and without my Lord and Savior I would be without purpose.
  In His infinite plan, He blessed me with a life that might be seen as hard, it was, but I wouldn't change it. My mother struggled most of her life but she was my angel. Her walk was hard and fraught with adversity but despite it all she persisted and planted a mustard seed of hope and faith in ME. I carry her every day in my smile, my laugh, my stubbornness and her legacy thrives in and through me and her grandchildren, Sean and Emily. That legacy is our intangible imprint on our short time here on earth.
  As for a legacy for me in this great organization, it is all of you...all those I have met, worked with, those who have inspired and given me hope and faith in our tomorrow's..
  I've actually thought about this moment a very long time and over the last year, it took me to a place where I was still. For those of you that are familiar, scripture tells us about being still. Psalm 46:10, "Be still, and know that I am God; I will be exalted

among the nations, I will be exalted in the earth." The

Hebrew word *raphe* means "to be weak, to let go, to release." Essentially, it means to surrender, and know.

Well I had no choice but to be still because I was dealing with an illness. In my stillness, there was no "chief" work because I was not well enough to do it. I resisted at first because stuff just doesn't stop...but as I settled in, I realized how ill I was, and I needed to rest and allow the process of stillness and healing to work. However, in the stillness I began to prioritize me and my life for me. How was my vertical alignment with God.

I will miss the many faces, voices, tears and laughs of so many of you who I've had a chance to share this journey here with our department. But I assure you, I am but a personal phone call away to be available to you whether a hello, or to continue to be the mentor you need. I am advocate for YOU and that will not change.

There are men and women in this room that have shaped my career. But there are women in this room that shaped my life. Proverbs 27:17.

"As iron sharpens iron, so one person sharpens another." Scripture magnifies the mutual benefit in the rubbing of two irons together and it is with this that we are to sharpen one another, in times of counsel, fellowship, conflict and devastating loss. Many of you have been by my side during some very difficult times for me professionally and personally... you sat with me, cried with me, laughed with me, encouraged me and helped me make it through those seasons and I'm sure many more. You are priceless and your strength is above reproach.

This calling we have chosen is hard but so worth it, this life we have been gifted to live is even harder. Without my personal village of beloved friends and family that I've been so blessed to have, I would be only be half of what I have become, so thank you.

My family, you must know how you have filled my life for all my days. My brother, sisters, Aunt, cousins - my very sweet daughter in law, there are no words but LOVE.

Kevin, God blessed me with a soulmate and knew he'd have to be unconditionally loving as you've been my rock these last several years. He sent you so my yoke would be easy. Thank you.

Last, but by no means the very least, my reasons for striving for excellence and seeking a life worthy of living, my children Sean Jr. and Emily. Publicly in front of everyone here today, I say to you both how proud of you I am in your character, of your hearts for God, your pursuits of your own excellence by graduating college and soon to graduate ;-), by being loving and kind. You two fill my life with such great joy and been on this journey the longest. I want you to know all the little notes, hugs, dance battles, late night tv, Saturday breakfasts, texts, and calls from when you were small to now, I carry in my spirit. They keep me rising every day to be better than the day before. Thank you for giving me LOVE and always believing I could do all things. Most importantly for persistently letting me know that what I've done is enough in this season so that I can be strong in the next. My hearts.

As I close, I look around today and my heart is full but more importantly, I see hope and promise in all of you who have and continue to serve. We work for an organization, and profession, that gives the very same hope and promise to those in the community when we arrive. For those of you still carrying the baton, take that seriously every day in the way you lead, mentor, and serve others both externally and to those who work alongside you. Every day, because it does matter. Remember this quote; "to the world you may be one person, but to one person you are their world." Live and model it every day.

Remember to give life to your journey by having compassion for others and contributing back to the community. Our gifts are not just given to us just for ourselves. All of us, we are nothing without each other. Remember that as you move forward.

Every day strive for excellence and never settle for mediocrity. Don't settle. Live your life with integrity. Be a trailblazer. Be BOLD.

Lastly, remember: Psalm 90:12, "Teach us to number our days, that we gain a heart of wisdom. Remember, each day is unique and irreplaceable, a gift from heaven above. You have been given time that can be invested or wasted; hours that can be used or misused." That's why the psalmist prayed to God, "Teach us to number our days." He was saying, "Teach us to value every moment we've been given." Do well with it. God bless you all, thank you!

The retirement luncheon had left me, and many of those in attendance speechless. Several commented about how they had never been to a law enforcement retirement celebration that was so…so, spiritual, and so beautifully touching. Feeling convinced of God's presence in the moment made my heart sing.

Drained of every last bit of vulnerable tears, and after seeing everyone out of the door, we headed home. At home, a few family and close friends came over and it was peaceful. Later that evening, after all had quieted down, I was able to finally exhale. My mind shifted to finishing preparations for the Christmas holiday which was right around the corner. I was able to smile after realizing that I didn't have to draw straws for which chief would have to take the "Con," *Star Trek* reference for those trekkies, on who would be handling the division for the holiday. Kevin came up behind me, wrapping his arms around my waist, whispering in my ear, "Let's get you on the couch and give you a nice bedtime foot massage." He got no resistance from me; it was a wrap.

Sifted, It Had to Happen

As my reflection of those moments faded into the immediate presence of the ongoing interview, I thought of Brené Brown's remarks that so eloquently describes my feelings, "I've worked to live with an unarmored heart as wholeheartedness in my leadership journey. Cultivating courage, compassion, and connection to wake up in the morning and think, no matter what gets done and how much is left undone, I am enough. It's going to bed at night thinking, Yes, I am imperfect and vulnerable and sometimes afraid, but that doesn't change the truth that I am brave, and worthy of love, belonging."

The spiritual battle has been real throughout my story of fighting my own darkness, loneliness, worthiness, right to love, being a mother, being a leader, being a friend, or simply just being. It was not easy learning to hear the rise of my collective voice by allowing myself to be different than others and being unapologetic in that sifting process. The navigation of my promotional ascension amid the strain of life was exhausting, an emotional Chernobyl, that could have easily unraveled the purpose of my life.

As Steven Furtick, pastor of Elevation Church, shares in a sermon he did on the sequel from "It Will Happen" to "It Had to Happen," a continuing series about faith and fear. In this series, it's about how the apostle Paul is in the middle of a miracle and a mistake. He goes on to deliver the message and saying how sometimes the two are the same thing. "Sometimes the things we go through aren't because there's something we did wrong, actually they may be connected to something you did right."

Within in his sermon, he explains that we can't always know the reason but if we stay stuck in the "needing to know" the reason we will miss our revelation and that is much more powerful. In the biblical context, he describes the island of Malta, located in the Mediterranean Sea, south of Italy and how Paul ended up there unintended. His correlation was asking all of us have any of you ever been to Malta. "Have you ever been somewhere you didn't plan on going? A place you never planned on staying. Have you ever been in a season you didn't plan on experiencing?" He explains that Malta is the emotional place you never felt you'd experience and gives examples of what our Malta might be. As I was listening mine were clear...broken childhoods, divorce, death, illness, unplanned locations, closed doors, being overlooked, feeling not enough, feeling different.

This sermon resonated so deeply. In essence, it doesn't matter what you've been through or the reason, it's your response, your release and how God will use you in your "Malta." And at the end of his sermon, he said something that anchored me in it all, "Maybe what you went through isn't even about you, it's generational." Furtick spoke about his father and his hard life, and he had told his father those chains had been broken and he didn't have to worry about his son. As the tears flowed from my face this time, they were not filled with pain, disappointment, and fear, they were filled with the revelation of hope, and of promise in seeing the future of my children, my grandchildren, and great grandchildren. I knew that the very place where my purpose has been found has been in the very place I'd been injured over my life. It had to happen. It has made me who I am and how I have led.

It has been through the survival of me being sifted as wheat, in all those moments of crisis and lack of faith, where I have come to know the value of my "Maltas." Through the threshing and the winnowing where I've been tossed in the air, the chaff being carried away and separated. What was left of me is valuable, worthy, enough.

As I was closing out my final thoughts for the interview, I again thought about that little girl in the mirror, thinking on what she might say to me today. Perhaps it would be something like, "This may be the day to begin to let the veil of shame, fear, and anxiety finally begin to recede. It might also finally be the day that you no longer have to hide from yourself." And she would be right – she would be so right.

Final Thoughts

The Interview After the Interview ~ "Real Talk"

As I took time to reflect on the interview I had just completed with this amazing doctoral student, I realized that during the interview there were certain questions and the resulting discussion that I felt were of great importance to all of us. I wanted to make sure to give them their proper emphasis considering the current climate in leadership in a number of industries, most especially in policing.

Recently, there has been a consistent drum beat for change advocating both reform and the defunding of police. These progressive measures are coming from the community, legislative leaders and even police executives in order to support better policing and governance across the country.

There are fundamental aspects of law enforcement that are steeped in a long history of police being agents for social control by way of the criminal justice system. Some of these have involved noble efforts in the enforcement of laws that are designed to protect individual civil rights from racist and discriminatory actions. Yet in actuality, some of these very efforts result in bringing society into increased contact with police. This puts additional pressure on the police profession to consistently grow and evolve to meet these moments.

As of this writing, there is legislation being presented in some states that is advocating for the removal of qualified immunity. This legislation goes further in wanting to reallocate funds from policing budgets and redirecting those funds to other social services. Chiefs of police are terminating officers for their misconduct and forwarding cases to the local district attorney's offices for charging faster than ever before. Precedents are being set with the charging and convicting of officers for criminal conduct while under the color of authority. All of which is creating a new landscape of accountability for police misconduct.

The arc of justice is being driven by the outcry from people from across the nation and the world. It is demanding trust and legitimacy in policing.

These were some of her final questions:

Law enforcement organizational culture I've heard eats strategy for lunch. What are your thoughts on real change in a police agency? Is it impossible?

I feel this is a timeless question on creating real organizational change in policing. It is difficult. It's easy to point at changing policies, practices, training, and talking about creating a culture of accountability. However, it takes more than talk. It takes leadership at all levels internally and externally. Of course, the chief and executive leadership, but leadership has levels within the organization and every level has a role. If all levels are not congruent anywhere within the organization on a message, a new directive, an approach, or simply identifying bad conduct from right conduct, that's a problem.

Ethics, morality, leadership and professionalism is often a learning domain in initial training and the expectation moving forward. These character traits support the integrity of the person and one without the other tarnishes the profession. However, what's modeled, tolerated or even allowed sets the stage for a pattern of behavior that erodes over time. I strongly believe, and evidence-based research affirms, early intervention systems (EIS) should be the requirement not a consideration. They provide a pathway for intervention, prevention and attention. Accountability matters, so using or creating systems that do that are critical.

Implementation of better use of force policies, escalation and de-escalation tactics, trauma informed care, implicit bias and emotional intelligence training are all important facets of behavioral and organizational change. The longer strides needed are increasing the hours, recency and frequency of behavioral training to match tactical training. Emotional Intelligence is not a training, it is a way of life. It shows you can connect and communicate in the world more effectively and compassionately. More work in this area is critical, although growing, more is needed.

Trust me, I get it. There are so many priorities in policing whether it's reducing crime, finding solutions for homelessness, minimizing liability around ever corner and then trying to find ways to squeeze in additional training. But here's a consideration, reprioritize. And place building leadership competencies, characteristics, and compassion in employees for true guardians over warriors higher on the list.

Additionally, there has to be priority given to creating holistic officers and first responders which includes better services and practices for mental and physical health and wellness. The psychological consequences that they face from exposure to trauma, as well as the cultural and pragmatic barriers that officers face in seeking mental health care are the very areas researchers are working on evidence-based solutions. Suicide, post post-traumatic stress disorder (PTSD) and depression are much more prevalent than in the general population. Researchers' emphasis the role of untreated depression in suicide estimating that approximately one out of every 15 police officers is currently experiencing depression or will at some point in their lives. This is the data. Law enforcement leaders have to create new paradigms in training, services and resources for front-line workers and their families, especially in law enforcement.

Well-rounded holistic employees includes overall personal and professional development. Another consideration, heavy consideration, is implementing a coaching service similar to having services through the Employee Assistance Program (EAP) for counseling sessions. Having the ability to have a coach creates a space to build personal awareness, hone skill sets, safe place to gain perspectives, achieve goals, increase engagement, improve performance, and create a talent pipeline for leadership succession. There is already a pathway with the services and sessions most agencies provide through EAP, just extend it toward personal and professional development of staff.

One of the other considerations for changing law enforcement culture is reassessing the influence and power of unions. Their political and organizational power dynamic creates difficulty for police leaders in removing problem employees and elongates termination processes for officers. Efforts to avoid retaining negligent employees is almost like a boomerang effect. This is a great opportunity to find a better balance between the benefits of unions and how they can better support all their membership and hold officers accountable for misconduct and criminal acts in a unified stance with law enforcement leaders.

I could really go on, but I heard a pastor in a community forum the other day say to the police chiefs in the meeting, "Change in policy and people isn't seen in the community until a change in action." It's time for action and glad to see it happening through many courageous leaders, against internal and external adversity, taking a stand.

How would you describe the organizational culture for your past law enforcement agency and does it have the capacity to evolve?

People are what make a large machine run. I recall a master's paper that I wrote where I critically assessed my organization, along with all of the law enforcement industry, in the context of its own dynamic environment using a spectrum of metaphors. One of those was the Machine Metaphor. The analysis through the Machine Metaphor considers the overarching strengths of the machine metaphor are the ability to set up a structure of clearly defined activities linked by clear lines of communication, coordination, and control. However, it limits innovation and flexibility to adapt in an exponentially changing environment.

Although, the machine metaphor has advantages and disadvantages, it is important that leaders stay grounded that the machine metaphor is just a metaphor. As I was evaluating the metaphor comparative to my organization, it was clear many in leadership operate in this paradigm. Often finding it hard to create real connection or tap into the capacity of our emotionally intelligent leadership. Tradition, as we always call it, is better stated in this Machine Metaphor. It has created a defined structure of responsibility and accountability which are strengths within this framework of efficiency, reliability, and predictability.

Although, in my leadership roles, I have an understanding and deep sense of purpose attached to our people, my organization operated more like a machine in so many ways. It had this innate ability to diminish your enthusiasm due to tradition, policy, and what I believe is fear of change in ways that shatter old ideologies. Not truly understanding that our organizational culture is an ongoing, proactive process. It will be hard to change mindsets with old guards throughout the organization still standing in the way. Yet there's still the ability to reshape those perspectives and continue building common values, ideas, vision and shared systems of meaning that are accepted, internalized, and are acted on at every level of the department. My past organization, and all those learning organizations, will need to embrace using a metaphoric lens as an analytical tool that encourages discovery as they balance competing priorities.

For agencies in California, the public safety industry will be challenged with a projected growing population of over 44 million by 2030, broader issues of economic inequality, social unrest, rebuilding from COVID-19, increased political rhetoric, generational demography and a rising homeless population. These disruptions will shift and change the landscape for the citizens being served and will force policing paradigms to evolve or possibly collapse.

Contemporary leaders still struggle with the ability to shift their archetype and understand the need to be able to embrace environmental change as a norm. They need to develop mindsets and skills that can invent new ways of doing business and without becoming defensive.

With honest assessment, organizations will realize the untapped potential within their personnel, create environments that develop leadership at all levels that will become self-organizing, with potential for new forms of intelligence to emerge. It positions the industry through shared values and mobilizing a culture capable of dealing with the new realities of policing.

Tell me how you feel about the challenges with recruitment, hiring and promotions regarding women of color. Why do you think there are not more women of color in the law enforcement profession over all?

Recruitment and Hiring

I've wondered myself for almost three decades. As we've touched on, and I'm sure your research has found, it is many things.

With regard to recruitment and entry level hiring, studies, you pick one, show that women coming into policing as sworn officers is stagnant at around 11-12% nationally with African American women estimated at less than a quarter of that number nationally. The challenges or barriers that most agencies face is similar to a large state agency. I will speak from my past state agency lens.

The variances that make it more challenging for a state agency is an applicant is not going to attend a local academy or more than likely return to an office close to home. There is only a central academy in Sacramento and upon graduation, new officers are given assignments throughout California. Some will be lucky enough to get close to home based on some criteria which has changed off and on over the years such as homeowners, school aged children, etc. Then you attend a six-month live-in, or longer, academy hundreds of miles from home if you don't live in Sacramento with no guarantee of where you'll be assigned is a big deterrent for women. Especially women with children, husbands and families that may not support them.

Other challenges that occur from the point of recruitment run the gamut from interested to uncertain. Many may be opposed to the strict uniform and grooming standards and don't necessarily like the aspect of the over masculinity of the profession even for women. Many women are interested in the entire body of work, but there are those who are more interested in on aspects correlated to problem solving, community relations, public relations, working in the community and not necessarily driving a car fast. However, most recruitment campaigns often focus on the militaristic aspects and special assignments like SWAT, K-9, Air Operations which only a small percentage attain, and most are men.

Once you move into a testing process for the entry level step toward a background becomes problematic and the attrition increases. A large number do not show up for the written test or physical fitness test for many reasons already noted. Many of those who do get to the physical fitness test don't pass. It's usually upper body strength and sometimes it's the running portion. For those that do pass, they will usually struggle in the Academy with physical training and don't feel like they can compete with the predominately male cadets.

After the written and physical tests, the backgrounds gauntlet will often weed out not just women, but most. In this aspect there are hard and fast disqualifying criteria and then there is an area that becomes discretionary. Discretionary in the sense of assessing an applicant's behaviors, patterns of conduct and maturity which are evaluated for consideration to move them forward in the process. This discretionary space is narrow or wide depending on the background investigator and their investigative approach on articulating their ability or inability to be a good candidate. Although there are review processes in place, there is still room for discretionary progress for candidates.

The background process becomes a "gate keeping" mechanism to articulate why a candidate is disqualified. One of my longest friends experienced this personally when we were both younger. I may not have really believed it was happening until his incident. He is an African American male, he was in his mid-20s, graduated from a prestigious local university, spoke fluent Spanish, and was disqualified from the hiring process for minor issues. It was articulated in the background investigation report as a part of his immaturity to become a cadet, or officer, at that time. He went on to get hired by another police agency and has been in law enforcement for over 25 years successfully.

Once I became the assistant chief over these units, I found them frustrating on many occasions. My battle was uphill most of the time on trying to find ways to improve the understanding of cultural differences for some candidates based on social, economic, and racial backgrounds. But the matrix for qualifying criteria is standardized, with that subjective gray space for things like poor payment history, bad credit, last employment performance incidents, and other behavioral issues background investigators uncover. Listen, I'm not advocating to allow people into law enforcement that are not qualified, but there needs to be more work in how and who is assessing the next generation of officers for diversity, equity and inclusion. Old ways of doing business do not translate into new ways of doing business, or better ways of serving communities. It is all so subjective.

There are more oversights in place, but if the overseers are not intentional about their role, it is just a check box. Engaged leadership is essential. Challenging the past practices, or current culture, must become a part of the dialogue to break bad habits of institutional and systemic divisive and obstructing roadblocks for people of color into law enforcement. Perhaps, new reforms will look at third parties as a part of the hiring and background process to remove any biases, conscious or unconscious, from those within the organization.

Once candidates squeeze through the background gauntlet, they move to a psychological and medical examination. This isn't one of the higher segments of the process that overly eliminate women. However, you must demonstrate a level of aptitude and capacity for becoming a cadet, not necessarily an officer yet, but to enter the Academy as a cadet. The Academy is the experience to prepare you to become an officer.

In the Academy, it will make you or break you. It stretches everyone and if you're not resilient, many will break. It has over 1,000 hours of learning domains covering the 664 hours of basic peace officer required training by California Commission on Peace Officer Training and Standards (POST) and departmental training. The training includes in the classroom, driving, physical training, firearms, and other curriculum. For us women, it can be isolating and can feel overwhelming because our self-talk begins to win. What's critical is having a good support group in family or friends to keep you encouraged and focused. Within the Academy, it becomes about survival. Survival includes leveraging relationships in the Academy to help you build your weaknesses into strengths. I was often reminded, "Every day is a new day to start all over again, better."

When you graduate, you may not make it on break-in out in the field as it becomes stressful, fast paced and often the training officers are male. There are organizational, or command, cultural issues you must navigate and those people within it. I scratch my head on the number of times I just wanted to quit and go home as I shared. But I didn't. Once you're on your own, you're tested by your male counterparts to see if you're strong enough (physically and emotionally) to do the work. If it's not that, the male officers may try to date you, harass you, intimidate you, or marry you. As a side note on getting married to another officer, sometimes women will either quit or remain in their officer rank to have the flexibility to take care of children or to accommodate the husband's schedule. Not all, but many.

Promotions and Leadership

Relative to promotions. It becomes political at all ranks for the positions you have an opportunity to interview for. Embedded in our agency is the difference between the field and administrative assignments. Up to the rank of lieutenant, if there is a field position, it is assigned based on your placement on the promotional list and your desire to accept the offer. If it's administrative, it is the "rule of three" on the list that can apply.

However, if its an administrative assignment, there might be screening criteria to eliminate interviewing 100 people. Once selected for the interview, it's a process with broad enough questions for the interviewer to be relatively subjective in their selection while appearing to be objective in the interview. This is where your leveraged network becomes important to help promote you to those in higher ranks. Remember those emotional dances I had to experience?

I believe all these challenges apply across the board for women despite ethnicity. However, culturally, there will be some very deep-rooted concerns about police relations and family dynamics that can contribute to seeking out the profession. There are not many families of color wanting to see their sons or daughters in policing traditionally. One it's dangerous, and two, those incidents of excessive force against other people of color is discouraging and disheartening in policing. I do want to be clear; I am not here to condemn police; I was one for many decades. What I will say is I do not condone illegal, unethical, and immoral behavior. Good leadership will be able to balance accountability to both their officers and the community they serve. It's a tough position, not one to become popular, but one to do the hard work.

What were the challenges with your rate of promotion, or promoting at all?

Honestly, there was a couple of promotions in there that could have happened sooner. I don't want to challenge God's timing, ever. However, if you watch the players in the game, those qualified and unqualified, the latter seemed to surpass the qualified. Promotional test don't necessarily define readiness for the job, for leadership, more than it might really identify good test takers. Additionally, I think I also got burned out on how the gray area of maneuvering around the "rule of three" or incumbent selections became unexplainable to me. It's a rabbit hole I can travel miles down when I reflect on some of those particular situations.

When I had to face some realties of the arena I was entering in at the executive level, I decided to meet with one of the commissioners, who was a white male, who would be the one selecting those high appointments to field chiefs. I was nervous but the "right fit" selections were bothering me. So, I requested that we meet. We met at a local popular local coffee spot and sat outside. After a little light banter, I directly asked him where he saw me in the leadership of the organization. He proceeded to tell me how I had a good reputation, exceptional work ethic, other commissioners liked me, and my "time" would come. He honestly told me there were other people on the list that were passed over on the last list that he felt should be promoted and they would be promoted before me despite my work ethic, good reputation, and placement on the list. Many of those were other white males. Then he asked me, "How old are you again?" "I'm 49, I've been on 28 years. I can retire with over 29 years at 50, or I can work another 12 years." He was shocked at my age because he told me I didn't look that old. I was perturbed. This man truly wasn't even considering me anytime in the near future. It was a big reminder of how people in positions of power often don't see your value, just the people they decide to. True, I wasn't in his buddy circle, but I was in the circles of work that should have mattered impacting large organizational change, strategic thinking and crisis management. I worked hard to do that. My misstep was expecting him to recognize it and reward me with a promotion.

It was a moment that redefined my priorities for me. As women, we must have the courage to face the elephant in the room, even if the elephant could trample you. I didn't want to continue to assume what logically would occur with the future of my career, so this conversation took much thought before I requested the meeting. He's a nice enough person from my brief interactions over the years, but this was about equity, equality, fairness for my career in this discussion. However, his response to me was less than I expected or hoped for, but he was clear and honest. I think it was the nonchalant way his honesty smacked me in my personal and professional integrity. Just reinforcing my frustrations with the internal past examples of promoting the wrong people for the wrong reasons and wondering why the same outcomes of problematic issues.

For high-ranking positions within the organization, that successional leadership chain, there's a problem. Handing out favors before retirements disadvantages the organization. Past practices and traditional approaches to promoting those who've been on the longest, trailed the closest behind your coat tails, or have leveraged a personal relationship, need to be changed. There needs to be better processes for promoting within the organization that create true objectivity, ethical and equitable boundaries versus the illusion of it. It is a peak behind the curtain of vulnerability when there is no active succession planning at the higher levels of the organization that leave often times limited choices for those very critical positions. If you look at most police agencies, how many of your executive teams could retire within three to five years? Who's in the pipeline to fill their roles? I hope it's not just one person.

On the issue of real or perceived barriers, it's a moving target depending on your personal lived experience with anyone's particular agency. This is the reality as you move up any corporate ladder. We as women must create provocative consideration on changing the complexion of organizational leadership. Learning to navigate blind spots in our social exchanges while identifying characteristics and traits of effective leadership in ourselves as well as others.

Relative to perceived barriers for black women in policing, what I mean by perceived, are those barriers we personally believe impact our ability to either gain employment or rise within it. Yes, there are very real barriers by individuals and the organization. But I must include those we create ourselves, those artificial barriers, or limiting beliefs. I have found for myself, and many I have spoken with, our own insecurities, fear and shame hold us back. They show up as a triad of suppressing feelings that can make us uncomfortable in "those spaces" that our male, or white female, peers are in. Within that, we get sucked into finding blame or excuses for what we have created by sitting around and complaining while we are not making any progress.

I had to face my blind spots and habits that needed to be broken for me to rise and influence change. Those included self-sabotaging myself with upper limiting beliefs about my ability to compete and be competent enough, waiting for others to notice my work and merit, and the most common, perfectionism.

There has to be something in each of us as individuals, as women, as women of color, to step up and push through our own pain, our own shame, our own stuff and get to where we want to go. We have to be willing to be open to people pouring in even if it's not what we want to hear. If you want to have anything, it will be uncomfortable. Stay open. Instead of finding blame, work to find your own name. There is breakthrough in releasing, there is freedom in running the race. But if you never get to the starting line, you can't even fail, or succeed.

The last thing I'll share on barriers, the actual real barriers, they can often be hard to truly quantify. Barriers are obstacles that block movement or access. There are those which many of us have lived or heard of from other female colleagues. The ones where you are considered not equal in your ability to perform the job as your male counterparts because they've actually said it to your face. Or the ones where male officers have left maxi pads in your pigeonhole at work while talking trash about you like you're not even in the room.

Ones where wives of the officers would not let them be your graveyard partner because she didn't trust him riding with a woman, so he was too weak to ride with you. I've already mentioned the ones that would flat out say they're not riding with you and go home for the shift. Then there are those where your sergeant would call you in and ogle you every night sexually harassing you because he could. Or your captain would walk right past you and never speak. I've experienced these and many others, while other women have dealt with far worse. The list goes on.

It took me so many years to feel comfortable in my own skin and that place, not just being a woman, being a woman of color. A woman that had no family history of law enforcement, only a high school diploma and my previous job as a secretary. I was a secretary, a typist clerk to be exact and then went to a nontraditional job dominated by men. I'm just blown away all the time how far God has brought me, what he continues to do in and through me.

In considering a few last thoughts, as I rose in the ranks, the challenges that really bothered me were not even being considered for promotions or positions because you are not like the guys. I wasn't in their academy class, or I didn't go to grab a drink and smoke cigars or didn't work on the specialized team they all got to work on together. It's all really unfortunate and there is research to support this like, likes, like behavior. This is not just my feelings or opinions as some might read and not truly grasp. Organizational leadership often overlook focusing on the qualities, emotional intelligence, and the curation of people that make up the tone, culture, and vision of the organization for qualities that are familiar and comfortable for them individually. This is simply implicit bias, or in some cases, discriminatory. Leadership biases unfortunately highlight how unconscious biases, along with those intentional, shape and redefine the leadership landscape. This social categorization disproportionately disadvantages women and women of color.

As a reminder, when you move up in leadership, remember, you become part of the problem solving and solutions. Bring your ideas and creativity to the table for consideration and changes. Be bold, be brave and be brief but show up. Evaluate your recruitment, hiring and succession planning within your organization and make changes.

Challenge the "past practices" and strive for something better, something more equitable and inclusive. Be innovative or borrow good ideas from other partners or industries. Establish partnerships with all aspects of the community and create formal mentoring and coaching programs within your organizations to help others succeed. Be transparent and open to a new paradigm for leadership in your organization. Leadership is both those entering the organization and those within the hierarchy.

And pivotal to root cause issues is where emotional intelligence is essential to our next generation of law enforcement. Why? Do your research. When you do, you'll find copious correlation to emotional intelligence to better performance and decision making with higher emotional self-awareness. There is an entire inventory of data and quantitative assessment of emotional intelligence relative to law enforcement officers. Various research will identify emotional competencies such as—intrapersonal, interpersonal, stress management, adaptability, and general mood. These all inter-relate with not only poor decision making with incidents of use of force but also their resilience in law enforcement overall.

Barriers, whether perceived or real, they are moveable.

Early on in your career as an officer you said you didn't even know what was available to help you prepare for promotion. Later, You even confirmed there still isn't anything formal for preparation. Is that still how it is for those wanting to take examinations?

There were no study groups in any structured or formal way as I was coming up in the ranks until lieutenant. Even then, it wasn't formally sanctioned by the department, it was a selfless leader on the department who wanted to help others be successful. There were pockets of these cohorts across the organization, but you had to find them usually. It has become more common place for study groups, but they are still organized by selfless people who want to contribute back to their people. More leaders, commanders, and chiefs have managers or supervisors host a study group, some volunteer to do it, and others are voluntold as a leadership development opportunity. Those outcomes will be quite different in all situations.

True promotional preparation is a journey and requires assessing readiness, identifying where and how to study and what to study. You need to do a self-inventory of your tangible work along with intangible soft and technical skills. Being aware of what the study, examination and actual promotion process requires.

I've always found my success has been derived through the sifting that has taken place over my life. We all need champions who are transcendental to our journey. Early in my law enforcement career, I had a desire to promote. Having a desire and an actual plan are two vastly different things. I stumbled across a mentor with promotional study sessions that were concise, systematic, and effective. Over the next three promotions and the next decade, I discovered how to navigate understanding how to "study" for promotions and becoming a leader on the way to them.

Due to that influence on my leadership ascension, I picked up the mantle of helping others promote and build their leadership. I created the *"Survival Guide" to Law Enforcement Promotional Preparation.* It is a resource to share what was always so secretly coveted in those private study groups...knowledge, understanding, championing. I outline the framework involved in promotional preparation. Helping identify and create study approaches and workshop environments that effectively help to manage the copious amounts of information within an organization that generate from policy, procedures and legal codes.

Within the chapters, I share strategies for time management; how to build your confidence and competence; why it's important to have mentors; how to cultivate skills to be a continual learner, and how to develop the skill of leveraging your life, personal and professional experience to expand your capacity for promotion. The framework includes how to develop your own self-paced training; and build collaborative learning cultures. Systems work, so I created one for myself and then modeled that for others. Reaching back and giving back, or paying it forward, is our leadership responsibility.

What the organization does do well is provide leadership opportunities for growing knowledge, skills, and capacity. There is formal leadership development training, growth assignments through committees and projects, and continual learning through education or leadership programs. So, understanding the importance of educating yourself on processes and finding good mentors and coaches is essential. These relationships leverage and amplify your voice at tables you're not at yet. They will become your champions for your successional growth.

Know what is available to you as an employee and tap into those resources. I remember learning what a career development plan was as a new sergeant. How? Because while I was studying for the test, I discovered it. Knowledge actually does create power, your own. Creating my own goals toward upward mobility was a huge Aha moment that gave me focus and intention. It also let my supervisors and managers know where I wanted to go in the organization when we conducted my annual appraisal. This is something I've made sure to share with any of my staff and encourage those I consult to develop. Many agencies also have leadership development plans that align with your leadership goals and career plans, complete them and then follow them.

There are many opportunities within your organization, and outside your organization, to grow knowledge, skills, and abilities, they are available if you are willing to say YES. I had to stretch myself beyond my comfort zone, my YES Zone, and risk my vulnerability to being imperfect and making mistakes while learning to lead, so must you.

Lastly, regarding promotional preparation, if there is no study group, create one. Once you promote, create one for others. If there's no support within the agency, seek outside of it. Always consider yourself, you are your best investment. You are also your best champion.

Really, this is my last question, or maybe questions…lol. How does it feel in retirement? Do you feel done, or is there more for you to do?

It's been almost four years since I retired. How has time flown so fast? I have no answer for it, none. But someone I love dearly said, "Since time will pass anyway, what will you do with your time?" Every day we have 86,400 seconds to make choices. I was listening to a video that went viral on what we choose to do with these seconds in our day. If we choose to sleep 8 hours instead of 6, we lose 7,200 seconds. Lol. I lost many seconds the first several months of my retirement! Time is funny that way, it does not stop or consider, it just keeps going.

My children have graduated college, my first grandson Canon James arrived safely last year, and my husband is by my side sharing those seconds in the day, I'm grateful. Wanting to find a balance of retirement and connectivity, I completed a lifelong dream of completing my graduate degree in the first year and blessed to receive an invitation to instruct for the same institution, the University of San Diego, and give back to executives and leaders in the law enforcement and public safety industry. At the other end of the leadership spectrum, I adjunct at the local junior college in a regional police academy instructing new cadets beginning their journey into law enforcement on professionalism, leadership and ethics.

I've found time to serve in my own community on the board of a nonprofit for childcare services and education, which serves the underserved. I bring my experience and perspective to the organization and get to keep living a purpose-driven life. I enjoy contributing to people to make lives better.

Being remarried has been absolutely amazing. Such a beautiful reminder to myself that life truly is a journey not a destination. It's been great finding my cadence in retirement which has led me to my coaching, consulting and speaking opportunities through my business, JL Consulting Solutions. I'm able to balance all the "work" if you even want to call it that with time for my husband, children, grandson and even golf on occasion.

When I first retired, things weren't as rosy as they are now. I often hear "I can't wait to retire," but that can change once one really does retire. It's scary to leave a career that you spent more than half your life doing. There's also so much accumulated trauma from the job that it took 6 to 12 months to get used to my personal phone ringing and not expecting to hear a notification on a tragedy. It's taken these three years to physically heal my body. I have lost over 80 lbs. since I started feeling significantly ill four or five years ago and had to create a new normal for my overall health. Over my career, I had to learn to guard my own heart from my life and career choices, even more so in retirement.

It's a tough transition when you retire, statistics validate the difficulties from depression to suicide. I came from an environment where you are over-exposed to people and challenges. Colleagues and community are the norm for your daily interactions. Then suddenly there is an abyss, a hard stop, so to speak, of interactions. It's a bit of a shock. People don't check in. Intended or unintended, it's a reality. The blog below was written with the intent of helping others understand that what they feel as they transition in retirement can create unexpected emotional vulnerability, and that's okay.

We just must learn how to set boundaries, give ourselves grace and remember there's a new day that will dawn. So, it is so important to guard your heart, mind, and spirit, as it never truly heals from the trauma of cumulative emotional strain of the profession. Being marred in the battle of policing leaves us fragile when we brush up against reminders of those spaces. We also leave behind an immense social network we create in decades of service which translates to a small fraction of those who actually stay connected to you once you retire.

"Guard your heart above all else, for it determines the course of your life." Proverbs 4:23

I had to be resilient during that time as I transitioned to my healthy normal. It wasn't just a new normal, it was a refreshing normal once I leaned in. Now, I'm only limited by myself so for me, there are only great opportunities, and I get to choose which ones. Expanding my footprint beyond these opportunities these past couple of years is the work on race relations, diversity, equity, and inclusion in a myriad of capacities. What a great way to bookend my passion for teaching, contributing, and building people for this incredible work they will do.

Retirement from the CHP was not retirement from my life. It just allowed me to step down from my calling for that season to move into my next. Serving on the department has been wonderful, I'm grateful. But in this next part of my life, this one life, I'm free to try the things

I've only thought of and longed to do.

It's an amazing feeling to continue soaring. I plan to continue to mentor, coach, consult, educate and empower myself and others to strive every day for excellence. Surviving my own sifting allows me to help others through their sifting. If I can persevere, stand steadfast, stay faithful, and breakthrough, so can you.

References

Bradberry, Travis. Greaves, Jean, et al. (2009, June 16). Emotional Intelligence 2.0. San Diego, CA: TalentSmart.

Tarver, Marsha. Walker, Steve. Wallace, Harvey. (2001). Multicultural Issues in the Criminal Justice System 1st Edition. Boston, MA: Allyn and Bacon.

Barton, Blair. (2021). California Association of Highway Patrolmen APB: Thriving in Retirement.

Brown, Brené. (2010). The Gifts of Imperfection: Letting Go of Who We Think We Should Be and Embracing Who We Are. Center City, MN: Hazelden.

Brown, Brené. (2012). Daring Greatly: How the Courage to Be Vulnerable Transforms the Way We Live. Love, Parent, and Lead. New York, NY: AVERY- an imprint of Penguin Random House.

Brown, Brené. (2017, April). Rising Strong: How the Ability to Reset Transforms the Way We Live, Love, Parent and Lead. New York, NY: Random House

Clear, James. (2018). Atomic Habits: An Easy & Proven Way to Build Good Habits & Break Bad Ones. New York: Avery, an imprint of Penguin Random House.

Collins, Jim. (2001). Good to Great: Why Some Companies Make the Leap and Others Don't. New York, NY: Harper Business.

Calls to End Qualified Immunity Boosted by Chauvin's Conviction. (2021, April 21).
Retrieved from https://news.bloomberglaw.com/social-justice/calls-to-end-qualified-immunity-boosted-by-chauvins-conviction

English, Tammy. Davis, Jordan. Wei, Melissa. Gross, James J.. (2017). Homesickness and Adjustment Across the First Year of College: A Longitudinal Study. Retrieved from https://www.ncbi.nlm.nih.gov/pmc/articles/PMC5280212/

Flynn, Jill. Holt, Mary D. Heath, Kathryn. (2011). Break Your Own Rules: How to Change the Patterns of Thinking that Block Women's Paths to Power. San Francisco, CA: Jossey-Bass.

Foster, Richard. (1999). Money, Sex, and Power: The Spiritual Disciplines of Poverty, Chastity and Obedience. New York: Harper Collins.

Gilmartin, Kevin. (2002). Emotional Survival for Law Enforcement. Arizona: E-S PRESS.

Hanna, Shebrena. (2018). Factors Impacting African American Women, Underrepresented in Executive Law Enforcement Positions. San Diego, CA: Argosy University.

Jerry Maguire Crowe, Cameron. TriStar Pictures, 1996. Retrieved from https://www.slashfilm.com/jerry-maguire-mission-statement/).

Katz, Charlie. (2021). Authority Magazine, Five Things You Need to Be a Highly Effective Leader During Turbulent Times. Retrieved from https://medium.com/authority-magazine/jonni-redick-of-jlconsulting-solutions-five-things-you-need-to-be-a-highly-effective-leader-during-73d70c4730cc.

Kwik, Jim. (2020, April) Limitless: Upgrade Your Brain, Learn Anything Faster, and Unlock Your Exceptional Life. New York: Hay House, Inc.

Larsen, Reif. (2009). The Selected Works of T.S.Spivet. New York: Penguin Press.

Llopis, G. (2012, July 23). 6 Types of People Build Your Mental Toughness. Forbes.Com. https://www.forbes.com/sites/glennllopis/2012/07/23/6-types-of-people-build-your-mental-toughness/?sh=f2f78ae561c2

Magny, Obed. (2021, April 7). Can Coaching be Beneficial in Policing? Retrieved from https://www.americansebp.org/blog/can-coaching-be-beneficial-in- policing.

Morgan, G. (2006). Images of Organization. Thousand Oaks (CA): Sage.

Morrison, Tony. (2007). The Bluest Eye, New York: Vintage Books, Penguin Random House.

Natan, Simcha. (2018). Dare to Ask. Retrieved from https://www.bible.com/es/reading-plans/10226-dare-to-ask/day/5

Pastor Glenn R. Shields. "A Slow Leak," "How to Bloom in Babylon," "Living Above the Level of Mediocrity," "Gates of Change, Save Your Strength." Sermons, Progressive Community Church. Stockton, CA.

Police Executive Research Forum, An Occupational Risk: What Every Police Agency Should Do To Prevent Suicide Among Its Officers. (2019). Retrieved from https://www.policeforum.org/assets/PreventOfficerSuicide.pdf

Popov, Igor. Salviati, Chris. (2019, May) "Traffic, Trains, or Teleconference? The Changing American Commute. Retrieved from https://www.apartmentlist.com/research/traffic-trains-or-teleconference-the-changing-american-commute

Redick, Jonni. (2019). Survival Guide to Law Enforcement Promotional Preparation. Independent Publishing: Amazon.

San Francisco-Oakland Bay Bridge. (n.d.). Wikepedia. Retrieved September 7, 2020, from https://en.wikipedia.org/wiki/Eastern_span_replacement_of_the_San_Francisco%E2%80%93Oakland_Bay_Bridge

Sinek, Simon. (2014). Leaders Eat Last: Why Some Teams Pull Together and Others Don't. New York: Penguin Group .

Souza, Pete. Picture with Barack Obama and Jonni Fenner, San Francisco, CA. November 25, 2013.

Swindoll, Charles. (1987). Living Above the Level of Mediocrity, A Commitment to Excellence. Waco, TX: Word Books.

Tatum, Beverly D. (1997). Why Are All the Black Kids Sitting Together in the Cafeteria? New York: Basic Books.

The Big Bang Theory: All seasons. Lorre, C., Prady, B., Molaro, S., Galecki, J., Parsons, J., Cuoco, K., Helberg, S., (2007-2014), Warner Home Video

The Final Report. (2015, May). The President's Task Force on 21st Century Policing. Retrieved from https://cops.usdoj.gov/pdf/taskforce/taskforce_finalreport.pdf

The Holy Bible, New International Version (NIV). 1986. Michigan: Zondervan.

Warren, Rick. (2013). The Purpose Driven Life: What on Earth Am I Here For? Michigan: Zondervan.